# COMPUTER ACCOUNTING APPLICATIONS

## Using Microsoft® Excel with a Mouse

*A Workbook to Be Used
With Financial/Managerial or
Accounting Principles Courses*

Roger A. Gee, MS, CPA
Associate Professor--Accounting
San Diego Mesa College
7250 Mesa College Drive
San Diego, California 92111

PRENTICE HALL, Englewood Cliffs, New Jersey 07632

Library of Congress Cataloging-in-Publication Data

Gee, Roger A.
   Computer accounting applications, using Microsoft Excel with a
mouse : a workbook to be used with financial/managerial or
accounting principles courses / Roger A. Gee.
       p.    cm.
   Includes index.
   ISBN 0-13-096157-4
   1. Accounting--Data processing.  2. Microsoft Excel (Computer
file)    I. Title.
HF5679.G433   1993
657'.0285'5369--dc20                                    92-23920
                                                           CIP

Acquisitions editor:  Terri Daly
Editorial/production supervision:  Brian Hatch
Cover design:  Ben Santora
Copy editor:  Terry Seng
Prepress buyer:  Trudy Pisciotti
Manufacturing buyer:  Patrice Fraccio
Supplements editor:  Lisamarie Brassini

Printed in the United States of America

10  9  8  7  6  5  4  3  2  1

ISBN 0-13-096157-4

Prentice-Hall International (UK) Limited, *London*
Prentice-Hall of Australia Pty Limited, *Sydney*
Prentice-Hall Canada Inc., *Toronto*
Prentice-Hall Hispanoamericana, S.A., *Mexico*
Prentice-Hall of India Private Limited, *New Delhi*
Prentice-Hall of Japan, Inc., *Tokyo*
Simon & Schuster Asia Pte. Ltd., *Singapore*
Editora Prentice-Hall do Brasil, Ltda., *Rio de Janeiro*

My thanks to

Two of my students at San Diego Mesa College,
Sherry Stock and John Trollinger,
who beta tested this workbook.

Two colleagues at San Diego Mesa College,
Doris Gartley and Raymond Hummell,
who tested this workbook in their classes.

Five reviewers from around the country:
Eric Carlson, Kean College of New Jersey;
Marilyn Fuller, Paris Junior College, Blossom, TX;
Roy E. Garris Jr., Tri-County Technical College
at Pendleton, South Carolina;
John A. Polk, Southwest Texas State University;
Martin Ward, DeVry Institute of Technology
at Kansas City.

Their comprehensive critiques
led to significant improvements
in this first edition.

To my editor,
Terri Daly,
who stood by me even when
the workbook got larger
and larger and larger.

And to my wife, Lynn,
who was home when I was home,
but wasn't really home.

# Table of Contents

# *To the Student:*

Your instructor probably selected this workbook because he or she felt that you needed to apply the principles taught in your first-year accounting class. You'll learn how to solve real-world problems using a computer spreadsheet software package and this workbook.

This workbook was written based upon the suggestions of students like yourself. You will notice that it requires you to create your own worksheets, financial statements and charts (or graphs). This approach was used because college students have told me that plugging numbers into preprogrammed templates was a waste of their time. Business students, no matter what their major, would rather learn how to organize data to solve problems. When they can do that, they'll have a marketable skill. Do you agree?

The primary emphasis of this workbook is on accounting. You will learn plenty about how to use a spreadsheet software package, but that is not the focus of this workbook. You will learn spreadsheet commands, functions and formulas as you need them to solve accounting problems. You will also see ideas from finance, marketing, economics, and management sprinkled throughout the workbook. Students have told me that these ideas make the chapters interesting. You tell me. Are the chapters interesting?

I have already started a collection of success stories associated with the workbook projects. One was from a student who had gotten a B.A. degree in economics but couldn't find a job in her major. She found an accounting job in a major hospital because she took her completed projects to a job interview. Great thinking!

Another success story was reported to me by a student who was already working in accounting. She learned how to do bank reconciliations one evening in class. The next day she did 40 bank reconciliations and impressed her boss. Great application!

A third success story comes from a student who took the computer accounting applications course at our community college and went on to a four-year institution to major in finance and minor in accounting. He was better prepared than his fellow students because he learned to think with a computer using this workbook. Great preparation for upper division courses!

I'd enjoy reading about your successes in computer accounting because of what you learned in this workbook. My address is on the first page. I'll also accept suggestions for improvement for the next edition.

--Roger A. Gee, CPA

# *To the Instructor:*

This workbook was developed at the request of the Accounting Advisory Committee to the San Diego Community College District. The committee members, who are controllers from around the San Diego metropolitan area, wanted business students to be exposed to real-world computer applications of the principles taught in the first-year accounting course. The focus is on how spreadsheet software can be used to help them solve day-to-day accounting problems encountered in the workplace.

You will notice that <u>this workbook specifically avoids the use of preprogrammed templates</u>. I found that the students prefer to create their own worksheets. They consider that plugging numbers into a template is a waste of their time.

The workbook was written to satisfy two needs. First, it can be used in computer labs that should be offered concurrently with your accounting principles course. Each chapter in the workbook has a tutorial where the students are shown how to create their own worksheets, databases, and/or charts (or graphs). There is also a project in each chapter where the students are expected to exercise their "critical thinking" skills. The instructor's manual has a table showing the chapter correlation between this workbook and five major accounting principles textbooks. The instructor's manual also shows the average number of lab hours required for each chapter.

Second, the workbook can also be used in a one semester three-unit computer accounting applications course. Course suggestions are in the instructor's manual. Optional project steps and a homework assignment are in each chapter to meet the needs of such a course.

The students should take an introduction-to-computers course as a prerequisite, but it is not mandatory. You can match students with computer experience with those who have never touched a keyboard. You'll be amazed at the amount of student-to-student teaching and learning that goes on.

If at all possible you should offer this workbook along with it's companion, **Computer Accounting Applications Using Lotus® 1-2-3 Release 2.2 Or Later.** The output is essentially the same. The students, who have Lotus® 1-2-3 at home or at work, are not interested in Microsoft® Excel. Students who are about to purchase a computer may get Lotus® 1-2-3 in a software package. Some students, who are seeking employment in accounting, have a need to know how to use both spreadsheet programs.

# Introduction: General Information

## Workbook Objectives:

This workbook was written so that you, the student, can learn how to use a computer spreadsheet program to create real-life practical applications of accounting principles. The workbook is designed to be integrated with the financial and managerial chapters of your first-year accounting text where spreadsheets would most effectively be used.

Each chapter in this workbook contains a tutorial. The tutorial shows the **Microsoft® Excel** command sequences needed to format a worksheet. Following each tutorial is a more difficult project to exercise your critical thinking abilities.

It is not the objective of this workbook to teach you all there is to know about **Microsoft® Excel**. The focus, instead, is on how this powerful software can be used to solve day-to-day accounting problems that you can expect to encounter in the workplace.

## Formatting a Data Disk:

You are asked to save your work to a data disk at the end of each tutorial and project. Your instructor will give you the commands needed to format a blank floppy disk. Please write them in the following box:

# Loading (Starting) Microsoft₀ Excel:

The first step in each chapter tutorial and project starts with the command: Load **Microsoft₀ Excel**. The sequence of actions leading up to this command varies from computer lab to computer lab. Therefore, the following box is offered as a "permanent home" where such preliminary steps (available from your instructor) can be written:

```


```

# Notational Conventions:

The tutorial section of each chapter in this workbook contains a series of steps which you will be carrying out. Each step performs a required command sequence for a particular process. Examples of some of the common commands are:

> Arrow to cell **C3** and press **<Ctrl> <Home>**
> Type **Accounting is the language of business** in cell **B2**
> and press **<Enter>**
> Drag cell **B2** to cell **B10** and drag **Edit** to **Fill Down**
> Drag **Edit** to **Clear** and click on **All** and **OK**

The best way to see how these commands work is to use them while watching the results on your computer screen.

1. Do the following step according to the instructions written in the box above:

> Load **Microsoft₀ Excel**

When the **Microsoft®** **Excel** software is properly loaded, a window appears on your computer screen with a worksheet called, Sheet1, in it. The worksheet consists of a set of columns that are lettered and a set of rows that are numbered. One of the cells in the worksheet is highlighted. It is identified as, cell A1, because it is located in the intersection of column A and row 1.

2. The first command is:

Arrow to cell **C3**

To carry out this command, you should press the necessary combination of independent <RightArrow> and <DownArrow> keys to get to cell C3. There are arrows on the number keys in the "10-key pad" section of your keyboard. DO NOT PRESS THESE KEYS. Since the <NumLock> key on your computer should be activated, numbers will appear in cell A1 if you press them. (Some laptop computers don't have independent arrow keys. If you are using this kind of computer, you must turn off the <NumLock> key each time you want to arrow to a specific cell location.)

3. The second command is:

and press **<Ctrl> <Home>**

To carry out the second command, press the <Ctrl> key and keep it down while you tap the <Home> key. Next, you should release the <Ctrl> key. Notice that cell A1 becomes the active cell again.

4. The third command is:

Type **Accounting is the language of business** in cell **B2**
and press **<Enter>**

First, arrow to cell B2. Next, type the sequence of letters, numbers, punctuation marks, or other symbols that appear in boldfaced type. Finally, press the <Enter> key. Notice that even though the active cell is B2, the text spills over into cell C2.

5. The fourth command listed on the previous page is:

Drag cell **B2** to cell **B10**

Move your mouse until the "cross icon" (the moving graphic image on your computer screen that looks like a cross) is in cell B2. Then, hold the left-hand button of the mouse down while you move the mouse until the "cross icon" is in cell B10. Finally, release the button.

6. Command number five is:

and drag **Edit** to **Fill Down**

"Edit" is one of the options listed on the menu bar that runs along the top of your computer screen. It is in the upper left-hand corner. Move your mouse until the point of the "arrow icon" is on the word, Edit. (The "cross icon" changes to the "arrow icon".) Hold the left-hand button of your mouse down while you move the mouse until the point of the "arrow icon" is on Fill Down. Release the button. Notice that the information in cell B2 is now repeated in cells B3 through B10.

7. The sixth command in the list on page I-2 is:

Drag **Edit** to **Clear**

Notice a box of choices on the screen. The last command:

and click on **All** and **OK**

deals with these choices. First, move your mouse until the point of the "arrow icon" is on the word *All*. Click the left-hand button on the mouse. Next, move your mouse until the point of the "arrow icon" is on OK. Click the left-hand mouse button again. Notice that all of the information in cells B2 through B10 is erased from the screen.

## *How to Handle Typing Errors:*

If you make a typing error and discover it before you press the <Enter> key, you have two choices. One choice is to press the <BackSpace> key as many times as you need to back up to the error. When you use the <BackSpace> key, the characters get erased as you back up.

The other choice is to click on the box with the X in it. The box sits just below the word, Format, in the upper left corner of your computer screen. When you click on that box, you erase everything you typed for that cell location.   About now you are saying to yourself, "What box?"  The box appears as you are entering information in a cell location.

Type **Debit or credit?  That is the question!** in cell **B2**

If you did not press the <Enter> key, you can click on that box with the X in it to erase what Shakespeare might have said.

If you discover your typing error <u>after</u> you press the <Enter> key, you have four choices that are most often used.  The first and easiest choice is to retype any information that goes in the cell.  The information that you retype will automatically replace the previous information the moment you press the <Enter> key.

The second choice is to press <F2> (the edit function key).  Notice that a vertical line (your cursor) appears next to the exclamation point up in the formula bar.  Use the <LeftArrow> key to move your cursor next to the error.  Then, use the <BackSpace> key to erase the error.

The third choice is used when you discover that you typed information in a cell location which should have been left blank.  Make sure the cell that you want to clear is highlighted, then:

Drag **Edit** to **Clear** and click on **OK**

The fourth choice is extreme.  You can "warm boot" your computer and reload the program, but CHECK WITH YOUR INSTRUCTOR FIRST.

Before you start the next section, you should have a formatted data disk in the A drive of your computer.

## *Recording the Info Macro:*

A macro is a set of instructions that you create in order to have your software program perform a certain repetitive task.  As you use this workbook, you will have to carry out such a task.  You will be entering a block of information in the upper left-hand corner of each worksheet you prepare.  In the following steps you will create the Info Macro.  Make sure your worksheet *Sheet1* is clear of all information before you start.

1.  Do the following:

Press **<Ctrl> <Home>** to get to cell **A1** and drag **Macro** to **Record**
Type **InfoMacro**  and click on **OK**

2. Set the widths of columns A and B:

> Press **< Ctrl > < Home >** and drag **Format** to **Column Width**
> Type **1** (the number one key) and click on **OK**
> Arrow to cell **B1** and drag **Format** to **Column Width**
> Type **11** in the column width box and press **< Enter >**

3. Enter the block of information as follows:

> Type <u>your name</u> in cell **B1** and press **< Enter >**
> Type <u>your student identification number</u> in cell **B2**
>     and press **< Enter >**
> Type <u>your course number</u> in cell **B3** and press **< Enter >**
> Type **Chapter ???** in cell **B4** and press **< Enter >**
> Type <u>today's date</u> in cell **B5** (using a 00/00/00 format)
>     and press **< Enter >**
> Drag **Format** to **Number** and click on the **DownArrow Symbol** in
>     the **Format Number Box** until **d-mmm-yy** appears
> Click on **d-mmm-yy** and **OK**
> Drag **Format** to **Alignment** and click on **Left** and **OK**

4. Stop the Macro Recorder and look at the Info Macro you just created:

> Drag **Macro** to **Stop Recorder** and drag **Window** to **Macro1**
> Drag **Format** to **Column Width**
> Type **20** in the column width box and press **< Enter >**
> Arrow to cell **A18** s l o w l y and press **< Ctrl > < Home >**

**Figure I-A: Your Info Macro Should Look Similar**

| | A | B | C |
|---|---|---|---|
| 1 | InfoMacro | | |
| 2 | =COLUMN.WIDTH(1) | | |
| 3 | =SELECT("R1C2") | | |
| 4 | =COLUMN.WIDTH(11) | | |
| 5 | =FORMULA("Student Name") | | |
| 6 | =SELECT("R2C2") | | |
| 7 | =FORMULA("999-99-9999") | | |
| 8 | =SELECT("R3C2") | | |
| 9 | =FORMULA("Acct150") | | |
| 10 | =SELECT("R4C2") | | |
| 11 | =FORMULA("Chapter ???") | | |
| 12 | =SELECT("R5C2") | | |
| 13 | =FORMULA("9/15/1993") | | |
| 14 | =FORMAT.NUMBER("d-mmm-yy") | | |
| 15 | =ALIGNMENT(2) | | |
| 16 | =RETURN() | | |

Correct minor errors by following the editing instructions on pages I-4 and I-5.

> Hint: Your macro will probably work even if it does have errors. Save your macro and see if it runs by following the directions at the bottom of this page.

## *Saving Worksheets, Macros, and Charts:*

Before you save a worksheet, macro, or chart, make sure you have your data disk in the A drive of your computer. In this example you will be saving your macro. SAVING A WORKSHEET OR A CHART IS DONE THE SAME WAY EXCEPT YOU WILL BE ENTERING A DIFFERENT FILE NAME.

Drag **File** to **Save As** and type  **a:\info**  and press **<Enter>**

Notice that the title of the worksheet has changed from Macro1 to INFO.XLM. The word *INFO* is the file name. It should be eight letters (or numbers) or less. The extension *XLM* identifies the file as a macro.

## *Exiting the Program:*

If there are no significant changes made to the worksheet, macro, or chart:

Drag **File** to **Exit** and click on **No**

Remove your data disk from the A drive. If you are in a computer lab, your instructor may provide commands to get you back to a main menu.

## *Running the Info Macro:*

To run **Info Macro** (after you have loaded Excel) do the following:

Drag **File** to **Open** and click on [-A-] in the Directories box
Click on **OK** and click on **INFO.XLM** and click on **OK**
Drag **Window** to **Sheet1** and drag **Macro** to **Run**
Click on **Info** in the Run box and click on **OK**

Your information block should appear in cells B1 through B5.

# *Printing the Worksheet:*

In the following chapters you will be asked to save your worksheet as some file name and then print it. Save first. Print second. This is a particularly good habit to adopt for any software program! After you have saved your worksheet, you can print it by doing the following steps.

1.  Set the printer for portrait or landscape orientation.

    Drag **File** to **Printer Setup** and click on **Setup**
    Click on either **Portrait** or **Landscape**

When you choose the portrait orientation, the page on which you print will look taller than it is wide. When you choose the landscape orientation, the page will look wider than it is tall.

    Click on **OK** and click on **OK** again

    Note: If you are printing with a dot matrix printer and are not using single sheets of paper, there is an extra choice you can make when you choose the landscape option. After you click on landscape, you can click on the DownArrow symbol in the Paper Height Box until 22 in appears. Click on 22 in and No Page Break before you click on OK. This choice will be particularly useful in the Chapter One project when you create a worksheet that is two pages wide.

2.  Set the page up for printing by doing the following:

    Drag **File** to **Page Setup**
    Press **<SpaceBar>** to remove the **&f** in the header box
    Click on **Row** to remove the X in the box next to Row & Column
    Click on **Gridlines** to remove the X in the box next to Gridlines
    Click on **OK**

3.  Set the font, size, and style of type that you want to use.

    Drag **Format** to **Fonts** and click on **Fonts >>**
    Click on **Printer Fonts**

Notice the names of the various fonts that work with your printer in the Font box. Boxes are provided on the next page for you to write the suggestions from your instructor.

A regular-sized font for a portrait orientation:

A regular-sized font for a landscape orientation:

A compressed-sized font for a portrait orientation:

A compressed-sized font for a landscape orientation:

In the style box there is a list of alternative styles that can be selected instead of the regular default style.

Click on any style that shows an X in the box next to it

In other words, don't chose the alternative styles for accounting worksheets.

Click on **Replace** and **OK**

I-9

4. In this step you will preview what you want to print:

Drag **File** to **Print**

An X should be in the box next to preview.  If the X is not there:

Click on **Preview** to get an X in the preview box and click on **OK**

There are two reasons why you preview a worksheet that you are about to print.  First, you should make sure that what appears on the page is really what you want.  If you forget to select a compressed type font, you may discover that you are missing columns.  Second, you need to be sure that the information you will print is properly positioned on the page.

You can get a closeup look at what you are about to print by either clicking on Zoom or by moving the "magnifying glass" icon over the text and clicking the left-hand button of the mouse.  Arrow around the page that you are about to print to see if the printer is going to produce what you expect.

If you see a string of ##### in a particular cell, the cell is not wide enough to accept the information you put there.  To correct the problem:

Click on **Cancel** and increase the column width.

Note:  You may have wondered why the Info Macro started putting text in cell B1 rather than cell A1.  People who often use this spreadsheet program leave column A empty.  The width of column A can then be adjusted to position the information on the page without affecting the information in the rest of the worksheet.  The latest versions of Excel allow you to position your worksheet automatically on the page without having to adjust the column A width.

When you are satisfied (and you know your instructor will be satisfied) with the information that you are going to print, make sure your printer is on line with your computer.  Then:

Click on **Print**

## *Printing the Chart:*

As with your worksheet, you should save your chart first and then print it.  The following steps should be followed to determine the size of your chart, to choose a portrait or landscape orientation, and to print the chart.

1.  The first step is to determine the size of the chart.  This is done by adjusting the margins.  The larger you make the margins, the smaller you make the chart.

> Drag **File** to **Page Setup** and click to the right of the numbers
>    in the **Left** margin box
> Press **<Backspace>** key enough times to clear the default width
> Type **2.00**  and click to the right of the numbers
>    in the **Right** margin box

Change the numbers in the rest of the margin boxes in a similar manner.  The number in the right margin box should be 2.00.  The number in the top and bottom margin boxes should be 3.00.

> Click on **Ok** when you are done

2.  To choose a portrait or landscape orientation:

> Drag **File** to **Printer Setup** and click on **Setup**
> Click on **Portrait** or **Landscape** and click on **Ok**
> Click on **Ok** again

3.  Print the chart:

> Drag **File** to **Print** and click on **Preview** to put X in box
> Click on **Ok** and inspect your chart
> Click on **Print**

# *Words of Advice:*

You can either choose to enjoy the tutorials and projects in this workbook, or you can choose to be stressed out by them.  No matter which choice you make, you will be making mistakes.  If you choose to enjoy this workbook, then figuring out how to correct your mistakes will be half the fun of learning about a new software package.  Allow yourself the time to play on the computer.  Make this learning experience fun!

Notes:

# Chapter One

# Accounting Equation

## Chapter Objectives:

A. Create worksheets (spreadsheets) that show typical business transactions for a professional practice.

B. Demonstrate the relationship the account column totals in the worksheets have with the accounting equation.

C. Emphasize the business entity concept when analyzing transactions.

## Tutorial:

Assume that T. B. Pickens, MD, brings you the financial records for her first month as the new owner of a medical practice. Please carry out the following steps to create a worksheet with account column names in financial statement order. You will use the accounting equation to prove the column totals.

1. Do the following according to the instructions in the Introduction chapter of this workbook:

Load **Microsoft**® **Excel** and run **Info Macro**

2. Edit the text in cell B4 by doing the following:

Arrow to cell **B4** and press **<F2>** (the edit function key)
Press **<BackSpace>** three times to erase the ???
Type **1** (the number one key) and press **<Enter>**

Edit the date in cell B5 to show today's date. Refer to page I-4 if you need instructions.

3. The heading for a worksheet should be in a "who, what, when" format:

> Type **T.B. PICKENS, MD** in cell **D1** and press **<Enter>**
> Type **WORKSHEET** in cell **D2** and press **<Enter>**
>
> Type **FOR THE MONTH ENDED** in cell **D3** and press **<Enter>**
> Type **="DECEMBER 31, 1993"** in cell **D4** and press **<Enter>**
>
> Note: You must add the **="** and the **"** to make the date appear in the heading as DECEMBER 31, 1993.

4. On December 5, Dr. Pickens opens a business checking account with a $75,000 deposit (representing her investment in the medical practice). Enter the details of this transaction as follows:

> Type **DATE** in cell **B7** and press **<Enter>**
> Type **DESCRIPTION** in cell **C7** and press **<Enter>**

Change the column C width by doing the following:

> Drag **Format** to **Column Width**
> Type **20** and press **<Enter>**

Continue with the column headings:

> Type **CASH** in cell **D7** and press **<Enter>**
>
> Type **PICKENS,** in cell **F6** and press **<Enter>**
> Type **CAPITAL** in cell **F7** and press **<Enter>**

You are now going to enter the details of the above transaction:

> Type **12/05** in cell **B9** and press **<Enter>**
> Type **Initial Investment** in cell **C9** and press **<Enter>**
>
> Type **75000** in cell **D9** and press **<Enter>**
> Type **75000** in cell **F9** and press **<Enter>**

5. On December 8, Dr. Pickens pays Medical Office Management $2,750 using check number 1001. The check amount includes $750 for the December rent (it's a partial month), $1,000 for the January rent, and the rest for a security deposit. Dr. Pickens signs a three-year lease.

Notice in the following command sequence that transactions are described differently in real life than in your textbook. One reason for this is that the textbook has a different purpose for the transaction description. Textbook authors are trying to get you to understand the various types of transactions. In real life, you would use the description to help you trace back to the source documents that show the objective evidence for the transaction. Also notice from the following commands that you add column (or account) names as new ones are needed:

> Type **PREPAID** in cell **E6** and press **<Enter>**
> Type **RENT** in cell **E7** and press **<Enter>**
>
> Click on the **F column header** (above cell F1)
> Drag **Edit** to **Insert**
>
> Type **SECURITY** in cell **F6** and press **<Enter>**
> Type **DEPOSIT** in cell **F7** and press **<Enter>**
> Type **RENT** in cell **H6** and press **<Enter>**
> Type **EXPENSE** in cell **H7** and press **<Enter>**

Now you can enter the information about the transaction:

> Type **12/08** in cell **B10** and press **<Enter>**
> Type **Ck1001 Med Off Mgt** in cell **C10** and press **<Enter>**

Your accounting textbook may have used "paid office rent and security deposit" as an explanation. In real life you would refer to Ck1001 as the source document which shows Medical Office Management as the payee. If you should ever need to look at the objective evidence for this transaction, you could look in the file cabinet for the paperwork referenced by the description above.

> Type **-2750** in cell **D10** (note the minus sign) and press **<Enter>**
> Type **1000** in cell **E10** and press **<Enter>**
> Type **1000** in cell **F10** and press **<Enter>**
> Type **-750** in cell **H10** and press **<Enter>**

The rent expense is entered with a minus sign because it represents a decrease in owner's equity.

6. On December l5, Dr. Pickens purchases Furniture and Equipment from MediQuip, Inc:

Total price including sales tax............................................ $90,122.75
Down payment (check number 1002)............................. 30,122.75
---------------
10-Year Note Payable to MediQuip............................... $60,000.00

Add two new columns as follows:

Drag cell **F1** to cell **F12**
Drag **Edit** to **Insert** and click on **OK**
Drag cell **H1** to cell **H12**
Drag **Edit** to **Insert** and click on **OK**

Add the new column headings:

Click on cell **F6**
Type **FURNITURE &** and press < **Enter** >
Type **EQUIPMENT** in cell **F7** and press < **Enter** >
Click on cell **H6**
Type **NOTE** and press < **Enter** >
Type **PAYABLE** in cell **H7** and press < **Enter** >

Now you can enter the details of the transaction:

Arrow to cell **B11**
Type **12/15** and press < **Enter** >
Type **Ck1002 MediQuip Inc** in cell **C11** and press < **Enter** >
Type **-30122.75** in cell **D11** and press < **Enter** >

First, if your computer has a 10-key pad, use  . (the period key) located there to place the decimal point in the above number. Second, use − (the minus key) that is located in the 10-key pad.  Third, GET USED TO ENTERING NUMBERS FROM THE 10-KEY PAD.

Click on cell **F11**
Type **90122.75** and press < **Enter** >

6. (continued)

Type **60000** in cell **H11** and press **<Enter>**
Arrow to cell **C13** and type **TOTALS** and press **<Enter>**

7. Enter the SUM function AS follows:

Arrow to cell **D13**
Type **=sum(** (do NOT press <Enter> here)
Drag cell **D8** to cell **D12**
Type **)** and press **<Enter>**

You could have typed the formula $=D9+D10+D11$ and you would have been correct. This is the formula style that most books teach, but it is not the one used in this situation in real life. One reason why the formula style is not used is because it is too easy to make a typing error. Another reason is because it is too easy to forget to change the formula if you want to add more numbers to the column. In actual situations there are a lot more numbers in most of the columns.

The SUM function is one of the statistical functions offered by **Microsoft**® **Excel**. It is easy to use and is flexible. If you want to add rows and numbers within the range of the function, **Microsoft**® **Excel** will automatically adjust the function range for the new cell locations containing the numbers.

Note: Excel versions 3.0 and later have a toolbar with an "AutoSum" tool on it. When you click on the "AutoSum" tool, it inserts the SUM function and a proposed sum range based upon the data above or to the left of the active cell.

8. Copy the SUM function in cell D13 to cells E13 through J13. Your active cell should still be cell D13. With the **<Shift>** key pressed down:

Arrow to cell **J13** and release the **<Shift>** key
Drag **Edit** to **Fill Right and drag Format** to **Column Width**
Type **13** and click on **OK**

9. Format the numbers in the worksheet so that they look like dollars and cents. Notice that the dollar sign is not used.

Drag cell **D9** to cell **J13**
Drag **Format** to **Number**
Click on **#,##0.00** and **OK**

10. Adjust your worksheet by aligning certain column headings and the transaction dates:

>    Drag cell **D6** to **J7** and drag **Format** to **Alignment**
>    Click on **Right** and **OK**
>
>    Arrow to cell **B9** and drag cell **B9** to cell **B11**
>    Drag **Format to Alignment** and click on **Left** and **OK**

11. Enter the accounting equation. Here the total of the asset columns should equal the total of the liability columns plus the owner's equity columns.

>    Type  **TOTAL ASSETS**  in cell **C16** and press <Enter>
>    Type  **LIABILITIES &**  in cell **C18** and press <Enter>
>    Type  **OWNER'S EQUITY**  in cell **C19** and press <Enter>
>
>    Arrow to cell **D16** and type  **=sum(**   Do not press <Enter> here
>    Arrow to cell **D13**

With the <Shift> key held down:

>    Arrow to cell **G13** then release the <Shift> key
>    Type  )  and press <Enter>
>    Arrow to cell **D19** and type  **=sum(**
>    Arrow to cell **H13**

With the <Shift> key held down:

>    Arrow to cell **J13** then release the <Shift> key
>    Type  )  and press <Enter>
>    Drag cell **D16** to cell **D19**
>    Drag **Format** to **Number**
>    Click on **#,##0.00** and **OK**

Total assets should equal liabilities and owner's equity. The worksheet should look similar to the one illustrated on the following page.

12. Save your worksheet as  **a:\tut1**  and print it using compressed type in a landscape orientation according to the instructions in the Introduction chapter. Exit the program.

# Figure 1-A: Completed Tutorial

Student Name
999-99-9999
Acct150
Chapter 1
15-Sep-93

T.B. PICKENS, MD
WORKSHEET
FOR THE MONTH ENDED
DECEMBER 31, 1993

| DATE | DESCRIPTION | CASH | PREPAID RENT | FURNITURE & EQUIPMENT | SECURITY DEPOSIT | NOTE PAYABLE | PICKENS, CAPITAL | RENT EXPENSE |
|---|---|---|---|---|---|---|---|---|
| 5-Dec | Initial Investment | 75,000.00 | | | | | 75,000.00 | |
| 8-Dec | Ck1001 Med Off Mgt | -2,750.00 | 1,000.00 | | 1,000.00 | | | -750.00 |
| 15-Dec | Ck1002 Mediquip Inc | -30,122.75 | | 90,122.75 | | 60,000.00 | | |
| TOTALS | | 42,127.25 | 1,000.00 | 90,122.75 | 1,000.00 | 60,000.00 | 75,000.00 | -750.00 |
| TOTAL ASSETS | | 134,250.00 | | | | | | |
| LIABILITIES & OWNER'S EQUITY | | 134,250.00 | | | | | | |

# *Project:*

Assume for the purpose of this project that you are in need of some tooth repair and Dr. Jose Morales is in need of some bookkeeping assistance for his new dental practice. Set up a spreadsheet similar to the tutorial you completed to clearly illustrate the accounting equation.

The account column names should be in financial statement order. The Asset column names should be in order of liquidity. The Owner's Equity column names should be in the following order: Capital, Drawing, Revenue, and Expenses. Be careful with the amounts in the Drawing and Expense columns. They are recorded as minus numbers because they represent reductions in the owner's equity.

1. Do the following according to the instructions in the Introduction chapter:

**Load Microsoft® Excel and run Info Macro**

2. On October 1, 1993, Jose Morales opened a business checking account with a $90,000 deposit. The $90,000 came from three sources unrelated to the business: $40,000 from personal savings, $30,000 from a second mortgage on his house, and $20,000 as a personal loan from his grandmother. Keep the business entity principle in mind when you enter his investment.

3. On October 3, Dr. Morales purchased some real estate from another dentist who retired. Check number 1001 was used for the down payment. The details of the transaction are as follows:

| | |
|---|---:|
| Land (add a Land column) | $ 75,000 |
| Building (add a Building column) | 150,000 |
| | ------------ |
| Total price | $225,000 |
| Down payment (to Fast Mortgage Company) | 45,000 |
| | ------------ |
| 20-year Mortgage (add a Mortgage Payable column) | $180,000 |

4. On October 6, Dr. Morales paid a $300 security deposit to Ma Bell Telephone Company with check number 1002. Since this is a short-term asset, a Security Deposit column should be inserted to the left of the Land column.

1-8

5. On October 15, Dr. Morales purchased furniture and equipment for his new practice from DDS Equipment Company:

Total Price including sales tax......................................... $104,872.33
Down Payment (check #1003)...................................... 35,000.00
----------------
Note Payable (short-term)............................................. $ 69,872.33

Note: There is a catchy little jingle to help you remember how to arrange long-term tangible assets: "You buy the land. You put the building on the land. The junk goes inside and the cars go around." The most common way to arrange these assets is: Land, Building, Furniture & Equipment, and Transportation Equipment.

6. On October 18, Jose purchased dental and office supplies on account from Zest Dental Products, Inc., for a total of $3,855.49 (invoice number 159753). Put the Supplies column between the Cash and Security Deposit columns.

7. On October 20, Jose paid a $434.86 telephone bill to Ma Bell Telephone Company with check number 1004. Add a Telephone Expense column.

8. On October 25, Dr. Morales paid a $208.10 bill to Coast Gas & Electric Company. He used check number 1005 for the utilities expense.

9. On October 26, Jose paid the mortgage company $1,990.00 with check number 1006. The major portion of the payment was interest expense in the amount of $1,722.50.

Note: There is an easy way to enter the principle reduction amount in the Mortgage Payable column: Enter the check amount and the interest expense amount. Arrow to the cell where you want the principle reduction amount to show and press = (the equal key). Arrow to the cell where you entered the $1,990.00. Then press - (the minus key), arrow to the cell where you entered the interest expense, and press <Enter>.

10. On October 27, Jose paid the first monthly payment on the DDS Equipment Company note. Of the $944.00 paid, $812.75 was interest expense. Check number 1007 was used.

11. On October 28, Jose Morales paid $1,900.00 on account to Zest Dental Products, Inc. He used check number 1008.

12.  On October 31, Dr. Morales deposited $4,251.00 in the business checking account.  All of the money was received in the form of checks from his patients or their insurance companies.  This deposit represented his Professional Fees Earned (a Revenue column name) during October.  A suggested description is:  Oct Rev Dep

13.  Also on October 31, Dr. Morales withdrew $3,300 using check number 1009.

> Hint:  After this transaction the total assets should equal 339,201.86 without a dollar sign.  The instructions for formatting numbers are on page 1-5.

14.  Save your worksheet as  **a:\proj1**  and print it in a landscape orientation with a compressed type font according to the instructions in the Introduction chapter.  If you are using a dot matrix printer, you may be able to improve the appearance of your worksheet by lengthening the page to 22 inches (see the Introduction chapter for guidance).  Exit the program.

15.  (Optional)  Jose Morales would like to see the cash receipts on one worksheet and the cash payments on another worksheet.  Your boss wants you to type a one-page report to Dr. Morales that discusses the advantages and disadvantages of a two-worksheet approach over a single-worksheet approach.

If you don't have access to a word processing package, use **Microsoft® Excel**.  Adjust the B column width to 72.  Save your report as  **a:\report1** and print it in a portrait orientation using a regular-sized type font.  Exit the program.

## Assignment:

Prepare by hand a proper looking worksheet showing the transactions explained in this chapter's project.  The worksheet should have a title that indicates the "who, what, and when" of the project.  The column names should be arranged in financial statement order.

Student Name:_____

Date:_____

# Chapter One Transmittal Sheet for Excel

A.  Hand this page in to your instructor with the following items attached on the back in the following order:

1.  Project worksheet
2.  Hand written assignment
3.  Project step 15 report (optional)

B.  Refer to your project worksheet to list the items requested:

1.  List the asset account names in financial statement order.

2.  List the liability account names in financial statement order.

3.  List the remaining account names in financial statement order.

4.  Write the formula or function that is in the cell location where the total interest expense is located in your project worksheet.

5.  Write the formula or function that is in the cell location where the total assets is located in your project worksheet.

Notes:

# Chapter Two

# Rules of Debit and Credit

---

## Chapter Objectives:

A. Create general journal printouts using spreadsheet software.

B. Analyze transactions according to the rules of "debit and credit" and record them in a computer file.

C. Explain the similarities and differences that you see between hand-prepared and computer-generated journals.

## Tutorial:

Assume that you move to Hollywood to be a star in the movies. You know, deep down, that you may never get that big break. On the other hand, you don't want to keep body and soul together by flipping burgers or waiting on tables. You scrape together the dollars to purchase a swimming pool maintenance business called Starving Actor's Pool Service.

1. Do the following according to the instructions in the Introduction chapter:

> Load **Microsoft**® **Excel** and run **Info Macro**

2. Edit the text in cell B4 as follows:

> Arrow to cell **B4** and press **<F2>** (the edit function key)
> Press **<BackSpace>** three times to erase the ???
> Type **2** and press **<Enter>**

Edit the date in cell B5 to show today's date.

3. Enter the page titles and column headings for a computer-generated journal. The journal page you create will look like one of the printouts from a well-known general ledger accounting software package, but will not act like one. You will not be able to post from the page you create to any ledger accounts. Since this journal would ordinarily be located in the general ledger module of the accounting software package, it is called the G/L Journal.

> Type **STARVING ACTOR'S POOL SERVICE** in cell **C7**
>       and press **<Enter>**
> Type **G/L JOURNAL** in cell **G7** and press **<Enter>**
> Type **PAGE 1** in cell **J7** and press **<Enter>**

Enter the following column headings in a similar manner:

| Cell Location | Column Heading Text |
| --- | --- |
| B9 and C9 | TRNS |
| B10 | NMBR |
| C10 | DATE |
| | |
| D9 | ACCT |
| D10 | NMBR |
| F10 | ACCOUNT |
| | |
| G9 | TRANSACTION |
| G10 | DESCRIPTION |
| H9 | DEBIT |
| I9 | CREDIT |
| | |
| H10 and I10 | AMOUNT |
| J9 | POSTED |
| J10 | YES/NO |

4. Change the column widths:

> Click on any cell in column **C**
> Drag **Format** to **Column Width**
> Type **9** and click on **Ok**

Change the widths of the following columns in a similar manner:

| Column | Width |
|--------|-------|
| D | 5 |
| E | 1 |
| F | 25 |
| G | 24 |
| H and I | 10 |
| J | 7 |

5.  Some of the column headings need to be aligned:

> Drag cell **B9** to cell **D10**
> Drag **Format** to **Alignment**
> Click on **Right** and on **Ok**

6.  Format the range of cells in column B so that the  transaction numbers (to be entered later) will be right aligned.  You must first establish the cell range to format, then carry out the formatting procedure.

> Arrow to cell **B12**
> Press < **Shift** > down  (keep the key down until
>     you are told to release it)
> Press < **DownArrow** > until you reach cell **B60**
> Release < **Shift** > and drag **Format** to **Alignment**
> Click on **Right** and on **Ok**

7.  Format the cells in column C so that the dates (to be entered later) will look OK.  Establish the cell range C12 through C60 as you did in step six, then:

> Drag **Format** to **Number**
> Click on the **Arrow** in the lower right corner of the
>     **Format Number Box** until **m/d/yy** appears
> Click on **m/d/yy** and on **Ok**

8.  You must also format the dollar amounts that will be entered later in columns H and I.  As you are entering transactions, note that the numbers you enter do not appear the same way on the screen.  They include commas,

periods, and extra zeros that you didn't type. Establish the cell range H12 through I60.

> Drag **Format** to **Number**
> Click on **#,##0.00** and on **Ok**

9. The column J information needs to be right aligned. Establish the cell range J12 through J60.

> Drag **Format** to **Alignment**
> Click on **Right** and on **Ok**

10. Enter SUM functions in cells H60 and I60 as follows:

> Type  = **sum(h12:h59)** in cell **H60** and press **<Enter>**
> Drag cell **H60** to cell **I60** and drag **Edit** to **Fill Right**

Note: You just created automatic footers in cells H60 and I60. These Debit and Credit column totals change as you enter transaction amounts.

11. It is time to enter your first transaction. Assume that you take $20,000 (all borrowed from your relatives) to your bank, and you open a business checking account. Notice that the dollar value of any promissory notes that you sign will not appear as liabilities in the journal of your business. You owe the money to your relatives. Your business does not. Enter the following information regarding this transaction:

| Cell Locations | Information |
|---|---|
| B12 and B13 | J001 |
| C12 and C13 | 10/1/93 |
| | |
| D12 | 1100 |
| D13 | 3100 |
| | |
| F12 | Cash |
| F13 | Your Last Name, Capital |
| G12 and G13 | Cash Investment In Bus |
| | |
| H12 and I13 | 20000 |
| J12 and J13 | No |

Note: In a computerized accounting system transaction numbers are used to identify entries in the journal and ledger. Entries are posted by transaction number. Account numbers tell the computer where to post the information, but they do not serve as posting references. A separate column is used to show "proof of posting."

12. Assume in the second transaction that you purchase an existing business from Hollywood actor Ima Starr. Ima got that big break in the movies. The full purchase price of the business is $22,000. You pay $4,200 with check number 101 and sign a short-term promissory note for the rest. Enter the following:

| Cell Locations | Information |
|---|---|
| B15 through B20 | J002 |
| C15 through C20 | 10/2/93 |
| | |
| D15 | 1700 |
| D16 | 1800 |
| D17 | 1200 |
| D18 | 1300 |
| D19 | 1100 |
| D20 | 2100 |
| | |
| F15 | Furniture & Equipment |
| F16 | Transportation Equipment |
| F17 | Accounts Receivable |
| F18 | Supplies |
| F19 | Cash |
| F20 | Notes Payable |
| | |
| G15 through G20 | Ck101 Ima Starr |
| | |
| H15 | 8000 |
| H16 | 8500 |
| H17 | 4500 |
| H18 | 1200 |
| | |
| I19 | 4200 |
| I20 | 18000 |
| | |
| J15 through J20 | No |

Note: In real life the transaction descriptions include numbers and names from the source documents. If you need information about a certain transaction, you would be able to find the source documents in the file cabinet based upon the journal description.

13. Assume in this transaction that you pay the first and last months' rent to Office Management Company. Check number 102 is used. The check amount is $4,000. Notice how the landlord's name is abbreviated to fit in the limited space. Enter the following:

| Cell Locations | Information |
| --- | --- |
| B22 through B24 | J003 |
| C22 through C24 | 10/2/93 |
| | |
| D22 | 5500 |
| D23 | 1400 |
| D24 | 1100 |
| | |
| F22 | Rent Expense |
| F23 | Prepaid Rent |
| F24 | Cash |
| | |
| G22 through G24 | Ck102 Off Mgt Co |
| | |
| H22 and H23 | 2000 |
| I24 | 4000 |
| | |
| J22 through J24 | No |

14. Go to cell I60. The total crebits (46,200.00) in cell I60 should equal the total debits in cell H60. If they are not equal, compare your results with the tutorial illustrated on the next page. If the entries on your screen look like the numbers in the tutorial, you may have entered the numbers as text. For example, if you typed 20,000.00 in cell H12 (instead of 20000), you entered the amount as text. Text information cannot be added to numbers or included in formulas. Make any necessary corrections.

15. Save your journal as **a:\tut2** and print it using a compressed type font in a portrait orientation. Instructions for doing this are in the Introduction chapter. Exit the program.

**Figure 2-A:  Journal Without Column Totals (Footers)**

Student Name
999-99-9999
Acct150
Chapter 2
15-Sep-93

STARVING ACTOR'S POOL SERVICE          G/L JOURNAL          PAGE 1

| TRNS NMBR | TRNS DATE | ACCT NMBR | ACCOUNT NAME | TRANSACTION DESCRIPTION | DEBIT AMOUNT | CREDIT AMOUNT | POSTED YES/NO |
|---|---|---|---|---|---|---|---|
| J001 | 10/1/93 | 1100 | Cash | Cash Investment In Bus | 20,000.00 | | No |
| J001 | 10/1/93 | 3100 | Your Last Name, Capital | Cash Investment In Bus | | 20,000.00 | No |
| J002 | 10/1/93 | 1700 | Furniture & Equipment | Ck101 Ima Starr | 8,000.00 | | No |
| J002 | 10/1/93 | 1800 | Transportation Equipment | Ck101 Ima Starr | 8,500.00 | | No |
| J002 | 10/1/93 | 1200 | Accounts Receivable | Ck101 Ima Starr | 4,500.00 | | No |
| J002 | 10/1/93 | 1300 | Supplies | Ck101 Ima Starr | 1,200.00 | | No |
| J002 | 10/1/93 | 1100 | Cash | Ck101 Ima Starr | | 4,200.00 | No |
| J002 | 10/1/93 | 2100 | Notes Payable | Ck101 Ima Starr | | 18,000.00 | No |
| J003 | 10/1/93 | 5500 | Rent Expense | Ck102 Off Mgt Co | 2,000.00 | | No |
| J003 | 10/1/93 | 1400 | Prepaid Rent | Ck102 Off Mgt Co | 2,000.00 | | No |
| J003 | 10/1/93 | 1100 | Cash | Ck102 Off Mgt Co | | 4,000.00 | No |

# Project:

Assume for the purpose of this project that you are still the owner of the swimming pool maintenance business. You will be entering additional transactions for the month of October 1993.

1. Do the following in accordance with the instructions in the Introduction chapter:

> Load **Microsoft**® **Excel** and open the file: **a:\tut2.xls**
> Save the file as **a:\proj2**

2. The chart of accounts on the next page is shown in a T format to help you analyze the transactions in this project. The account names appear in the columns that would show their normal account balances. The asset accounts are shown on the debit side of the T because they normally have debit balances. The liability accounts are shown on the credit side because they normally have credit balances.

The Owner's Equity accounts are shown on both sides of the T. The Capital and Revenue accounts are shown on the credit side because they indicate increases in owner's equity. The Drawing and Expense accounts are shown on the debit side because they show decreases.

3. The following events are typical when you purchase an existing business. Most of them result in transactions. Some do not. Record the transactions on the G/L Journal page starting with transaction number J004:

> Note: The G/L Journal is the same as the General Journal discussed in your accounting textbook. It is called the G/L Journal because it is located in the General Ledger module of most accounting software packages.

Oct. 3    You apply for a sales tax permit (resale permit) in the name of the business at the State Office Building. No deposit is required.

You apply for a business license at City Hall and a fictitious name permit at the County Administration Building. You pay a total of $85 out of your pocket. Later in the morning you write check number 103 to yourself to cover those expenses. The debit is to Taxes and Licenses Expense. This is transaction number J004.

Note: A fictitious name permit identifies Starving Actor's Pool Service as a fictitious name. The permit also identifies who owns the business.

Oct. 4    You decide to purchase a pickup truck so that there will be one for you and one for the employee who came with the business. The purchase price of the truck is $8,000. You pay 25% down (check number 104) to Freeway Motors and finance the rest with a note.

**Figure 2-B:  Accounts in Financial Statement Order**

CHART OF ACCOUNTS

| | | | | |
|---|---|---|---|---|
| 1100 | Cash | | | |
| 1200 | Accounts Receivable | | | |
| 1300 | Supplies | | | |
| 1400 | Prepaid Rent | | | |
| 1450 | Prepaid Insurance | | | |
| 1500 | Security Deposit | | | |
| 1700 | Furniture & Equipment | | | |
| 1800 | Transportation Equipment | | | |
| | | 2100 | Notes Payable | |
| | | 2200 | Accounts Payable | |
| | | 2400 | Payroll Taxes Payable | |
| | | 3100 | Owner's Name, Capital | |
| 3500 | Owner's Name, Drawing | | | |
| | | 4100 | Service Revenue | |
| 5100 | Advertising Expense | | | |
| 5300 | Insurance Expense | | | |
| 5350 | Interest Expense | | | |
| 5400 | Meals & Entertainment Expense | | | |
| 5500 | Rent Expense | | | |
| 5550 | Repairs Expense | | | |
| 5600 | Salaries Expense | | | |
| 5650 | Supplies Expense | | | |
| 5700 | Taxes & Licenses Expense | | | |
| 5750 | Telephone Expense | | | |
| 5800 | Truck Expense | | | |
| 5900 | Utilities Expense | | | |

Oct. 4   You go with Ima Starr, the previous owner of the business, to his insurance broker to get a business liability insurance policy. The broker advises you to also get workers' compensation insurance to cover your employee since it is required by law. You write check number 105 to Metro Insurance Company in the amount of $3,600 for the one-year policies.

The rest of the day is spent visiting the clients on Ima Starr's pool route. He introduces you as the new owner of the business and assures the clients that the quality of service will remain the same. They appreciate the fact that Ima Starr's one employee will be working for you.

Oct. 5   You meet your employee at Discount Maintenance Supplies. You establish credit and purchase $210 worth of chemicals on account. Their invoice is number 7582.

While your employee heads off to clean pools, you go to Hollywood Speedy Print to purchase some business cards. You take a coffee break and go back to pick up your cards. Check number 106 is written in the amount of $120. Since it will take you about a year to pass out all of the cards, an asset account (Supplies) is debited.

The rest of the day is spent knocking on doors. Ima Starr was kind enough to leave you his list of homes and businesses that have pools. Your goal is to double the size of your pool route. Call it beginner's luck--you sign up Mrs. Bit Parts as a new client. You will begin cleaning her pool next week for $120 per month. No advance payment is collected.

Oct. 8   You call Pacific Bell Telephone Company to inform them that you are the new owner of Starving Actor's Pool Service. The existing phone service and yellow page advertising will remain unchanged.

You also call Pacific Gas & Electric Company to inform them of a change in ownership. Since you are new to the Hollywood area, they request a $200 security deposit. It will be returned to you in six months if you maintain good credit with them. You mail them check number 107.

You pay Terri Daly, your only employee, her wages for the first half of the month. Her gross pay (Salaries Expense) is $700. Payroll taxes amounting to $200 are withheld. You owe those taxes to the federal and state governments. Check number 108 is written for the net amount (her take-home pay). Make sure the total debits equal the total credits in this compound journal entry. She thanks you for paying her a week early.

Oct. 9    The mail arrives at 9:30 a.m. Checks from some of your clients amounting to $2,400 are received on account. Enter each check separately:

Ck852 University Apts....................................................... $900
Ck753 Bev Hills Shp Ctr.................................................... $650
Ck951 Sunset Condos....................................................... $850

Go to cell I60. The Debit and Credit columns should total 61,515.00. You deposit the checks at your bank and head for the Internal Revenue Service. You apply for a federal employee identification number and pick up some payroll tax deposit coupons. You then head for the State Government Building to get a state employee identification number. You pick up payroll tax deposit coupons there too.

The rest of the day you spend knocking on doors. Nobody is home. You come up with no new clients. After supper you attend a pool service management seminar sponsored by Discount Maintenance Supplies. One of the tips you pick up is that pool builders are a good source of leads for new maintenance contracts. You plan to call on them in the near future.

4. Create a second page of the G/L Journal by doing the following:

Arrow to cell **A7**
Press the **<Shift>** key down and keep it down
Arrow to cell **J10** then release the **<Shift>** key
Drag **Edit** to **Copy** and arrow to cell **A67**
Press the **<Shift>** key down and keep it down
Arrow to cell **J70** then release the **<Shift>** key
Drag **Edit** to **Paste**
Type **PAGE 2** in cell **J67** and press **<Enter>**

5.  Record the following transactions on G/L Journal page 2:

Oct. 15    You take the office manager of one of the swimming pool contracting companies to lunch. The bill at the Cozy Corner Restaurant totals $65, which you pay for with check number 109.

Oct. 30    You invoice your clients for services rendered during the month of October. Each invoice is entered separately on account.

> Inv456 Sunset Condos.......................................................  $850
> Inv457 Hollywood Office..................................................  $975
> Inv458 Vine Street Apts...................................................  $750
> Inv459 University Apts......................................................  $900
> Inv460 Hollywood Hotel...................................................  $880
> Inv461 Bev Hills Shp Ctr.................................................  $650
> Inv462 Mrs. Bit Parts........................................................   $90

Oct. 31    You receive the statement from Pacific Bell Telephone Company. The telephone charges amount to $120, and yellow page advertising costs $280 for the month of October. You question the value of the yellow page advertising, but you record the bill as a liability.

You also receive the Pacific Gas & Electric Company statement. The October charges for this utility amount to $140. You will pay the bill in November.

You pay your loyal employee the same amount for the last half of the month as the first half. Check number 110 is used.

You write check number 111 to yourself in the amount of $300 to cover some personal expenses.

You write check number 112 to Terri Daly in the amount of $90 to cover gasoline purchased and an oil change done on the company truck during October.

6.  Foot (total) the Debit and Credit columns of page 2 using SUM functions. Your column totals should equal 6,790.00. Save your journal as **a:\proj2** and print it. Exit the program.

7. (Optional) Type a memo to your instructor explaining the similarities and differences between hand-prepared and computer-prepared journals.

## *Assignment:*

Do the journal entries called for in the tutorial and the project by hand.

# Chapter Two Transmittal Sheet for Excel

A. Hand in this page to your instructor with the following items attached in the order requested:

    1. Project G/L Journal
    2. Hand written assignment
    3. Project step 7 memo to instructor (optional)

B. Refer to your project G/L Journal to determine total assets, total liabilities and total owner's equity:

| ASSETS | LIABILITIES | OWNER'S EQUITY |
|--------|-------------|----------------|
|        |             |                |

Hint: Total assets should equal total liabilities plus total owner's equity. The owner's equity T account should include Capital, Withdrawals, Revenue, and Expenses.

## Chapter Three

# Service Business Worksheet

## Chapter Objectives:

A. Create six-column worksheets (spreadsheets) that show the trial balance, adjusting entries, and adjusted trial balance for a service business.

B. Apply the revenue (or realization) principle when preparing period-end adjusting entries.

C. Apply the matching principle when preparing period-end adjusting entries.

D. Review the rules of debit and credit.

## Tutorial:

Assume that you recently landed a job with a local CPA firm. You are asked to prepare the year-end adjusting entries for a client, Uptown Playhouse. Your boss tells you that this client was instructed to use a "checkbook" (cash basis) method of accounting. You know the other employees call it the KISS (Keep It Simple Stupid) method. You soon discover that the volunteers, who help out with the Uptown Playhouse financial records used no particular method at all.

1. Do the following according to the instructions in the Introduction chapter:

### Load **Microsoft**® **Excel** and run **Info Macro**

2. Make sure your information block shows Chapter 3 and today's date.

3. Change the width of column B as follows:

> Click on **Column B Header** (above cell B1)
> Drag **Format** to **Column Width**
> Type **24** and click on **OK**

Change the widths of columns C and D to 10, F and H to 9, I and J to 12, and E and G to 4. Make sure your <CapsLock> light is on. It is above the 10-key pad on most computers.

4. Enter the "who, what, and when" in the worksheet heading:

> Type **UPTOWN PLAYHOUSE** in cell **D1** and press **<Enter>**
> Type **WORKSHEET** in cell **D2** and press **<Enter>**
> Type **="DECEMBER 31, 1993"** in cell **D3** and press **<Enter>**

> Note: the **="  "** allows you to enter the date as a string of text.

5. Enter the following column headings:

> Type **TRIAL BALANCE** in cell **C7** and press **<Enter>**
> Type **ADJUSTING ENTRIES** in cell **E7** and press **<Enter>**
> Type **ADJUSTED TRIAL BALANCE** in cell **I7** and press **<Enter>**

> Type **DEBIT** in cells **C8, F8**, and **I8** and press **<Enter>** each time
> Type **CREDIT** in cells **D8, H8**, and **J8** and press **<Enter>** each time

6. To place a line under the column headings:

> Arrow to cell **B9**

> With the **<Shift>** Key Pressed Down,
> Arrow to cell **J9** and release the **<Shift>** key

> Drag **Format** to **Border**
> Click on **Top** and **OK**
> Drag **Format** to **Row Height**
> Type **2** and click on **OK**

Make sure your <CapsLock> light is off.

7.  Enter the following information from the Uptown Playhouse financial records starting in cell B10:

| | | |
|---|---|---|
| Cash | 8523.11 | |
| Prepaid Insurance | 2644.44 | |
| Lighting Equipment | 15240.00 | |
| Accum Deprn--Light Equip | | 3048.00 |
| Unearned Ticket Revenue | | 12300.00 |
| E. Scrooge, Capital | | 6221.98 |
| E. Scrooge, Drawing | 24000.00 | |
| Ticket Revenue | | 192150.00 |
| Advertising Expense | 11080.00 | |
| Payroll Taxes Expense | 11641.10 | |
| Rent Expense | 36000.00 | |
| Salaries Expense | 97000.00 | |
| Utilities Expense | 7591.33 | |

Note: Be sure to type the Accumulated Depreciation--Lighting Equipment account in the abbreviated form shown above.

8.  Create a line in cells B23 through J23, as you did in step 6, but DO NOT CHANGE THE ROW HEIGHT.

9.  Notice that when you copy the SUM function in cell C24 to the adjoining cell locations, the cell references automatically change for each column total.

Type **TOTALS** in cell **B24** and press **< Enter >**
Type **= sum(** in cell **C24** BUT DO NOT PRESS **< Enter >**

Drag cell **C10** through **C22**
Type **)** and press **< Enter >**

The amount, 213719.98, should appear in cell C24.

With the **< Shift >** key pressed down:
Arrow To cell **J24** and release the **< Shift >** key

Drag **Edit** to **Fill Right**

Your trial balance credit column total should also equal 213719.98.

10. The following matrix, which illustrates the rules of debit and credit, may be of help to you in this chapter:

| INCREASE ACCOUNT BALANCE | | | | |
|---|---|---|---|---|
| Debit | Credit | Credit | Credit | Debit |
| ASSETS | LIABILITIES | EQUITY | REVENUE | EXPENSE |
| Credit | Debit | Debit | Debit | Credit |
| DECREASE ACCOUNT BALANCE | | | | |

The matrix above is easy to use when you prepare adjusting entries. First, decide what type of account you are planning to change. In other words, is it an Asset, Liability, Owner's Equity, Revenue, or Expense account? Next, decide whether you want the account balance increased or decreased. Finally, use the matrix above to decide whether the increase or decrease requires a debit or credit entry.

11. An analysis of the Prepaid Insurance account indicates that $1,322.22 should be written off to the Insurance Expense account. You can use the above matrix to decide whether to debit or credit Prepaid Insurance. Prepaid Insurance is an asset account. You want to decrease the balance. The adjusting entry to that account must be a credit.

Since debits must equal credits, the adjusting entry to the Insurance Expense account must be a debit. The matrix above indicates that a debit to an expense account increases the balance in that account.

> Press <Ctrl> <Home> and arrow to cell **A19**
> Click on **row 19 header** (next to cell A19)
> Drag **Edit** to **Insert**
> Type **Insurance Expense** in cell **B19** and press <Enter>
>
> Type **(a)** in cell **E19** and press <Enter>
> Type **1322.22** in cell **F19** and press <Enter>
> Type **(a)** in cell **G11** and press <Enter>
> Type **1322.22** in cell **H11** and press <Enter>
> Type **(a) Ins Exp Adj** in cell **B27** and press <Enter>

12. The next adjusting entry is for Depreciation Expense in the amount of $3,048.00. The matrix on page 3-4 indicates that you must debit the Depreciation Expense account to increase its balance. The credit will go to Accumulated Depreciation--Lighting Equipment. Even though this account is in the asset range, it is not debited. It is called a *contra-asset account.* *Contra* means opposite. A *contra-asset account* shows the decrease from historical cost (shown in the companion asset account) to book value.

> Press **<Home>** and click on **row 19 header**
> Drag **Edit** to **Insert**
> Type **Depreciation Expense** in cell **B19** and press **<Enter>**
> Type **(b)** in cell **E19** and press **<Enter>**
>
> Type **3048** in cell **F19** and press **<Enter>**
> Type **(b)** in cell **G13** and press **<Enter>**
> Type **3048** in cell **H13**
> Type **(b) Deprn Exp Adj** in cell **B29** and press **<Enter>**

13. An analysis of the Unearned Ticket Revenue account indicates that $1,200 (ticket sales for next season) is mixed in with ticket sales for this season. An analysis of the Ticket Revenue account indicates that $800 (ticket sales for next season) is mixed in with ticket sales for this season. Some adjusting entries, like the following, can also be correcting entries:

> Type **(c)** in cell **E14** and press **<Enter>**
> Type **10300** in cell **F14**
> Type **(c)** in cell **G17** and press **<Enter>**
> Type **10300** in cell **H17** and press **<Enter>**
> Type **(c) Ticket Rev Adj** in cell **B30** and press **<Enter>**

14. Format the numbers in the Debit and Credit columns of the worksheet:

> Arrow to cell **C10** and drag cell **C10** to cell **J26** (you can do it)
> Drag **Format** to **Number** and click on **#,##0.00** and **OK**

15. You can produce the correct numbers in the Adjusted Trial Balance Debit column using a tool provided by **Microsoft® Excel**. It is called the IF function. In the IF function a logical test is set up. If the result of the test is positive (or true), then one answer happens. If the result of the test is negative (or false), then another answer happens.

In the worksheet you are preparing, an Adjusted Trial Balance debit entry (on a particular line) should happen only if a Trial Balance debit plus any Adjusting Entry debit minus any Trial Balance credit minus any Adjusting Entry credit yields a number greater than zero. Otherwise, nothing should go in the Adjusted Trial Balance debit cell on that line.

Arrow to cell **I7** then arrow to cell **I10**

Type  **= if(0 < c10 + f10-d10-h10,c10 + f10-d10-h10,"**
         (DO NOT PRESS **<Enter>** AFTER THE **"**)

Press **<SpaceBar>** instead
Type  **")**  and press **<Enter>**

Note: The balance, 8523.11, should appear in cell I10.

```
┌─IF Function Test For A Debit Entry In Cell I10─┐
│                                                │
│     0<C10+F10-D10-H10 is the logical test      │
│                                                │
│     C10+F10-D10-H10 is the answer if the       │
│              test is positive                  │
│                                                │
│     " " (or a blank space) is the answer       │
│              if the test is negative           │
└────────────────────────────────────────────────┘
```

16. To copy the function to other cells in column I:

    Drag:        **cell I10 to cell I24**
    Drag:        **Edit to Fill Down**

Slowly arrow down to cell I24 and notice how the IF function changes for each cell in the Adjusted Trial Balance Debit column. The Debit column total should be 216,767.98.

17. The IF function for the Credit column cells in the Adjusted Trial Balance is similar except you are looking for a positive number when the sum of the credits is greater than the sum of the debits.

    Arrow to cell **J7** then arrow to cell **J10**
    Type  **= if(0 < d10 + h10-c10-f10,d10 + h10-c10-f10," ")**  and press
            **<Enter>** (nothing should appear in cell J10)

```
┌─ IF Function Test For A Credit Entry In Cell J10 ─┐
│                                                   │
│        0<D10+H10-C10-F10 is the logical test      │
│                                                   │
│        D10+H10-C10-F10 is the answer if the       │
│                test is positive                   │
│                                                   │
│        " " (or a blank space) is the answer       │
│                if the test is negative            │
│                                                   │
└───────────────────────────────────────────────────┘
```

18. Copy the IF function to cells J11 through J24. The total in cell I26 should equal the total in cell J26. In other words, the total debits in the Adjusted Trial Balance columns should equal the total credits.

19. Center the labels (column headings) in cells C8 through J8:

> Arrow to cell **C8**
> With **< Shift >** Key Pressed Down,
> Arrow to **J8** and release the **< Shift >** key
> Drag **Format** to **Alignment** and click on **Center** and **OK**

Also, make sure the letters in columns E and G are right aligned.

20. You should also move the labels *Trial Balance* and *Adjusting Entries* so that they are centered over the Debit and Credit columns. You cannot drag Format to Alignment for these labels, because they span more than one cell. Use the <F2> edit key, arrow to the left side of each label, press the <SpaceBar> a few times, then press <Enter> when you think you have what you want. Getting these labels centered properly requires a "trial-and-error" approach. Also, clear the ### in cells E26 and G26.

> Hint: Arrow to each cell and drag Edit to Clear.

21. In this step you are creating a double rule below the column totals:

> Arrow to cell **C27**
>
> With the **< Shift >** Key Pressed Down:
> Arrow to cell **J27** and release the **< Shift >** key
> Drag **Format** to **Border**
> Click on **Top, Bottom,** and **OK**

## Figure 3-A:  Six-Column Worksheet

Student Name
999-99-9999
Acct150
Chapter 3
15-Sep-93

UPTOWN PLAYHOUSE
WORKSHEET
DECEMBER 31, 1993

| | TRIAL BALANCE | | ADJUSTING ENTRIES | | ADJUSTED TRIAL BALANCE | |
|---|---|---|---|---|---|---|
| | DEBIT | CREDIT | DEBIT | CREDIT | DEBIT | CREDIT |
| Cash | 8,523.11 | | | | 8,523.11 | |
| Prepaid Insurance | 2,644.44 | | | (a) 1,322.22 | 1,322.22 | |
| Lighting Equipment | 15,240.00 | | | | 15,240.00 | |
| Accum Deprn--Light Equip | | 3,048.00 | | (b) 3,048.00 | | 6,096.00 |
| Unearned Ticket Revenue | | 12,300.00 | (c) 10,300.00 | | | 2,000.00 |
| E. Scrooge, Capital | | 6,221.98 | | | | 6,221.98 |
| E. Scrooge, Drawing | 24,000.00 | | | | 24,000.00 | |
| Ticket Revenue | | 192,150.00 | | (c) 10,300.00 | | 202,450.00 |
| Advertising Expense | 11,080.00 | | | | 11,080.00 | |
| Depreciation Expense | | | (b) 3,048.00 | | 3,048.00 | |
| Insurance Expense | | | (a) 1,322.22 | | 1,322.22 | |
| Payroll Taxes Expense | 11,641.10 | | | | 11,641.10 | |
| Rent Expense | 36,000.00 | | | | 36,000.00 | |
| Salaries Expense | 97,000.00 | | | | 97,000.00 | |
| Utilities Expense | 7,591.33 | | | | 7,591.33 | |
| TOTALS | 213,719.98 | 213,719.98 | 14,670.22 | 14,670.22 | 216,767.98 | 216,767.98 |

(a) Ins Exp Adj
(b) Deprn Exp Adj
(c) Ticket Rev Adj

21. (continued)

Drag **Format** to **Row Height**
Type **2** and click on **OK**

22. Save your worksheet as **a:\tut3** and print it using a portrait orientation and condensed type according to the instructions in the Introduction chapter. Exit the program.

# *Project:*

Ms. French, owner of the Good Earth Travel Agency, gives you a trial balance that was taken from her general ledger as of December 31, 1993. You are to prepare a six-column worksheet.

1. Do the following according to the instructions in the Introduction chapter:

Load **Microsoft**® **Excel** and run **Info Macro**

2. The following accounts and their balances are listed in alphabetical order. Please arrange them in financial statement order on the worksheet:

| | | |
|---|---|---|
| Accounts Receivable | 6502.76 | |
| Accum Deprn--Furn & Fix | | 11077.00 |
| Cash | 3122.33 | |
| Commissions & Fees | | 97830.55 |
| Furniture & Fixtures | 19335.00 | |
| Insurance Expense | 455.00 | |
| Office Supplies | 1040.88 | |
| Office Supplies Expense | 2812.93 | |
| Payroll Taxes Expense | 2055.37 | |
| Prepaid Insurance | 1200.00 | |
| Rent Expense | 7200.00 | |
| Salaries Expense | 18255.66 | |
| Telephone & Utilities Expense | 11802.44 | |
| Tina French, Capital | | 152.82 |
| Tina French, Withdrawals | 36000.00 | |
| Unearned Revenue | | 722.00 |

3. Prepare adjusting entries based on the following information:

a. The Cash account should be reduced by $450 for bank service charges. The high dollar amount is due to heavy use of bank credit cards.

b. A one-year business insurance policy was purchased on April Fool's Day. The total amount of this policy was put into Prepaid Insurance. The amount in Insurance Expense is from the policy purchased the year before and is an expired cost.

c. The cost of office supplies on hand on December 31 is $708.

d. The depreciation for the year amounts to $6,323.

e. Of the customer deposits sitting in the Unearned Revenue account, $550 have not yet been earned. Also a Commissions Receivable account must be set up for $2,945 in overrides earned but not yet received from the airlines. Make one compound journal entry for the two revenue adjustments.

4. Save your worksheet as **a:\proj3** and print it in a portrait orientation with compressed type according to the instructions in the Introduction chapter. Exit the program.

5. (Optional) Tina French will be hiring a new bookkeeper in two months. She needs a typed list of six questions with answers (not three of each) about the accounting cycle that she can ask the job applicants. Prepare the list for her in good form.

6. (Optional) Compare and contrast a computer-prepared worksheet with a hand-prepared worksheet.

## Assignment:

Prepare by hand the worksheet described in the project. Don't be afraid to use your accounting textbook to find accounts in financial statement order.

Student Name:_____

Date:_____

# *Chapter Three Transmittal Sheet for Excel*

A. Hand in this page to your instructor with the following items attached in the order requested:

1. Project six-column worksheet
2. Hand-written assignment
3. Project step 5 job applicant questions (optional)
4. Project step 6 comparing and contrasting a computer-prepared worksheet with a hand-prepared worksheet (optional)

B. Refer to your project worksheet to answer the following questions:

1. Write the formula or function that is in the cell where the 36,000 figure appears in the Adjusted Trial Balance Debit column.

2. Write the formula or function that provides the total for the Adjusting Entries Credit column.

3. If you were to use the same worksheet again for December 31, 1994, what cell range would you erase or clear so that you could enter new numbers?

Notes:

# Chapter Four

# *Automatic Financial Statements*

---

## *Chapter Objectives:*

A. Create a classified balance sheet, a statement of owner's equity, and an income statement for a service business.

B. Show how formulas are used to automate the transfer of information from a "six-column worksheet" window to "financial statement" windows.

C. Show the importance of arranging accounts on the worksheet in financial statement order.

## *Tutorial:*

Ms. E. Scrooge, owner of Uptown Playhouse, wants to see financial statements that are based on the six-column worksheet you created in the Chapter 3 tutorial. You decide (or this workbook decides for you) that if you are going to prepare financial statements, they should be designed so that they can be easily updated at the end of each new accounting period.

You may have noticed, in Chapter 3, that you placed new account names in financial statement order on the worksheet you prepared. The advantage of placing all account names in financial statement order will become apparent to you as you create the balance sheet, statement of owner's equity, and the income statement.

1. Do the following according to the instructions in the Introduction chapter:

**Load Microsoft® Excel but do not run the Info Macro**

2. To retrieve the worksheet that you completed in the Chapter 3 tutorial make sure your data disk is in the A drive:

> Drag **File** to **Open** and click on **[-A-]** in the Directories box
> Click on **OK, TUT3.XLS** and **OK**
> Press **<Ctrl> <Home>** to move the curser to cell **A1**

3. Change the chapter number in cell B4 to Chapter 4. Change the date in cell B5 to today's date. Save this worksheet as **a:\tut4iws** at this time.

The worksheet saved as a:\tut4iws.xls is now in a window designated as the independent window. The balance sheet you will be creating will be in a window designated as the dependent window. You will be setting up external cell references that will link cell locations in the dependent window to cell locations in the independent window.

The time advantage of linking two windows is tremendous when financial statements are prepared over and over again. Each time you change dates and dollar amounts, this new information is automatically transferred to the dependent financial statements.

4. Set up the first dependent window as follows:

> Drag **Window** to **Sheet1** and click on column **A Header** (above cell A1)
> Drag **Format** to **Column Width**
> Type **1** and click on **OK** (if you didn't already press <Enter>)

5. Set the widths of the following columns:

| Column | Width |
|--------|-------|
| B | 13 |
| C | 15 |
| D | 1 |
| E | 12 |
| F | 2 |
| G | 1 |
| H | 12 |

6. Transfer the information block in TUT4IWS.XLS (containing your name) to Sheet1.

Type **=tut4iws.xls!b1** in cell **B1** of Sheet1

What you just typed in cell B1 is called an "external cell reference". It references a cell location that is outside your active window. The portion of the external cell reference after the exclamation point (the "b1") is called a *relative cell address*. It will change as the information you typed in cell B1 is copied to new cells:

Drag cell **B1** to cell **B5** in Sheet1
Drag **Edit** to **Fill Down** and arrow to cell **B5**  s l o w l y

Notice the change in the relative cell address? Most of the information originally created by the Info Macro should now appear on Sheet1. The exception is the date. The number that appears in cell B5 is a *date index number*. You need to convert it to a recognizable date and to a left-justified alignment:

Click on cell **B5 and** drag **Format to Number**
Click on the **DownArrow** in the Format Number box until
d-mmm-yy appears
Click on **d-mmm-yy** and **OK**
Drag **Format** to **Alignment** and click on **Left** and **OK**

7. Save *Sheet1* as **a:\tut4dbs** at this time. The letters *dbs* stand for dependent window--balance sheet.

8. Exit the program. You are asked to exit the program so that you can learn that there is a protocol you must follow when you open independent and dependent windows. You must always open an independent window first. Then, when you open a dependent window, the external cell references in that window have the independent cells available for data transfer.

```
┌──────The Rule For Opening Windows──────────────────┐
│                                                    │
│     Always Open The Independent Window             │
│                                                    │
│     Before You Open The Dependent Window(s)        │
└────────────────────────────────────────────────────┘
```

8. (continued)

> Load **Microsoft**® **Excel**
> Open **A:\TUT4IWS.XLS**  (the independent window)
>
> Note:  You may have to click on the DownArrow in the Files Box until you find the above file name.
>
> Open  **A:\TUT4DBS.XLS**  (the dependent window)
> Drag **Window** to **Sheet1** and drag **File** to **Close**
> Drag **Window** to **Arrange All**

The dependent window should be on the left-hand side of your computer screen.  The independent window should be on the right.

9.  Make the balance sheet heading as follows:

> Arrow to cell **E1** in **TUT4DBS.XLS** then arrow to cell **D3**
> Press  =  BUT DO NOT PRESS <**Enter**> here!
> Click on any cell in **TUT4IWS.XLS** and arrow to cell **D1**

The moving bank of dots going around cell D1 is called a *marquee*.  It looks like a movie theatre marquee.  It is used to designate a cell or range of cells when a different cell is active.

> Press <**Enter**>  (Uptown Playhouse should appear in cell D3)
> Type  **BALANCE SHEET**  in cell **D4** of **TUT4DBS.XLS**
>     and press <**Enter**>
>
> Arrow to cell **D5** and press   =   (the equal key)
> Click on any cell in **TUT4IWS.XLS**
> Arrow to cell **D3** and press <**Enter**>

The heading in TUT3DBS.XLS should be centered:

> Drag cell **D3** to cell **D5**
> Drag **Format** to **Alignment** and click on **Center** and **OK**

The "who, what, and when" of your balance sheet heading should look properly centered.

14. (continued)

      Arrow to cell **B15** and press **< SpaceBar >** twice
      Type **PROPERTY, PLANT & EQUIPMENT** and press **< Enter >**

      Arrow to cell **B16**, press = BUT DO NOT PRESS < Enter > here
      Click on any cell in **TUT4IWS.XLS**
      Arrow to cell **B12** and press **< Enter >**
      Type **Less: Accumulated Depreciation** in cell **B17** of
          **TUT4DBS.XLS** and press **< Enter >**

      Type **$** in cell **D16** of **TUT4DBS.XLS** and press **< Enter >**
      Arrow to cell **E16** and press =

Transfer the dollar amount for the Lighting Equipment as in step 13. The amount *15240* should come from cell I12 of the independent window.

The dollar amount for the accumulated depreciation is a positive figure in the Adjusted Trial Balance Credit column. It has to appear as a negative figure in the balance sheet.

      Arrow to cell **E17** in **TUT4DBS.XLS**
      Press **–** (the minus key)

Transfer the dollar amount as in step 13. The minus amount *-6096* should appear in cell E17 of TUT4DBS.XLS.

      Drag cell **D18** to cell **E18**
      Drag **Format** to **Border** and click on **Top** and **OK**

      Drag **Format** to **Row Height**, type **3** and click on **OK**
      Arrow to cell **B19** and press **< SpaceBar >** twice

      Type **TOTAL PROP., PLANT & EQUIP.** and press **< Enter >**
      Type **=e16+e17** in cell **H19** and press **< Enter >**

15. To format the amounts in the monetary columns:

      Drag cell **E11** to cell **H19**
      Drag **Format** to **Number** and click on **#,##0.00** and **OK**

16. In this step you will be placing a rule under 9,144.00. Notice that the rule is put at the top of the cells below the numbers rather than in the cells that the numbers occupy. Also the row height of the cells with the line in them is reduced.

> Drag cell **G20** to cell **H20**
> Drag **Format** to **Border** and click on **Top** and **OK**
> Drag **Format** to **Row Height**, type **2** and click on **OK**

17. Complete the Asset section of the balance sheet.

> Arrow to cell **B21** and press **< SpaceBar >** twice
> Type **TOTAL ASSETS** and press **< Enter >**
>
> Type **$** in cell **G21** and press **< Enter >**
> Type **= sum(h14:h19)** in cell **H21** and press **< Enter >**
>
> Drag **Format** to **Number** and click on **#,##0.00** and **OK**

18. To put a double rule in the cells under $18,989.33:

> Drag cell **G22** to cell **H22**
> Drag **Format** to **Border** and click on **Top, Bottom** and **OK**
> Drag **Format** to **Row Height**
> Type **4** and press **OK**

19. Complete the rest of the balance sheet so that it looks similar to the one on the next page. The Capital account balance is from the equation:

> Assets – Liabilities = Owner's Equity

20. Save the balance sheet as **a:\tut4dbs.xls** and replace the existing file. Print it using a portrait orientation and regular-sized type. Use your Preview Option. Adjust the A column width until the balance sheet is correctly positioned on the page (with equal left and right margins).

## Figure 4-A: Dependent Balance Sheet

```
Student Name
999-99-9999
Acct150           UPTOWN PLAYHOUSE
Chapter 4         BALANCE SHEET
15-Sep-93         DECEMBER 31, 1993


                        ASSETS


  CURRENT ASSETS:
Cash                       $     8,523.11
Prepaid Insurance                1,322.22
  TOTAL CURRENT ASSETS                        $     9,845.33
  PROPERTY, PLANT & EQUIPMENT:
Lighting Equipment         $    15,240.00
Less: Accum. Depreciation       -6,096.00
  TOTAL PROP., PLANT & EQUIP.                       9,144.00
  TOTAL ASSETS                                $    18,989.33


            LIABILITIES & OWNER'S EQUITY


  CURRENT LIABILITIES:
Unearned Ticket Revenue                       $     2,000.00
  OWNER'S EQUITY:
E. Scrooge, Capital                               16,989.33
  TOTAL LIABILITIES & OWNER'S EQUITY          $    18,989.33
```

## *Project:*

It is a year later.  Ms. Esther Scrooge brings her financial records for Uptown Playhouse in to your office and offers her usual request:  "I need these financial statements YESTERDAY!"  You say that you will get them to her as soon as possible.

1.   Do the following in accordance with the instructions in the Introduction chapter:

**Load Microsoft® Excel but do not run Info Macro**

2. Open two windows and save them to new file names:

> Drag **File** to **Close** (to close Sheet1)
> Open **TUT4IWS.XLS** (from your data disk in the A drive)
> Open **TUT4DBS.XLS**
> Click on cell **B11** (where the word *cash* is displayed)
>    in **TUT4DBS.XLS**

Notice that the external cell reference is **=tut4iws.xls!b10**

> Click on any cell in **TUT4IWS.XLS**

Save your independent worksheet as **a:\proj4iws** at this time.

> Click on cell **B11** in **TUT4DBS.XLS** again

Notice that the external cell reference was automatically changed to the new independent worksheet name. If you arrow around the balance sheet, you'll notice that all of the external cell references were changed. Save your dependent worksheet as **a:\proj4dbs** at this time.

3. Change the financial information in the trial balance to the following:

| | | |
|---|---:|---:|
| Cash | 29375.42 | |
| Prepaid Insurance | 2908.40 | |
| Lighting Equipment | 15240.00 | |
| Accum Deprn--Light Equip | | 6096.00 |
| Unearned Ticket Revenue | | 14760.00 |
| E. Scrooge, Capital | | 16989.33 |
| E. Scrooge, Drawing | 30000.00 | |
| Ticket Revenue | | 218242.14 |
| Advertising Expense | 13288.00 | |
| Payroll Tax Expense | 12805.10 | |
| Rent Expense | 37800.00 | |
| Salaries Expense | 106700.00 | |
| Utilities Expense | 7970.55 | |

4. Input adjusting entries for the year ended **December 31, 1994,** based on the information at the top of the next page:

a. Insurance Expense for the year................................. $1,454.20

b. Depreciation Expense for the year........................... $3,048.00

c. Portion of the balance in the Unearned Ticket
   Revenue account that was earned...................... $12,885.00

5. Show the net income (loss) for the year in the lower right corner of the worksheet as follows:

Type **NET INCOME (LOSS)** in cell **H29** and press **<Enter>**
Type **=sum(j17:j24)-sum(i17:i24)** in cell **J29** and press **<Enter>**
Drag **Format** to **Number** and click on **#,##0.00** and **OK**

The check figure for cell J29 is: 48,061.29

6. Arrow around the balance sheet. Notice that you don't have to make any changes. All of the numbers and dates have been automatically transferred from the worksheet. The total assets should now equal $36,925.62. Save the balance sheet as **a:\proj4dbs.xls** and replace the file previously saved. Print the balance sheet--you shouldn't have to make any changes.

7. Change the balance sheet heading to one that would be suitable for a statement of owner's equity:

UPTOWN PLAYHOUSE
STATEMENT OF OWNER'S EQUITY
FOR THE YEAR ENDED
DECEMBER 31, 1994

Clear cells **B8** through **H33**. Reset the cell range to a standard row height. The statement of owner's equity should show the Capital account beginning balance that is transferred in from the worksheet. The net income comes from the lower right corner of the worksheet. The capital account ending balance should equal (but not come from) the amount shown in the balance sheet.

Save the statement of owner's equity as **a:\proj4doe** and print the statement.

8.   Create an automatic income statement for Uptown Playhouse. Subtract the expense amounts from the revenue amount to get the net income shown in the worksheet.  Save the income statement as  **a:\proj4dis**  and print it.  Exit the program.

9.  (Optional) Ms. Scrooge is considering purchasing the Playhouse.  The present owner has made the following offer:

| | |
|---|---|
| Land........................................................................ | $172,000 |
| Building................................................................... | 148,000 |
| | |
| Total Price............................................................... | $320,000 |
| Cash Down Payment................................................. | 20,000 |
| | |
| Mortgage Payable..................................................... | $300,000 |

Assume that the theatre and land could be hers (if she wants them) in early January 1995.  Also assume that the percentage increase in revenue and expenses will be the same in 1995 over 1994 as 1994 was over 1993.  The building should be depreciated over 30 years using the straight line method and no residual (or salvage) value.  Interest-only payments at 10% will be made for the first four years.  Will Ms. Scrooge be better off accepting the offer or remaining a tenant?  Support your conclusion (without considering the impact of income taxes) in a typed letter to her.

## *Assignment:*

Prepare by hand the worksheet and the three financial statements that are discussed in the project.  Models for the statement of owner's equity and income statement can be found in your accounting principles textbook.

# Chapter Four Transmittal Sheet for Excel

A. Hand in this page to your instructor with the following items attached in the order requested:

1. Project balance sheet
2. Project statement of owner's equity
3. Project income statement
4. Hand written assignment
5. Project step 9 letter to Ms. Scrooge (optional)

B. Refer to the dependent financial statement windows on your computer screen to answer the following questions:

1. The formula or function in the cell where the 29,375.42 figure appears in the balance sheet.

2. The formula or function providing the amount for the E. Scrooge, Capital account in the balance sheet.

3. The formula or function showing withdrawals as a minus number in the statement of owner's equity.

4. The formula or function providing the Utilities Expense account name in the income statement.

Notes:

# Chapter Five

# Merchandising Business

---

## Chapter Objectives:

A. Compare the adjusting process with the closing process to record inventory change in a periodic inventory system.

B. Format and analyze an income statement with a percent column for a merchandising business, a statement of owner's equity, and a classified balance sheet.

C. Compute the amount of a short-term loan request assuming a current ratio limit of two-to-one.

## Tutorial:

Most accounting principles textbooks address the issue of inventory change in a periodic inventory system by showing the traditional use of closing entries. The balance in the Inventory account at the beginning of the accounting period is usually transferred within the worksheet from the Adjusted Trial Balance Debit column to the Income Statement Debit column. The ending inventory is usually entered in the Income Statement Credit column and the Balance Sheet Debit column. Then all of the account balances showing up in the income statement columns are brought to zero through the use of closing entries.

This traditional method works well enough when ledger accounts are posted by hand; however, when the accounting work is done using a general ledger software package, adjusting entries are generally used. This method requires the addition of two new accounts in the Cost of Goods Sold section of the general ledger. These accounts are Beginning Inventory and Ending

Inventory. The use of adjusting entries is especially helpful when the computer software can be set up to close ranges of accounts automatically.

1. Do the following in accordance with the instructions in the Introduction chapter:

Load **Microsoft® Excel**

2. You formatted a six-column worksheet in Chapter 3, and you should have saved it to your data disk. To open that tutorial file:

Drag **File** to **Open** and click on **[-A-]** and **OK**
Click on **TUT3.XLS** and **OK**

3. Make some changes to the worksheet as follows:

Change the information in cell **B4** to **Chapter 5**
Enter today's date in cell **B5**

Type **POST CARDS 'N STUFF** in cell **D1** and press **<Enter>**

Note: The date in cell D3 should be December 31, 1993.

4. To clear some of the existing information in the worksheet:

Arrow to cell **B10** (where Cash is displayed)

With the **<Shift>** key pressed down,
Arrow to cell **H24**
Drag **Edit** to **Clear** and click on **OK**

Notice that the numbers in the Adjusted Trial Balance columns also disappear. Also clear the cells B28 through B30.

5. You need to make space for additional accounts as follows:

Click on **Row 11 Header** (next to cell A11)

With the **<Shift>** key pressed down,
Arrow to **Row 18 Header**
Drag **Edit** to **Insert**

6. Enter the following Trial Balance starting with cell B10:

| | | |
|---|---:|---:|
| Cash | 7881.10 | |
| Accounts Receivable | 12400.00 | |
| Merchandise Inventory | 130050.45 | |
| Prepaid Insurance | 3600.60 | |
| Furniture & Fixtures | 6600.00 | |
| Less: Accum Depreciation | | 4400.00 |
| Goodwill | 162000.00 | |
| Accounts Payable | | 32410.22 |
| Payroll Taxes Payable | | 2510.90 |
| P.C. Kujawski, Capital | | 245281.35 |
| P.C. Kujawski, Drawing | 66040.00 | |
| Gross Sales | | 441130.00 |
| Sales Returns & Allow | 4312.00 | |
| Sales Discounts | 5127.00 | |
| Purchases | 213491.50 | |
| Purchase Returns & Allow | | 6121.88 |
| Purchase Discounts | | 4013.44 |
| Freight-In | 9788.66 | |
| Commissions Expense | 66000.00 | |
| Payroll Taxes Expense | 9587.14 | |
| Rent Expense | 15000.00 | |
| Salaries Expense | 21150.00 | |
| Utilities Expense | 2839.34 | |
| | -------------- | -------------- |
| | 735867.79 | 735867.79 |

Note: The Goodwill account indicates that P.C. Kujawski purchased the business from someone else. The Goodwill account is classified as an Other Asset.

7. The Merchandise Inventory account balance, amounting to $130,050.45, represents the scenic postcards on hand at the beginning of the year. If the owner of this business is a good distributor, he has sold this inventory and has replaced it with new merchandise purchased during the year. This amount needs to be transferred to a Cost of Goods Sold account called Beginning Inventory:

Arrow to cell **B7** to bring the Trial Balance heading into view
Type **(a)** in cell **G12** and press **<Enter>**
Type **130050.45** in cell **H12** and press **<Enter>**
Click on the **Row 24 Header** and drag **Edit** to **Insert**

Note: The "Row 24 Header" is the number 24 on the left-hand side of the worksheet next to cell A24. The Purchases account should have moved to cell B25.

Type **Beginning Inventory** in cell **B24** and press < **Enter** >
Type **(a)** in cell **E24** and press < **Enter** >

Type **130050.45** in cell **F24** and press < **Enter** >
Type **(a) Beg Inv Adj** in cell **B38** and press < **Enter** >

8.  A physical count of the scenic postcards not sold was taken at the end of the year. This ending inventory, amounting to $134,234.77, has to be put into the asset account called Merchandise Inventory:

Arrow to cell **B7**
Type **(b)** in cell **E12** and press < **Enter** >
Type **134234.77** in cell **F12** and press < **Enter** >

Click on the **Row 29 header** and drag **Edit** to **Insert**
Type **Ending Inventory** in cell **B29** and press < **Enter** >
Type **(b)** in cell **G29** and press < **Enter** >

Type **134234.77** in cell **H29** and press < **Enter** >
Type **(b) End Inv Adj** in cell **B40** and press < **Enter** >

**Figure 5-A:  Selected T Accounts**

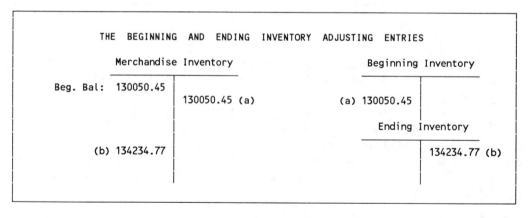

9.  Do an adjusting entry for Depreciation Expense in the amount of $1,100.00. Also adjust the Prepaid Insurance account to show that $1,800.30 has expired. These are adjusting entries (c) and (d) and should be explained in the lower-left corner of the worksheet.

# Figure 5-B:  Tutorial Worksheet (Without Company Heading)

| | TRIAL BALANCE DEBIT | TRIAL BALANCE CREDIT | ADJUSTING ENTRIES DEBIT | ADJUSTING ENTRIES CREDIT | ADJUSTED TRIAL BALANCE DEBIT | ADJUSTED TRIAL BALANCE CREDIT |
|---|---|---|---|---|---|---|
| Cash | 7,881.10 | | | | 7,881.10 | |
| Accounts Receivable | 12,400.00 | | | | 12,400.00 | |
| Merchandise Inventory | 130,050.45 | | (b) 134,234.77 | (a) 130,050.45 | 134,234.77 | |
| Prepaid Insurance | 3,600.60 | | | (d) 1,800.30 | 1,800.30 | |
| Furniture & Fixtures | 6,600.00 | | | | 6,600.00 | |
| Less: Accum Depreciation | | 4,400.00 | | (c) 1,100.00 | | 5,500.00 |
| Goodwill | 162,000.00 | | | | 162,000.00 | |
| Accounts Payable | | 32,410.22 | | | | 32,410.22 |
| Payroll Taxes Payable | | 2,510.90 | | | | 2,510.90 |
| P.C. Kujawski, Capital | | 245,281.35 | | | | 245,281.35 |
| P.C. Kujawski, Drawing | 66,040.00 | | | | 66,040.00 | |
| Gross Sales | | 441,130.00 | | | | 441,130.00 |
| Sales Returns & Allow | 4,312.00 | | | | 4,312.00 | |
| Sales Discounts | 5,127.00 | | | | 5,127.00 | |
| Beginning Inventory | | | (a) 130,050.45 | | 130,050.45 | |
| Purchases | 213,491.50 | | | | 213,491.50 | |
| Purchase Returns & Allow | | 6,121.88 | | | | 6,121.88 |
| Purchase Discounts | | 4,013.44 | | | | 4,013.44 |
| Freight-In | 9,788.66 | | | | 9,788.66 | |
| Ending Inventory | | | | (b) 134,234.77 | | 134,234.77 |
| Commissions Expense | 66,000.00 | | | | 66,000.00 | |
| Depreciation Expense | | | (c) 1,100.00 | | 1,100.00 | |
| Insurance Expense | | | (d) 1,800.30 | | 1,800.30 | |
| Payroll Taxes Expense | 9,587.14 | | | | 9,587.14 | |
| Rent Expense | 15,000.00 | | | | 15,000.00 | |
| Salaries Expense | 21,150.00 | | | | 21,150.00 | |
| Utilities Expense | 2,839.34 | | | | 2,839.34 | |
| TOTALS | 735,867.79 | 735,867.79 | 267,185.52 | 267,185.52 | 871,202.56 | 871,202.56 |
| | | | | NET INCOME (LOSS) | | 105,253.70 |

(a) Beg Inv Adj
(b) End Inv Adj
(c) Deprn Exp Adj
(d) Ins Exp Adj

10. Arrow to the totals in the Adjusted Trial Balance columns. Notice that they are not equal because the formulas for the automatic debit and credit amounts did not fill down to the new rows that you created. Make the totals equal by doing the following:

> Drag cell **I10** to cell **I36** and drag **Edit** to **Fill Down**
> Drag cell **J10** to cell **J36** and drag **Edit** to **Fill Down**

Change the formula in cell J42 so that you can see the net income indicated in Figure 5-B on the previous page. Format the number.

11. Save your worksheet as **a:\tut5iws** at this time. Before you print the worksheet, you must reset the print area.

> Drag cell **A1** to cell **J43** and drag **Options** to **Set Print Area**

Print it in a portrait orientation with a condensed type style.

12. Prepare your screen for doing an income statement:

> Drag **File** to **Open** and click on **INFO.XLM** and **OK**
> Drag **Window** to **Sheet1** and run **Info Macro**
> Drag **Window** to **INFO.XLM** and drag **File** to **Close**

Don't forget to change the information in cell B4 of Sheet1 to Chapter 5. Also make sure that today's date is in cell B5.

13. Set the widths for the following columns:

| Column | Width |
| --- | --- |
| C | 2 |
| D | 2 |
| E | 26 |
| F | 1 |
| G | 12 |
| H | 11 |

14. You will be formatting an income statement that will probably look different from the statements that are illustrated in the merchandising chapter

of your textbook. In this income statement the dollar amounts (including totals) are arranged in a single column. There is also a column for percentages. This statement style is particularly useful if you want to add current month dollars (with percentages).

Drag **Window** to **Arrange All**

Set up the income statement heading in cells **F6** through **F9** and center it. The "who" and "when" of your heading should come from your independent window.

15. Set up the column headings as follows:

Type **YEAR-TO-DATE** in cell **G11** and press **<Enter>**
Type **AMOUNT** in cell **G12** and press **<Enter>**
Drag **Format** to **Alignment** and click on **Center** and **OK**
Type **PERCENT** in cell **H12** and press **<Enter>**
Drag **Format** to **Alignment** and click on **Right** and **OK**

16. In this step you will center the YEAR-TO-DATE label over AMOUNT and PERCENT:

Click on cell **G11**

Move your mouse pointer until it is to the left (but within a hair's length) of the word YEAR in the formula bar. The pointer will change shape from an "Arrow" to an "I-Beam" when you position the mouse pointer correctly. The formula bar is above the Sheet1 window, and it looks like this:

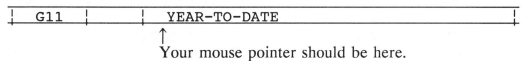

Your mouse pointer should be here.

Click the **left-hand button** of your mouse
Press **<SpaceBar>** six times and press **<Enter>**

The words YEAR-TO-DATE may not look centered on your screen, but should be centered when you print the income statement.

Drag cell **F13** to cell **H13**
Drag **Format** to **Border** and click on **Top** and **OK**

**Drag Format to Row Height and type 3 and press <Enter>**

17. Format the revenue section of the income statement. The dollar amounts in the two contra revenue accounts, Sales Returns & Allowances and Sales Discounts, appear as negative numbers.

Type **NET SALES:** in cell **C14** and press **<Enter>**
Type **=tut5iws.xls!b21** in cell **D15** and press **<Enter>**

Note: You are welcome to use the easier way to transfer information from the worksheet to the income statement, but you must remember to edit the dollar signs out of the cell reference.

Drag cell **D15** to cell **D17** and drag **Edit** to **Fill Down**
Type **TOTAL NET SALES** in cell **E19** and press **<Enter>**
Type **=tut5iws.xls!j21** in cell **G15** and press **<Enter>**
Type **=-tut5iws.xls!i22** in cell **G16** and press **<Enter>**
Drag cell **G16** to cell **G17**
Drag **Edit** to **Fill Down**
Type **=sum(g15:g17)** in cell **G19** and press **<Enter>**
Drag cell **G15** to cell **G19** and drag **Format** to **Number**
Click on **#,##0.00** and **OK**
Type **$** in cell **F15** and press **<Enter>**
Type **$** in cell **F19** and press **<Enter>**

18. In this step you will be typing a formula containing a relative cell reference and an absolute cell reference. The formulas you have typed up until this point have contained relative cell references. Relative cell references identify cells by their position in relation to an active cell location. You have probably noticed that when you "fill down" a formula, the relative cell references change as the active cell locations change.

Absolute, or fixed, cell references don't change as you "fill down" to new cell locations. Absolute cell references are identified by the dollar signs next to the column and row position indicators of the cells. For example, $A$1 is an absolute cell reference. A1 is a relative cell reference.

There are also mixed cell references. $A1 is a mixed cell reference where the column is absolute and the row is relative. A$1 is a mixed cell reference where the column is relative and the row is absolute.

Type **=g15/$g$19** in cell **H15** and press **<Enter>**

The numerator *G15* is the relative cell reference and the denominator

*$G$19* is the absolute cell reference.  Note the number *1.021865177* in cell H15.  Do the following to convert this formula to a percent and copy it down to other cells:

> Drag cell **H15** to cell **H19** and drag **Edit** to **Fill Down**
> Drag **Format** to **Number**
> Arrow to **0.00%** using the < DownArrow > key and press **< Enter >**
> Click on cell **H18** and drag **Edit** to **Clear** and click on **OK**

Arrow slowly up to cell H15.  You will see that the relative cell reference in the formula bar changes as you move to a new active cell location.  You'll see no change at all in the absolute cell reference.

19.  Finish the rest of the income statement.  If you need help, refer to Figure 5-C on the next page.

20.  Save your income statement as **a:\tut5dis** and print in a portrait orientation with a compressed type font.  Exit the program.

# Figure 5-C: Tutorial Income Statement

Student Name
999-99-9999
Acct150
Chapter 5
15-Sep-93

POST CARDS 'N STUFF
INCOME STATEMENT
FOR THE YEAR ENDED
DECEMBER 31, 1993

|  | | YEAR-TO-DATE | |
|---|---|---|---|
|  | | AMOUNT | PERCENT |
| NET SALES: | | | |
| Gross Sales | $ | 441,130.00 | 102.19% |
| Sales Returns & Allow | | -4,312.00 | -1.00% |
| Sales Discounts | | -5,127.00 | -1.19% |
| TOTAL NET SALES | $ | 431,691.00 | 100.00% |
| COST OF GOODS SOLD: | | | |
| Beginning Inventory | $ | 130,050.45 | 30.13% |
| Purchases | | 213,491.50 | 49.45% |
| Purchase Returns & Allow | | -6,121.88 | -1.42% |
| Purchase Discounts | | -4,013.44 | -0.93% |
| Freight-In | | 9,788.66 | 2.27% |
| Ending Inventory | | -134,234.77 | -31.10% |
| TOTAL COST OF GOODS SOLD | $ | 208,960.52 | 48.41% |
| GROSS PROFIT | $ | 222,730.48 | 51.59% |
| OPERATING EXPENSES: | | | |
| Commissions Expense | $ | 66,000.00 | 15.29% |
| Depreciation Expense | | 1,100.00 | 0.25% |
| Insurance Expense | | 1,800.30 | 0.42% |
| Payroll Taxes Expense | | 9,587.14 | 2.22% |
| Rent Expense | | 15,000.00 | 3.47% |
| Salaries Expense | | 21,150.00 | 4.90% |
| Utilities Expense | | 2,839.34 | 0.66% |
| TOTAL OPERATING EXPENSES | $ | 117,476.78 | 27.21% |
| NET INCOME (LOSS) | $ | 105,253.70 | 24.38% |

# Project:

Rose Lee, the owner of Gypsy's Costume Shop, brings her financial records for the year ended December 31, 1993, to you. She is proud of her business that specializes in weird looking "get-ups" for strange occasions, but since she needs to go to the bank for a short-term business loan, she does not want you to prepare weird-looking financial statements.

1. Do the following in accordance with the instructions in the Introduction chapter:

**Load Microsoft® Excel and retrieve A:\TUT5IWS.XLS**

2. Enter the following Trial Balance:

| | | |
|---|---:|---:|
| Cash | 3940.53 | |
| Accounts Receivable | 6210.10 | |
| Merchandise Inventory | 55025.40 | |
| Prepaid Insurance | 7201.20 | |
| Store Fixtures & Equipment | 19800.00 | |
| Less: Accum Depreciation | | 13200.00 |
| Security Deposit | 4000.00 | |
| Accounts Payable | | 16205.72 |
| Sales Tax Payable | | 2745.10 |
| Payroll Taxes Payable | | 423.96 |
| Rose Lee, Capital | | 47386.36 |
| Less: Withdrawals | 33020.00 | |
| Costume Rentals | | 252904.00 |
| Costume Sales | | 117634.00 |
| Less: Sales Ret & Allow | 3412.00 | |
| Purchases | 207410.38 | |
| Less: Pur Ret & Allow | | 5120.40 |
| Less: Purchase Discounts | | 4403.55 |
| Advertising Expense | 28714.00 | |
| Delivery Expense | 6210.59 | |
| Payroll Taxes Expense | 5550.15 | |
| Rent Expense | 24000.00 | |
| Salaries Expense | 46250.00 | |
| Store Supplies Expense | 3600.40 | |
| Utilities Expense | 5678.34 | |

3. The balance in the Merchandise Inventory account in the Trial Balance represents the beginning inventory on January 1, 1993. Rose Lee and her employees took a physical count of the costumes on December 31, 1993. The cost of those costumes amounted to $59,394.82.

4. The Prepaid Insurance account contains the cost of a one-year business package insurance policy that became effective February 1, 1993. That cost is $6,240. The remaining amount in the account is the January 1993 portion of the premium from last year's insurance policy.

5. The depreciation expense write-off for the year is $1,980. Accrued salaries amount to $2,250.

6. You notice that Ms. Lee has not been taking a physical count of the Store Supplies on hand at the end of the year. She tells you that her previous accountant never told her that she had to do it. (You could see that the Store Supplies Expense account on previous income statements never had much in it.) You ask her to estimate the cost of the store supplies she had on hand on December 31. She says, "About $1,200 worth!" Create a new Current Asset account called Store Supplies.

7. Make sure your debit column totals equal your credit column totals. Save your worksheet as **a:\proj5**. (Yes, you will replace the previous proj5 file.) Reset the print range and print it in a portrait orientation using a compressed type style.

8. Format a <u>complete</u> income statement that looks similar to the <u>partial</u> one illustrated on the following page. Also prepare a statement of owner's equity that is formatted similar to the models illustrated in your accounting principles textbook. Do a balance sheet that has the following classifications: Current Assets, Long-Term Assets, Other Assets, Current Liabilities, and Owner's Equity. Save your work as **a:\proj5** and print your financial statements in a portrait orientation. Select an appropriate type font.

9. (Optional) When you compare the current year income statement with the statement from last year, you notice that costume rentals are up 2%, costume sales are down 12%, and purchases are up 23%. (You also notice that on the balance sheet, there is no Long-Term Asset account called Rental Costumes.) The rest of the income statement items appear to be about the same as last year. Type a report to Ms. Lee that indicates what appears to be going on in her business.

## Figure 5-D: Partial Income Statement

```
Student Name
999-99-9999
Acct150
Chapter 5
15-Sep-93

                              GYPSY'S COSTUME SHOP
                               INCOME STATEMENT
                              FOR THE YEAR ENDED
                              DECEMBER 31, 1993
```

|  | YEAR-TO-DATE | |
|---|---|---|
|  | AMOUNT | PERCENT |
| **NET SALES & RENTALS:** |  |  |
| Costume Rentals | $ 252,904.00 | 68.89% |
| Costume Sales | 117,634.00 | 32.04% |
| Less: Sales Ret & Allow | (3,412.00) | -0.93% |
| TOTAL NET SALES & RENTALS | $ 367,126.00 | 100.00% |
| **COST OF GOODS SOLD:** |  |  |
| Beginning Inventory | $ 55,025.40 | 14.99% |
| Purchases | 207,410.38 | 56.50% |
| Less: Pur Ret & Allow | (5,120.40) | -1.39% |
| Less: Purchase Discounts | (4,403.55) | -1.20% |
| Ending Inventory | (59,394.82) | -16.18% |
| TOTAL COST OF GOODS SOLD | $ 193,517.01 | 52.71% |
| GROSS PROFIT | $ 173,608.99 | 47.29% |

10. (Optional) For how large of a short-term business loan can Ms. Lee apply? Type a letter advising her of the probable maximum loan amount. Base your answer on the information in the balance sheet and the bank's two-to-one current ratio policy.

## Assignment:

Prepare by hand the worksheet and the three financial statements that are discussed in the project above. Models for the statement of owner's equity and the income statement can be found in your accounting principles textbook.

Student Name:_____

Date:_____

# Chapter Five Transmittal Sheet for Excel

A. Hand in this page to your instructor with the following items attached in the order requested:

1. Project worksheet
2. Project income statement
3. Project statement of owner's equity
4. Project balance sheet
5. Hand written assignment
6. Project step 9 letter to Ms. Lee (optional)
7. Project step 10 current ratio letter (optional)

B. Below write the journal entries to close the temporary accounts indicated on the project worksheet:

*Chapter Six*

# Bank Reconciliation

---

## Chapter Objectives:

A. Format a bank reconciliation worksheet that has a Balance per Bank column and a Balance per Books column.

B. Prepare a bank reconciliation using a computer printout of the Cash in Bank--Checking account and a bank statement.

## Tutorial:

You have probably already figured out from the accounting lectures that what accountants call "cash" is more than coins and currency (the jingle in your pocket).

Most of the cash that accountants are thinking about when they talk about "cash" is sitting in a checking account at the bank. It is technically a receivable from the bank as far as the depositor is concerned. A depositor's checking account is a liability as far as the bank is concerned. Some bank statements make the idea of the checking account being a liability perfectly clear. Deposits are shown on those statements as credits; and checks that have been paid (or have cleared the account) are shown as debits.

There are two different business records of the cash deposited at the bank. One record is the general ledger. In many general ledgers that are produced using accounting software packages, the Cash account shows a listing of deposits made and checks written. The balance in this general ledger account is often adjusted at the end of the month because certain monetary items that appear in the bank statement were not recorded as transactions in the general ledger. The bank service charge is a common example because it appears in the bank statement, but it has not been recorded on the company books.

The other record of a firm's Cash account is the bank statement. The bank statement rarely contains the same balance as the Cash account, because of the time lag in recording deposits made and checks written. The bank statement ending balance is, then, modified on a worksheet by deposits in transit and outstanding checks. Deposits in transit are defined as deposits that are recorded on the company books, but not yet on the bank books. Outstanding checks are defined as checks that are recorded on the company books, but not yet on the bank books.

Assume that you are asked to do a bank reconciliation for a new client doing business as Bunkhouse Motel, Inc. The management of this corporation has developed an interesting concept. They plan to provide rooms with a king-size bed for mom and dad and bunk beds for the children. They are about to start construction on the first unit near an Orlando, Florida, theme park.

Also assume that your program does not have a bank reconciliation feature, although many other accounting software programs do. You have to create a separate worksheet.

1. Do the following:

   Load **Microsoft**® **Excel** and run **Info Macro**

2. Adjust the widths of the following columns:

   | Column | Width |
   | --- | --- |
   | B | 30 |
   | C | 10 |
   | D | 12 |
   | E | 12 |

When you print your bank reconciliation worksheet, you need to adjust the width of column A so that the worksheet is properly positioned on the page.  Don't forget to change the information in cell **B4** to Chapter 6 and to change the date in cell **B5** to today's date.

3.  In this step you will type the who, what, and when in the title:

> Type **BUNKHOUSE MOTEL, INC.** in cell **C1** and press **<Enter>**
> Type **BANK RECONCILIATION** in cell **C2** and press **<Enter>**
> Type **="MARCH 31, 1993"** in cell **C3** and press **<Enter>**

4.  Two monetary columns *Balance Per Bank* and *Balance Per Books* are next to each other in the worksheet.  It is easy to see when the two records are in agreement since the column totals are next to each other.

> Type **BALANCE** in cells **D5** and **E5** and press **<Enter>** each time
> Type **PER BANK** in cell **D6** and press **<Enter>**
> Type **PER BOOKS** in cell **E6** and press **<Enter>**
>
> Drag cell **D5** to cell **E6**
> Drag **Format** to **Alignment** and click on **Right** and **OK**

5.  Note that much of the information typed in column B is used over and over again.  The dates, numbers, and dollar amounts found in columns C through E can be erased and replaced each month.

> Type **BALANCES:** in cell **B7** and press **<Enter>**
> Type **Bank Statement Balance** in cell **B8** and press **<Enter>**
> Type **03/28/93** in cell **C8** and press **<Enter>**
> Type **9345.66** in cell **D8** and press **<Enter>**
>
> Type **General Ledger Balance** in cell **B9** and press **<Enter>**
> Type **03/31/93** in cell **C9** and press **<Enter>**
> Type **9988.54** in cell **E9** and press **<Enter>**
>
> Type **ADD TO BALANCE PER BANK:** in cell **B11** and press **<Enter>**
> Type **Deposit in Transit** in cell **B12** and press **<Enter>**
> Drag cell **B12** to cell **B13** and drag **Edit** to **Fill Down**
> Type **03/30/93** in cell **C12** and press **<Enter>**
> Type **1234.56** in cell **D12** and press **<Enter>**
> Type **SUBTRACT FROM BALANCE PER BANK:** in cell **B15** and press **<Enter>**

Type **Outstanding Check** in cell **B16** and press **<Enter>**
Drag cell **B16** to cell **B21** and drag **Edit** to **Fill Down**

Type **245** in cell **C16** and press **<Enter>**
Type **-123.45** in cell **D16** and press **<Enter>**
Type **246** in cell **C17** and press **<Enter>**
Type **-456.78** in cell **D17** and press **<Enter>**
Type **ADD TO BALANCE PER BOOKS:** in cell **B23** and
          press **<Enter>**
Type **Interest Revenue** in cell **B24** and press **<Enter>**

Type **03/01/93** in cell **C24** and press **<Enter>**
Type **23.45** in cell **E24** and press **<Enter>**

Type **SUBTRACT FROM BALANCE PER BOOKS:** in cell **B26**
          and press **<Enter>**
Type **Bank Service Charge** in cell **B27** and press **<Enter>**

Type **03/25/93** in cell **C27** and press **<Enter>**
Type **-12** in cell **E27** and press **<Enter>**

Drag cell **D30** to cell **E30** and drag **Format** to **Border**
Click on **Top** and **OK**
Drag **Format** to **Row Height**, type **4** and press **<Enter>**

Type **ADJUSTED BALANCES:** in cell **B31** and press **<Enter>**
Type **=sum(** in cell **D31** BUT DO NOT PRESS **<Enter>** HERE
Click on cell **D29**

With the **<Shift>** key pressed down, arrow to cell **D8**
Type **)** and press **<Enter>**
Drag cell **D31** to cell **E31** and drag **Edit** to **Fill Right**

Drag cell **D32** to cell **E32** and drag **Format** to **Border**
Click on **Top, Bottom** and **OK**
Drag **Format** to **Row Height** and type **4** and press **<Enter>**

Drag cell **C8** to cell **C31** and drag **Format** to **Alignment**
Click on **Right** and **OK**
Drag cell **D8** to cell **E31** and drag **Format** to **Number**
Click on **#,##0.00** and **OK**

## Figure 6-A: Bank Reconciliation Worksheet

| | | BALANCE PER BANK | BALANCE PER BOOKS |
|---|---|---|---|
| Student Name | BUNKHOUSE MOTEL, INC. | | |
| 999-99-9999 | BANK RECONCILIATION | | |
| Acct150 | MARCH 31, 1993 | | |
| Chapter 6 | | | |
| 15-Sep-93 | | | |
| BALANCES: | | | |
| Bank Statement Balance | 3/28/93 | 9,345.66 | |
| General Ledger Balance | 3/31/93 | | 9,988.54 |
| | | | |
| ADD TO BALANCE PER BANK: | | | |
| Deposit in Transit | 3/30/93 | 1,234.56 | |
| Deposit in Transit | | | |
| | | | |
| SUBTRACT FROM BALANCE PER BANK: | | | |
| Outstanding Check | 245 | -123.45 | |
| Outstanding Check | 246 | -456.78 | |
| Outstanding Check | | | |
| Outstanding Check | | | |
| Outstanding Check | | | |
| Outstanding Check | | | |
| | | | |
| ADD TO BALANCE PER BOOKS: | | | |
| Interest Revenue | 3/1/93 | | 23.45 |
| | | | |
| SUBTRACT FROM BALANCE PER BOOKS: | | | |
| Bank Service Charge | 3/25/93 | | -12.00 |
| | | | |
| ADJUSTED BALANCES: | | 9,999.99 | 9,999.99 |

6. Save your bank reconciliation worksheet as **a:\tut6** and print it in a portrait orientation using a regular-sized type font. Exit the program.

## *Project:*

Mr. J. W. Campbell, owner of Body Tech Health Spa, brought in his general ledger printout for the month of August 1993. Your usual job is to look over the ledger accounts and recommend adjusting entries which his bookkeeper will input on the computer. This was an unusual month for Mr. Campbell's business. It was closed for remodeling for all but the last few days of the month.

A part of your monthly analysis of Mr. Campbell's business includes preparing a bank reconciliation of the Cash in Bank--Checking account. Illustrated below is the bank statement. On the next page is a portion of the general ledger computer report showing account number 1120.

**Figure 6-B: Project Bank Statement**

# Commerce National Bank     Statement

------------------------------------------------------------

**10290 Scripps Ranch Blvd.**
**San Diego, CA 92131**
**Phone: 619-345-6789**

```
                         BODY TECH HEALTH SPA
                         ATTEN: J.W. CAMPBELL
                         9210 CAMINITO BURRITO
                         SAN DIEGO CA 92126
```

```
CHECKING ACCOUNT: 10740-05678              TAX ID: 12-345-6789
- - - - - - - - - - - - - - - - - - - - - - - - - - - - - - - -
SUMMARY:   PREVIOUS BALANCE 07-31-93.................  21,877.21
           DEPOSITS & OTHER CREDITS.................. 204,547.43
           CHECKS & OTHER DEBITS..................... 204,341.69
           THIS BALANCE 08-30-93.....................  22,082.95
- - - - - - - - - - - - - - - - - - - - - - - - - - - - - - - -
```

CHECKS & OTHER DEBITS:

| CHECK# | AMOUNT | CHECK# | AMOUNT | CHECK# | AMOUNT |
|--------|--------|--------|--------|--------|--------|
| 4217 | 1610.45 | 8853 | 4000.00 | 8854 | 355.46 |
| 8855 | 8933.74 | 8856 | 31000.00 | 8857 | 18237.46 |
| 8858 | 65410.90 | 8860 | 25644.00 | 8861 | 12400.00 |
| 8862 | 36610.00 | NSF | 125.10 | SERVCH | 14.58 |

DEPOSITS & OTHER CREDITS:

| DATE | AMOUNT | DATE | AMOUNT | DATE | AMOUNT |
|------|--------|------|--------|------|--------|
| 08-02 | 3210.50 | 08-02 | 4592.87 | 08-03 | 3590.80 |
| LOAN | 185000.00 | 08-29 | 3910.42 | 08-30 | 4242.84 |

Note: The statement above shows the bank's liability to the depositor. Notice that the deposits are credits and the cleared checks are debits.

# Figure 6-C: Page 1 of the General Ledger

```
BODY TECH HEALTH SPA                   PRINT DATE:  09-02-93              PAGE 001
================================================================================
TRNS    TRNS    JRNL  ACCT  REF   ACCOUNT NAME -OR-        CURRENT          YEAR-
NMBR    DATE    CODE  NMBR  NMBR    ENTRY DESCRIPTION      PERIOD         TO-DATE
----    --------  ----  ----  ----  -----------------------  -------------  -------------

                      1110        CASH ON HAND

        07-31-93      1110        BALANCE                                 1,000.00

                      1120        CASH IN BANK-CHECKING

        07-31-93      1120        BALANCE                                19,477.26
4053    08-01-93  CR  1120  DEP   CASH REPORT               4,592.87
4060    08-01-93  CP  1120  8854  PAC WEST ELECTRIC           355.46-
4062    08-01-93  CP  1120  8855  UPTOWN INSURANCE AGENCY   8,933.74-
4064    08-02-93  CR  1120  DEP   CASH REPORT               3,590.80
4066    08-05-93  CR  1120  DEP   SIX MO BANK LOAN        185,000.00
4070    08-09-93  CP  1120  8856  GLEN'S COMMERCIAL CARPETS 31,000.00-
4072    08-15-93  CP  1120  8857  SOUTHWEST GYM EQUIPMENT  18,237.46-
4077    08-16-93  CP  1120  8858  MIKE'S INTERIOR DESIGN   65,410.90-
4082    08-21-93  CP  1120  8859  VOID                          0.00
4083    08-21-93  CP  1120  8860  KENT CONSTRUCTION        25,644.00-
4087    08-21-93  CP  1120  8861  SWAN PLUMBING CORP       12,400.00-
4089    08-28-93  CR  1120  DEP   CASH REPORT               3,910.42
4093    08-29-93  CR  1120  DEP   CASH REPORT               4,242.84
4095    08-30-93  CR  1120  DEP   CASH REPORT               2,860.22
4098    08-31-93  PR  1120  4218  ANN THOMPSON              1,610.45-
4105    08-31-93  PR  1120  4219  GEORGE WARING             1,786.39-
4110    08-31-93  PR  1120  4220  NICOLE BENTLEY            1,356.00-
4115    08-31-93  PR  1120  4221  JENNIFER MORINO           1,443.40-
4120    08-31-93  PR  1120  4222  JIM ANDREWS               1,302.53-
4126    08-31-93  CR  1120  DEP   CASH REPORT               2,104.00
4131    08-31-93  CP  1120  8862  KENT CONSTRUCTION        36,610.00-

        08-31-93      1120        BALANCE                     210.82   19,688.08

                      1130        CERTIFICATES OF DEPOSIT

        07-31-93      1130        BALANCE                                15,000.00

                      1140        UNEXPIRED INSURANCE

        07-31-93      1140        BALANCE                                   655.00
4061    08-01-93  CP  1140  8855  UPTOWN INSURANCE AGENCY   8,933.74

        08-31-93      1140        BALANCE                   8,933.74    9,588.74

                      1160        SPA SUPPLIES

        07-31-93      1160        BALANCE                                 1,293.17
```

The first difference between this computer printout and the traditional general ledger is that there is more than one account on a page. You will also see that the printout doesn't have debit and credit monetary columns. Instead it has Current Period and Year-to-Date columns. The numbers in these columns with the minus signs are the credits. The rest of the numbers are debits.

Notice that there are three different journal codes: CR stands for the Cash Receipts Journal; CP stands for the Cash Payments Journal; and PR stands for the Payroll Register. Journal page numbers are not included as a posting reference. Instead, there are transaction numbers.

1. Do the following:

Load **Microsoft**® **Excel** and open **a:\tut6.xls**

2. Change the "who" and the "when" in the worksheet title. Clear (erase) the information in the range of cells C8 through E29. Enter the Balance per Bank amount and the Balance per Books amount (with appropriate dates). Add to or subtract from the Balance per Bank amount those monetary items that appear in the general ledger printout, but not on the bank statement.

3. Add to or subtract from the Balance per Books amount those monetary items that appear on the bank statement, but not on the general ledger printout. Be careful here. There is a deposit in transit and two outstanding checks that were on the previous month's bank reconciliation and on this month's bank statement. The NSF check is from G. Bush (not related to the President). It was used to pay a tab run up in the spa's restaurant.

4. Save the worksheet as **a:\proj6** and print it in a portrait orientation using a regular-sized type font. Exit the program.

5. (Optional) Type a memo to Mr. Campbell that suggests the adjusting entry which will correct the August 31, 1993, book balance.

## Assignment:

Prepare the project bank reconciliation by hand in accordance with the steps outlined in your accounting principles textbook.

# Chapter Six Transmittal Sheet for Excel

A. Hand in this page to your instructor with the following items attached in the order requested:

1. Project bank reconciliation
2. Hand written assignment
3. Project step 5 memo to Mr. Campbell (optional)

B. Assume that a month has passed and that you are ready to prepare another bank reconciliation worksheet.

1. What deposits will appear on the bank statement for the month of September 1993 but not on the general ledger computer report (at least during that period)?

2. What checks will appear on the bank statement for the month of September 1993 but not on the general ledger computer report (at least during that period)?

3. Assume that during the month of September 1993, Ms. Bush stops by to replace the NSF check with a money order. Indicate below the general journal entry that would show that transaction.

Notes:

*Chapter Seven*

# Accounts Receivable Aging Report

---

## *Chapter Objectives:*

A. Analyze invoices and prepare an accounts receivable aging report.

B. Use the Nested IF function to test if invoice due dates fall within current and past due date ranges.

C. Compare and contrast two types of accounts receivable aging reports.

## *Tutorial:*

The accounts receivable aging report is an excellent example of how a computer spreadsheet program can be used to save time and avoid making errors. This report is seldom prepared by hand anymore, except by students. Usually this report is prepared using the automatic features of a general ledger accounting software package. Even the inexpensive "off-the-shelf" accounting packages include this report option.

Invoices are still typed without the aid of a computer at many smaller businesses, yet in these same businesses, a computer is used to produce the report that you are going to learn how to format. In this tutorial you will be formatting a report that is equipped with the IF function, the Nested IF function, and the SUM function.

1. Do the following according to the instructions in the Introduction chapter:

**Load Microsoft® Excel and run Info Macro**

2. Change the information in cell B4 to "Chapter 7" and change the date in cell B5 to today's date.

3. Adjust the widths of the following columns:

Columns C - K        Width = 11
Column L             Width = 14

4. The heading of this report is unusual because it contains several dates.

Type  **JAMAICA COFFEE BEAN IMPORTERS**  in cell **H1** and press **<Enter>**
Type  **ACCOUNTS RECEIVABLE AGING REPORT**  in cell **H2** and press **<Enter>**

Drag cell **H1** to cell **H2** and drag **Format** to **Alignment**
Click on **Right** and **OK**

Type  **DATE THIS REPORT:**  in cell **G3** and press  **<Enter>**
Type  **30 DAYS BEFORE:**  in cell **G4** and press  **<Enter>**
Type  **60 DAYS BEFORE:**  in cell **G5** and press  **<Enter>**
Type  **90 DAYS BEFORE:**  in cell **G6** and press  **<Enter>**

Drag cell **G3** to cell **G6** and drag **Format** to **Alignment**
Click on **Right** and **OK**

Type  **05/31/94**  in cell **H3** and press  **<Enter>**
Type  **=h3-30**  in cell **H4** and press  **<Enter>**
Type  **=h3-60**  in cell **H5** and press  **<Enter>**
Type  **=h3-90**  in cell **H6** and press  **<Enter>**

The numbers that appear in cells H4 through H6 are called "date index numbers." You can see that older dates have lower numbers.

Drag cell **H3** to cell **H6** and drag **Format** to **Number**
Arrow to **d-mmm-yy** and click on **OK**

Notice how the dates in cells H4 through H6 automatically change when you do the following:

Type  **01/31/94**  in cell **H3** and press  **<Enter>**

5. Enter the headings: CUSTOMER, INVOICE, INVOICE, INVOICE, INVOICE, INVOICE, CURRENT, 1-30 DAYS, 31-60 DAYS, 61-90 DAYS, and OVER 90 DAYS in cells B8 through L8. Also enter: NAME, NUMBER, DATE, TERMS, AMOUNT, DUE DATE, INVOICE, PAST DUE, PAST DUE, PAST DUE, and PAST DUE in cells B9 through L9.

> Arrow to cell **C8**
> With the **<Shift>** key pressed down,
> Arrow to cell **L9**
> Drag **Format** to **Alignment** and click on **Right** and **OK**

6. Enter: Coffee Co, 12345, 12/15/93, 60, 7500, and +d11+e11 in cells B11 through G11.

> Click On cell **D11** and drag **Format** to **Number**
> Arrow to **d-mmm-yy** and click on **OK**

Do the same procedure with cell **G11**.

7. In this step you will be putting an automatic feature in cell H11. You need to test that the invoice due date in cell G11 is later than or equal to the report date located in cell H3. If it is, then your automatic feature should copy the amount in cell F11 to cell H11. If not, you don't want anything in cell H11. The automatic feature is nothing more than the IF function: =IF( Test, True, False ).

> Type **=if(g11>=$h$3,f11," ")** in cell **H11** and press **<Enter>**

**Figure 7-A: Current Date Test**

| | |
|---|---|
| The Test: | G11>=$H$3. Is the date in cell G11 later than or equal to the date in cell H3? Remember that the $$'s make cell H3 an absolute cell reference. |
| If True: | The amount in cell F11 is copied to cell H11 (where the IF function is written). |
| If False: | " " means that nothing goes into cell H11. |

8. A similar IF function is used for cell L11 except in this location, you are testing for a due date that is earlier than 90 days before the report date.

Type  =if(g11<$h$6,f11," ")  in cell **L11** and press **<Enter>**

9. The test for cell I11 is different. Here you need to see if the invoice due date in cell G11 is within a range of dates with an upper limit (later date) and a lower limit (earlier date).

The upper limit in cell I11 is one day past due, which is one day before the report date in cell H3. The lower limit is 30 days past due, which is the same as 30 days before the report date. That date can be found in cell H4.

This two-limit test requires something called a Nested IF function. What you will be doing here is nesting an IF function with a lower limit test in the "true" location of an IF function with an upper limit test. If this all sounds complicated, maybe the following diagram will help:

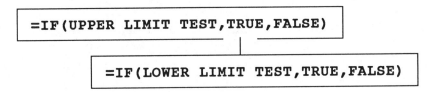

Type  =if(g11<$h$3,if(g11>=$h$4,f11," ")," ")  in cell **I11** and
      press **<Enter>**

**Figure 7-B: 1-30 Days Past Due Test**

| Upper Limit Test: | G11<$H$3. The due date in cell G11 must be before the report date in cell H3. If that is true, the lower limit test is activated. If that is false, then nothing goes in cell I11. |
|---|---|
| Lower Limit Test: | G11>=$H$4. The due date in cell G11 must be later than (with a higher date index number) or equal to the date in cell H4. If that is true, then the amount in cell F11 is copied to cell I11. If that is false, then nothing goes in cell I11. |

10. Similar thinking is used for cells J11 and K11:

   Type  = if(g11 < $h$4,if(g11 > = $h$5,f11," ")," ")  in cell **J11**
        and press **<Enter>**
   Type  = if(g11 < $h$5,if(g11 > = $h$6,f11," ")," ")  in cell **K11**
        and press **<Enter>**
   Drag cell **H11** to cell **L11** and drag **Format** to **Number**
   Click on **#,##0.00** and **OK**

Also, format the invoice amount in cell F11.

11. Test your automatic features by doing the following:

   Type  **09/15/93**  in cell **D11** and press **<Enter>**

Make the following changes in cell E11:

| Change Invoice Terms To: | 7,500.00 Should Appear In: |
|---|---|
| 150 | Current Invoice Column |
| 120 | 1-30 Days Past Due Column |
| 90 | 31-60 Days Past Due Column |
| 60 | 61-90 Days Past Due Column |
| 30 | Over 90 Days Past Due Column |

12. See the effect of different report dates by making the following changes in cell H3:

| Change Report Date To: | 7,500.00 Should Appear In: |
|---|---|
| 12/31/93 | 61-90 Days Past Due Column |
| 11/30/93 | 31-60 Days Past Due Column |
| 10/31/93 | 1-30 Days Past Due Column |
| 09/30/93 | Current Invoice Column |

13. Copy (fill down) all of the information in row 11 (including labels, numbers, formulas, functions and formats) to rows 12 through 17:

   Arrow to cell **B11**
   With the **<Shift>** key pressed down,
   Arrow to cell **L17** and drag **Edit** to **Fill Down**

14. Change the invoice information in columns **B** through **F** so that it agrees with the illustration on the next page. Complete the rest of the accounts receivable aging report so that it looks like the illustration.

# Figure 7-C:  Accounts Receivable Aging Report

Student Name
999-99-9999
Acct150
Chapter 7
15-Sep-93

JAMAICA COFFEE BEAN IMPORTERS
ACCOUNTS RECEIVABLE AGING REPORT
DATE THIS REPORT: 30-Sep-93
30 DAYS BEFORE: 31-Aug-93
60 DAYS BEFORE: 1-Aug-93
90 DAYS BEFORE: 2-Jul-93

| CUSTOMER NAME | INVOICE NUMBER | INVOICE DATE | INVOICE TERMS | INVOICE AMOUNT | INVOICE DUE DATE | CURRENT INVOICE | 1-30 DAYS PAST DUE | 31-60 DAYS PAST DUE | 61-90 DAYS PAST DUE | OVER 90 DAYS PAST DUE |
|---|---|---|---|---|---|---|---|---|---|---|
| Coffee Co | 12345 | 15-Sep-93 | 30 | 7,500.00 | 15-Oct-93 | 7,500.00 | | | | |
| Cup Cafe | 12330 | 15-Aug-93 | 45 | 200.00 | 29-Sep-93 | | 200.00 | | | |
| Dan's Rest | 12319 | 1-Sep-93 | 30 | 5,400.00 | 1-Oct-93 | 5,400.00 | | | | |
| Emporium | 12301 | 29-Aug-93 | 45 | 6,000.00 | 13-Oct-93 | 6,000.00 | | | | |
| Grove Mkt | 12280 | 31-Jul-93 | 30 | 4,500.00 | 30-Aug-93 | | | 4,500.00 | | |
| Inn Diner | 12253 | 25-Jun-93 | 30 | 1,100.00 | 25-Jul-93 | | | | 1,100.00 | |
| That Hole | 12236 | 5-May-93 | 30 | 2,100.00 | 4-Jun-93 | | | | | 2,100.00 |
| COLUMN TOTALS: | | | | 26,800.00 | | 18,900.00 | 200.00 | 4,500.00 | 1,100.00 | 2,100.00 |
| PERCENT UNCOLLECTIBLE: | | | | | | 2.00% | 5.00% | 12.00% | 25.00% | 55.00% |
| AMOUNTS UNCOLLECTIBLE: | | | | | | 378.00 | 10.00 | 540.00 | 275.00 | 1,155.00 |
| ALLOW FOR DOUBTFUL ACCOUNTS BAL: | | | | | | 2,358.00 | | | | |

14. Remember to input the percent uncollectible amounts as decimals so that they will look right when you format them as percentages.

15. Save your accounts receivable aging report as **a:\tut7** and print it in a landscape orientation using a compressed style. Exit the program.

## *Project:*

Assume that you are the new controller for Express Print, Inc., dba (doing business as) EXPRESS YOURSELF!! The board of directors recently approved the purchase of a high-tech German printing press. The quality and quantity of greeting cards and boxed notes that the company publishes improved dramatically.

The board of directors did not look at the accounting department until it started to have problems keeping up with the flow of paperwork generated by increased sales. Then the board approved the purchase of only one computer and an inexpensive general ledger software package. You notice that the accounts receivable module part of the package is missing some of the important "whistles and bells."

You decide to take a representative sample of invoices and do a couple of accounts receivable aging reports dated 7/31/93 and 8/31/93. Your goal is to see which reports show off the company in the more favorable light: the reports generated by you or the reports generated by the software bought at the discount computer store.

1.    Load **Microsoft® Excel** and open  **a:\tut7.xls**

2. Clear the range of cells that shows the invoice information (customer name, invoice number, date, terms, and amount). Change the company name in the report heading. Remember that there will be two report dates.

3. Enter the invoice information available on the next four pages. Limit the customer names to eleven characters. Arrange the customer names in alphabetical order. Disregard the 2% discount days.

## 7-D: Invoices (next four pages)

**EXPRESS YOURSELF!!**  **Greeting Card Publisher**
*169 Camino Taco, San Diego, CA 92126  (619)765-4321*

**Sold To:**

Cheers Gifts & Gags
210 W. State Street
Zebulon, GA 30295

**Ship To:**

Same

| DATE | SHIP VIA | YOUR P.O. NUMBER | F.O.B. | TERMS | INVOICE NUMBER |
|------|----------|------------------|--------|-------|----------------|
| 02-10-93 | UPS | 7085 | DEST | 2/10 N/30 | 13005 |

| QUANTITY | DESCRIPTION | PRICE | AMOUNT |
|----------|-------------|-------|--------|
| 25 dz | 1.25 Studio Cards | 7.50 | 187.80 |
| 15 dz | 1.25 Get Well Cards | 7.50 | 112.50 |
| 7 dz | 1.25 Birthday Cards | 7.50 | 52.50 |
| | TOTAL | | -------- |
| | | | 352.50 |

**EXPRESS YOURSELF!!**  **Greeting Card Publisher**
*169 Camino Taco, San Diego, CA 92126  (619)765-4321*

**Sold To:**

Ladybug Cards & Gifts
Downtown Mall, Suite 107W
Ithaca, NY 14850

**Ship To:**

Same

| DATE | SHIP VIA | YOUR P.O. NUMBER | F.O.B. | TERMS | INVOICE NUMBER |
|------|----------|------------------|--------|-------|----------------|
| 03-15-93 | UPS | 924A | DEST | 2/10 N/60 | 13374 |

| QUANTITY | DESCRIPTION | PRICE | AMOUNT |
|----------|-------------|-------|--------|
| 20 dz | 1.25 Mother's Day Cards | 7.50 | 150.00 |
| 15 dz | 1.25 Birthday Cards | 7.50 | 112.50 |
| 7 dz | 1.25 Anniversary Cards | 7.50 | 52.50 |
| | TOTAL | | -------- |
| | | | 315.00 |

## EXPRESS YOURSELF!!   Greeting Card Publisher
### 169 Camino Taco, San Diego, CA 92126   (619)765-4321

*Sold To:*                                    *Ship To:*

Just For The Halibut
Fisherman's Village Shopping Center          Same
Pistol River, OR 97444

| DATE | SHIP VIA | YOUR P.O. NUMBER | F.O.B. | TERMS | INVOICE NUMBER |
|------|----------|------------------|--------|-------|----------------|
| 05-20-93 | UPS | 17-5830 | DEST | 2/10 N/30 | 13759 |

| QUANTITY | DESCRIPTION | PRICE | AMOUNT |
|----------|-------------|-------|--------|
| 25 dz | 1.25 Friendship Cards | 7.50 | 187.50 |
| 15 dz | 1.25 Get Well Cards | 7.50 | 112.50 |
| 10 dz | 1.25 Anniversary Cards | 7.50 | 75.00 |
| | | | -------- |
| | TOTAL | | 375.00 |

---

## EXPRESS YOURSELF!!   Greeting Card Publisher
### 169 Camino Taco, San Diego, CA 92126   (619)765-4321

*Sold To:*                                    *Ship To:*

Drugs-R-Us Pharmacy
940 Main Street                              Same
Green Hut Park, NJ 07801

| DATE | SHIP VIA | YOUR P.O. NUMBER | F.O.B. | TERMS | INVOICE NUMBER |
|------|----------|------------------|--------|-------|----------------|
| 06-12-93 | UPS | RG10 | DEST | 2/10 N/30 | 14025 |

| QUANTITY | DESCRIPTION | PRICE | AMOUNT |
|----------|-------------|-------|--------|
| 25 dz | 1.25 Birthday Cards | 7.50 | 187.50 |
| 15 dz | 1.25 Get Well Cards | 7.50 | 112.50 |
| 12 dz | 1.25 Anniversary Cards | 7.50 | 90.00 |
| | | | -------- |
| | TOTAL | | 390.00 |

## EXPRESS YOURSELF!!  Greeting Card Publisher
### 169 Camino Taco, San Diego, CA 92126   (619)765-4321

**Sold To:**

Terri's Hallmark Palace
R.D.#2, Mountain Summit Road
Pocono Park, PA 18360

**Ship To:**

Same

| DATE | SHIP VIA | YOUR P.O. NUMBER | F.O.B. | TERMS | INVOICE NUMBER |
|---|---|---|---|---|---|
| 06-25-93 | UPS | X743 | DEST | 2/10 N/30 | 14338 |

| QUANTITY | DESCRIPTION | PRICE | AMOUNT |
|---|---|---|---|
| 25 dz | 1.25 Studio Cards | 7.50 | 187.50 |
| 15 dz | 1.25 Get Well Cards | 7.50 | 112.50 |
| 18 dz | 1.25 Friendship Cards | 7.50 | 135.00 |
| | | | -------- |
| | TOTAL | | 435.00 |

---

## EXPRESS YOURSELF!!  Greeting Card Publisher
### 169 Camino Taco, San Diego, CA 92126   (619)765-4321

**Sold To:**

Get-It-On Gifts
15 Oyster Harbor Heights
Cummaquid, MA 02637

**Ship To:**

Same

| DATE | SHIP VIA | YOUR P.O. NUMBER | F.O.B. | TERMS | INVOICE NUMBER |
|---|---|---|---|---|---|
| 07-02-93 | UPS | | DEST | 2/10 N/30 | 14416 |

| QUANTITY | DESCRIPTION | PRICE | AMOUNT |
|---|---|---|---|
| 30 dz | 1.25 Friendship Cards | 7.50 | 225.00 |
| 15 dz | 1.25 Get Well Cards | 7.50 | 112.50 |
| 15 dz | 1.25 Anniversary Cards | 7.50 | 112.50 |
| | | | -------- |
| | TOTAL | | 450.00 |

## EXPRESS YOURSELF!!          Greeting Card Publisher
### 169 Camino Taco, San Diego, CA 92126   (619)765-4321

**Sold To:**                              **Ship To:**

Great News--Papers, Mags & Cards
120 Jump River Station                    Same
St Croiz Falls, WI 54024

| DATE | SHIP VIA | YOUR P.O. NUMBER | F.O.B. | TERMS | INVOICE NUMBER |
|------|----------|------------------|--------|-------|----------------|
| 07-15-93 | UPS | | DEST | 2/10 N/150 | 14682 |

| QUANTITY | DESCRIPTION | PRICE | AMOUNT |
|----------|-------------|-------|--------|
| 40 dz | 1.25 Christmas Cards | 7.50 | 300.00 |
| 10 dz | 1.25 Thanksgiving Cards | 7.50 | 75.00 |
| 4 dz | 1.25 Halloween Cards | 7.50 | 30.00 |
| | | | -------- |
| | TOTAL | | 405.00 |

---

## EXPRESS YOURSELF!!          Greeting Card Publisher
### 169 Camino Taco, San Diego, CA 92126   (619)765-4321

**Sold To:**                              **Ship To:**

Mesa Bookstore of Higher Education
7250 Mesa University Dr.                  Same
San Diego, CA 92111

| DATE | SHIP VIA | YOUR P.O. NUMBER | F.O.B. | TERMS | INVOICE NUMBER |
|------|----------|------------------|--------|-------|----------------|
| 07-25-93 | UPS | 7250 | DEST | 2/10 N/60 | 14941 |

| QUANTITY | DESCRIPTION | PRICE | AMOUNT |
|----------|-------------|-------|--------|
| 45 dz | 1.25 Studio Cards | 7.50 | 337.50 |
| 15 dz | 1.25 Friendship Cards | 7.50 | 112.50 |
| 7 dz | 1.25 Anniversary Cards | 7.50 | 52.50 |
| | | | ------- |
| | TOTAL | | 502.50 |

4. Save your report dated 7/31/93 as **a:\proj7a** and print it in a landscape orientation using compressed type. Change the report date to 8/31/93. Save it as **a:\proj7b** and print it again. Exit the program.

5. (Optional) The following two illustrations are the reports generated by the existing accounting software package at EXPRESS YOURSELF!!

**Figure 7-C: Reports From Inexpensive Accounting Software**

```
REPORT DATE:  07/31/93
REPORT NAME:  A/R AGING
-----------------------------------------------------------------------------
                                  | ACCOUNT |---------DAYS FROM INVOICE DATE--------|
NAME OF CUSTOMER                  | BALANCE |  1-30  |  31-60 |  61-90 | OVER 90 |
-----------------------------------------------------------------------------
CHEERS GIFTS & GAGS               |  352.50 |        |        |        |  352.50 |
LADYBUG CARDS & GIFTS             |  315.00 |        |        |        |  315.00 |
JUST FOR THE HALIBUT              |  375.00 |        |        |  375.00|         |
DRUGS-R-US PHARMACY               |  390.00 |        |  390.00|        |         |
TERRI'S HALLMARK PALACE           |  435.00 |        |  435.00|        |         |
GET-IT-ON GIFTS                   |  450.00 |  450.00|        |        |         |
GREAT NEWS--PAPERS, MAGS & CARDS  |  405.00 |  405.00|        |        |         |
MESA BOOKSTORE OF HIGHER EDUCATION|  502.50 |  502.50|        |        |         |
-----------------------------------------------------------------------------
ACCOUNTS RECEIVABLE BALANCE       | 3225.00 | 1357.50|  825.00|  375.00|  667.50 |
UNCOLLECTIBLE ACCOUNTS PERCENTAGES|=========|   2.00%|   5.00%|  12.00%|  55.00% |
-----------------------------------------------------------------------------
ALLOW FOR D/A BALANCE             |  480.53 |   27.15|   41.25|   45.00|  367.13 |
=============================================================================
```

```
REPORT DATE:  08/31/93
REPORT NAME:  A/R AGING
-----------------------------------------------------------------------------
                                  | ACCOUNT |---------DAYS FROM INVOICE DATE--------|
NAME OF CUSTOMER                  | BALANCE |  1-30  |  31-60 |  61-90 | OVER 90 |
-----------------------------------------------------------------------------
CHEERS GIFTS & GAGS               |  352.50 |        |        |        |  352.50 |
LADYBUG CARDS & GIFTS             |  315.00 |        |        |        |  315.00 |
JUST FOR THE HALIBUT              |  375.00 |        |        |        |  375.00 |
DRUGS-R-US PHARMACY               |  390.00 |        |        |  390.00|         |
TERRI'S HALLMARK PALACE           |  435.00 |        |        |  435.00|         |
GET-IT-ON GIFTS                   |  450.00 |        |  450.00|        |         |
GREAT NEWS--PAPERS, MAGS & CARDS  |  405.00 |        |  405.00|        |         |
MESA BOOKSTORE OF HIGHER EDUCATION|  502.50 |        |  502.50|        |         |
-----------------------------------------------------------------------------
ACCOUNTS RECEIVABLE BALANCE       | 3225.00 |   0.00 | 1357.50|  825.00| 1042.50 |
UNCOLLECTIBLE ACCOUNTS PERCENTAGES|=========|   2.00%|   5.00%|  12.00%|  55.00% |
-----------------------------------------------------------------------------
ALLOW FOR D/A BALANCE             |  740.26 |   0.00 |   67.88|   99.00|  573.38 |
=============================================================================
```

5. (continued) Write a report to the board of directors that compares and contrasts your "days past due aging schedules" with the "days from invoice date aging schedules" illustrated on the previous page. Which schedules show the company in a more favorable light? Which are more useful to the credit manager? Which schedules take into account extended dating (net due in more than 30 days) for seasonal greeting cards?

## *Assignment:*

Prepare by hand the accounts receivable aging reports discussed in this chapter project.

Student Name:_____

Date:_____

# Chapter Seven Transmittal Sheet for Excel

A. Hand in this page to your instructor with the following items attached in the order requested:

1. Two project accounts receivable aging reports
2. Hand-written assignment
3. Project step 5 report to the board of directors (optional)

B. Use the accounts receivable aging report dated 8/31/93 as the basis for your answers to the following questions:

1. The amount receivable from Ladybug Cards & Gifts should be more than 90 days past due. What is the formula or function that places the $315.00 in that column?

2. The amount receivable from Terri's Hallmark Palace should be 31-60 days past due. What is the formula or function that places the $435.00 in that column?

3. Assume that the 8/31/93 trial balance indicates that there is a $200.00 credit balance in Allowance For Doubtful Accounts. Write below the appropriate adjusting entry based upon the 8/31/93 aging report.

4. Assume that the 8/31/93 trial balance indicates a $100.00 debit balance in Allowance For Doubtful Accounts. Write below the appropriate adjusting entry based upon the 8/31/93 aging report.

# Chapter Eight

# *Inventory Valuation*

---

## *Chapter Objectives:*

A. Format partial income statements for two consecutive years that compare first-in, first-out; average cost; and last-in, first-out assumptions in a periodic inventory system.

B. Use what-if analysis to decide which of the three assumptions would best suit a new company if prices are expected to change.

## *Tutorial:*

In this tutorial, Hungry Dog Food, Inc., a new company, must decide how to value its ending inventory. This company purchases dog food in 250-pound drums from a private label cereal company. It then repackages it in five-pound bags to sell under the "Gourmet Crunchy Meal" label.

Since the dog food is held for resale, the people at Hungry Dog must take a physical count of it at least once a year. They use the periodic inventory system, so they must do that physical count at (or near) the end of their fiscal year (which is December 31).

Once the drums of dog food are counted, you (the company bookkeeper) must assign unit costs to the inventory items based on one of the following three assumptions: first-in, first-out (FIFO); average cost (AVCO); or last-in, first-out (LIFO). These assumptions concern the flow of costs through a firm. The assumptions do not necessarily parallel the physical movement of merchandise.

The idea of merchandise costs flowing through a firm can be illustrated with water and a bucket. The FIFO assumption is illustrated by water going into a bucket that has a hole in the bottom:

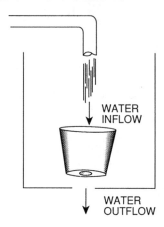

The first water to go into the bucket is the first water to leave through the hole. The water left at the end (meaning ending inventory) is the last water to flow into the bucket. If you are assigning costs to the Ending Inventory under the FIFO assumption, look at the last items purchased to get those per unit costs.

The LIFO assumption is illustrated by water going into a bucket that has a hole near the top:

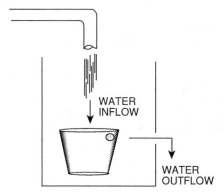

In this illustration, the first water to enter the bucket goes to the bottom and stays there. The water flowing out of the bucket is the last water entering the bucket after the water level has gone up to the height of the hole.

If you are assigning costs to the ending inventory for a company that uses the LIFO assumption, you must look at the beginning inventory (which was last year's ending inventory) and the early purchases to get the per-unit costs.

When the bucket analogy is applied to the AVCO assumption, the water goes into a bucket that has no hole in it. Water can be drawn from this bucket using a cup. Each time you stick the cup in the bucket full of water, you will get some water that first flowed in the bucket, some water that last flowed in the bucket, and water from in between the first and last flows.

When you are assigning costs to the ending inventory using the AVCO assumption, figure the total units and the total cost of those units available for sale (in other words: what did the whole bucket of water cost?). Then, divide the total cost by the total number of units to get the average unit cost.

1. Do the following according to the Introduction chapter:

   Load **Microsoft® Excel** and run **Info Macro**

2. Set up an inventory worksheet similar to the one in Figure 8-A. Save the inventory worksheet as **a:\tut8ws** but do not exit the program.

3. Open another window by doing the following:

   Drag **File** to **New**, click on **OK**, and run **Info Macro**

Set up the window to look like the income statement in Figure 8-B. Save the income statement as **a:\tut8is** and close the macro window.

   Drag **Window** to **Arrange All** and activate **TUT8WS.XLS** by clicking on any cell in that window

   Note: With later versions of Excel you should drag Window to Arrange and Click on Ok to accept the Tiled option.

4. Multiply the number of units by the unit cost to get the extended cost in cell G9. For example the extended cost for the physical inventory is derived with the following formula: =e9*f9. The formula is then filled down to the last invoice line. Use the SUM function to get the column totals in the Available for Sale row.

   Type **300** in cell **E17** and press **<Enter>**

# Figure 8-A: Inventory Worksheet Model

| | A | B | C | D | E | F | G | H | I | J | K | L | M | N | O |
|---|---|---|---|---|---|---|---|---|---|---|---|---|---|---|---|
| 1 | | Student Name | | "HUNGRY DOG" FOOD, INC. | | | | | | | | | | | |
| 2 | | 999-99-9999 | | INVENTORY WORKSHEET | | | | | | | | | | | |
| 3 | | Acct150 | | DECEMBER 31, 1993 | | | | | | | | | | | |
| 4 | | Chapter 8 | | | | | | | | | | | | | |
| 5 | | 15-Sep-93 | | | | FIRST-IN, FIRST-OUT | | | | AVERAGE COST | | | | LAST-IN, FIRST-OUT | |
| 6 | | | | | NO. OF | UNIT | EXTENDED | | NO. OF | UNIT | EXTENDED | | NO. OF | UNIT | EXTENDED |
| 7 | | DATE | DESCRIPTION | | UNITS | COST | COST | | UNITS | COST | COST | | UNITS | COST | COST |
| 8 | | | | | | | | | | | | | | | |
| 9 | | 12/31/92 | Physical Inventory | | 200 | 90.00 | | | | | | | | | |
| 10 | | 3/25/93 | Invoice #74588 | | 300 | 100.00 | | | | | | | | | |
| 11 | | 5/19/93 | Invoice #74923 | | 150 | 110.00 | | | | | | | | | |
| 12 | | 8/21/93 | Invoice #75471 | | 250 | 110.00 | | | | | | | | | |
| 13 | | 9/26/93 | Invoice #75964 | | 100 | 120.00 | | | | | | | | | |
| 14 | | | | | | | | | | | | | | | |
| 15 | | | Available for Sale | | | | | | | | | | | | |
| 16 | | | | | | | | | | | | | | | |
| 17 | | 12/31/93 | Physical Inventory | | | | | | | | | | | | |

## Figure 8-B: Income Statement Model

| | A | B | C | D | E | F | G | H | I | J | K |
|---|---|---|---|---|---|---|---|---|---|---|---|
| 1 | | Student Name | | | | | | | | | |
| 2 | | 999-99-9999 | | | PARTIAL INCOME STATEMENT | | | | | | |
| 3 | | Acct150 | | | FOR THE YEAR ENDED | | | | | | |
| 4 | | Chapter 8 | | | | | | | | | |
| 5 | | 15-Sep-93 | | | | | | | | | |
| 6 | | | | | FIRST-IN, | | | AVERAGE | | | LAST-IN, |
| 7 | | | | | FIRST-OUT | | | COST | | | FIRST-OUT |
| 8 | | | | | | | | | | | |
| 9 | | NET SALES | | $ | 252,000.00 | | $ | 252,000.00 | | $ | 252,000.00 |
| 10 | | COST OF SALES: | | | | | | | | | |
| 11 | | Beginning Inventory | | | | | | | | | |
| 12 | | Purchases | | | | | | | | | |
| 13 | | Less: Ending Inventory | | | | | | | | | |
| 14 | | | | | | | | | | | |
| 15 | | TOTAL COST OF SALES | | | | | | | | | |
| 16 | | | | | | | | | | | |
| 17 | | GROSS PROFIT | | | | | | | | | |

5. There is an easy way to copy a block of information from one range of cells to another:

> Drag cell **E9** to cell **G17** and drag **Edit** to **Copy**
> Drag cell **I9** to cell **K17** and drag **Edit** to **Paste**
> Drag cell **M9** to cell **O17** and drag **Edit** to **Paste**
> Press **<Escape>**

6. Figure the extended cost of the ending inventory under the FIFO assumption. Under this assumption, as you recall, the cost of the first drums of dog food purchased is the first cost to go. The ending inventory cost is that of the last 300 drums purchased, which you have to determine (at least in this example) from TWO DIFFERENT INVOICES. The trick is to get the computer (which is almost as dumb as a box of rocks) to understand it.

> Type  **=if(e17<=e13,f13*e17,e13*f13+(e17-e13)*f12)**  in cell **G17**
> and press **<Enter>**

The above IF function can be used if the ending inventory total cost can be gotten from the last two purchases. A Nested IF function is required if the ending inventory must be obtained from the last three or more purchases.

To figure the UNIT COST:

Type  $=g17/e17$  in cell **F17** and press **<Enter>**

Figuring the ending inventory cost using the FIFO assumption should make sense to you. It should parallel the physical movement of goods through a merchandising business. The first items purchased should be the first items sold, especially when there is a chance that the product could spoil or get stale. This assumption, however, does not match the most recent costs with the most recent selling prices. Your formatted unit cost should be 113.33, and your extended cost should be 34,000.00. Dollar signs aren't necessary in worksheets.

7. In this step you will be coming up with the formulas that determine the extended cost (or total cost) of the ending inventory using the average cost (AVCO) assumption.

Type  $=k15/i15$  in cell **J17** and press **<Enter>**
Type  $=i17*j17$  in cell **K17** and press **<Enter>**

When formatted, the unit cost is 104.00 and the extended cost is 31,200.00.

8. The IF function is also required to determine the total cost of the ending inventory using the LIFO assumption. In this case, however, the last drums of dog food are assumed to be the first ones to go.

Type  $=if(m17<=m9,n9*m17,m9*n9+(m17-m9)*n10)$  in cell **O17**
and press **<Enter>**
Type  $=o17/m17$  in cell **N17** and press **<Enter>**

You can see that the LIFO assumption has some problems reflecting the actual flow of dog food through the distributorship. If this assumption were applied to the physical flow of goods, the people at Hungry Dog wouldn't be able to sell anything until the last drums of dog food were purchased. (The last drum in has to be "in" before it can be the first drum out.) Also the early purchases of dog food would get stale after a while.

You must keep in mind that the LIFO assumption is merely an assumption. It does an effective job of matching the most recent costs with the most recent revenue. It also holds the lid on net income during periods of rising prices. The check figures are 93.33 and 28,000.00 (see Figure 8-C).

8-6

# Figure 8-C:  Completed Inventory Worksheet

Student Name
999-99-9999
Acct150
Chapter 8
15-Sep-93

"HUNGRY DOG" FOOD, INC.
INVENTORY WORKSHEET
DECEMBER 31, 1993

| DATE | DESCRIPTION | FIRST-IN, FIRST-OUT | | | AVERAGE COST | | | LAST-IN, FIRST-OUT | | |
|---|---|---|---|---|---|---|---|---|---|---|
| | | NO. OF UNITS | UNIT COST | EXTENDED COST | NO. OF UNITS | UNIT COST | EXTENDED COST | NO. OF UNITS | UNIT COST | EXTENDED COST |
| 12/31/92 | Physical Inventory | 200 | 90.00 | 18,000.00 | 200 | 90.00 | 18,000.00 | 200 | 90.00 | 18,000.00 |
| 3/25/93 | Invoice #74588 | 300 | 100.00 | 30,000.00 | 300 | 100.00 | 30,000.00 | 300 | 100.00 | 30,000.00 |
| 5/19/93 | Invoice #74923 | 150 | 110.00 | 16,500.00 | 150 | 110.00 | 16,500.00 | 150 | 110.00 | 16,500.00 |
| 8/21/93 | Invoice #75471 | 250 | 110.00 | 27,500.00 | 250 | 110.00 | 27,500.00 | 250 | 110.00 | 27,500.00 |
| 9/26/93 | Invoice #75964 | 100 | 120.00 | 12,000.00 | 100 | 120.00 | 12,000.00 | 100 | 120.00 | 12,000.00 |
| | Available for Sale | 1000 | | 104,000.00 | 1000 | | 104,000.00 | 1000 | | 104,000.00 |
| 12/31/93 | Physical Inventory | 300 | 113.33 | 34,000.00 | 300 | 104.00 | 31,200.00 | 300 | 93.33 | 28,000.00 |

9. Save your inventory worksheet as **a:\tut8ws** and activate the income statement window. In some of the next steps you will be transferring information to the income statement window from the inventory worksheet window as you did in chapter 4's tutorial.

10. Complete the income statement heading by doing the following:

> Type = in cell **E1** of the income statement (don't press <Enter> here)
>
> Click on any cell in the inventory worksheet window, arrow to cell **D1** and press **<Enter>**

Carry out a similar step for the heading date.

11. The beginning inventory is the same dollar amount for all three assumptions for this year, but the following will be needed for future years.

> Type **=tut8ws.xls!g9** in cell **E11** and press **<Enter>**

Identify the cell locations for the beginning inventory under the AVCO and LIFO columns and transfer them to the appropriate cells in the income statement window.

12. Record the purchases from TUT8WS.XLS. Be careful. This SUM function is complicated by the fact that you have to identify the cell range in the TUT8WS.XLS worksheet. When you enter the formulas correctly, you will see 86,000.00 appear in cells E12, H12 and K12. The purchase amount is the same for FIFO, AVCO and LIFO.

> Type **=sum(tut8ws.xls!$g$10:$g$13)** in cell **E12** and press **<Enter>**

Copy and paste the formula to cells H12 and K12.

13. Transfer the ending inventory amounts from TUT8WS.XLS to TUT8IS.XLS. Start your formulas with a minus sign since you are subtracting the ending inventories to compute the cost of sales amounts. Enter appropriate gross profit formulas.

14. The completed income statement should look like the one in Figure 8-C on the next page.

## Figure 8-D: Completed Income Statement

| | "HUNGRY DOG" FOOD, INC.<br>PARTIAL INCOME STATEMENT<br>FOR THE YEAR ENDED<br>DECEMBER 31, 1993 | | |
|---|---|---|---|
| Student Name<br>999-99-9999<br>Acct150<br>Chapter 8<br>15-Sep-93 | FIRST-IN,<br>FIRST-OUT | AVERAGE<br>COST | LAST-IN,<br>FIRST-OUT |
| NET SALES | $ 252,000.00 | $ 252,000.00 | $ 252,000.00 |
| COST OF SALES: | | | |
| Beginning Inventory | 18,000.00 | 18,000.00 | 18,000.00 |
| Purchases | 86,000.00 | 86,000.00 | 86,000.00 |
| Less: Ending Inventory | -34,000.00 | -31,200.00 | -28,000.00 |
| TOTAL COST OF SALES | $ 70,000.00 | $ 72,800.00 | $ 76,000.00 |
| GROSS PROFIT | $ 182,000.00 | $ 179,200.00 | $ 176,000.00 |

Save the worksheet and the income statement to the A drive and print them in a landscape orientation. Use compressed print for the inventory worksheet and regular-sized print for the income statement. Exit the program.

## Project:

Richard Growl, your boss at Hungry Dog, looks at the partial income statement you completed in the tutorial and likes what he sees! He wants you to do some what-if analysis for the year 1994. You are to create two pro forma income statements and help him pick which assumption (LIFO, FIFO, or AVCO) is best for the company.

The term *pro forma* comes from Latin and means "as a matter of form." It concerns the presenting of data where at least some of thc figures are hypothetical. Any budgetary analysis concerning future accounting periods is hypothetical because it is not based on transactions that have actually occurred.

1. Do the following in accordance with the instructions in the introduction of this workbook:

**Load Microsoft® Excel**

Close the **Sheet1** window.  Open **A:\TUT8WS.XLS** and **A:\TUT8IS.XLS**.

2.  Mr. Growl gives you the following information about 1994:

a.  The company plans to purchase 1,600 drums of dog food during 1994.  The expected purchase is 400 drums each quarter.  The cereal company has indicated that the following price schedule is anticipated for 1994:

| | |
|---|---|
| Jan-March | $122.50 per drum |
| April-June | $125.00 per drum |
| July-Sept | $127.50 per drum |
| Oct-Dec | $130.00 per drum |

b.  An ending inventory of 500 drums is planned for 12/31/94.

c.  Mr. Growl is negotiating a quantity discount schedule with the cereal company sales representative.  The cereal company hasn't approved the schedule yet, but if it does, the following discounts will apply:

| QUANTITY PER ORDER | DISCOUNT |
|---|---|
| 0-599 drums | None |
| 600-799 drums | 6% |
| 800-999 drums | 8% |
| Over 999 drums | 10% |

d.  If the discount schedule becomes effective before March 31, 1994, Hungry Dog will purchase 800 drums of dog food during March and 800 drums during September.  Be careful here.  A quantity discount is not the same as a purchase discount.  Do not change the format of the income statement.  You only have to reduce the per-drum cost by the amount of the discount.

e.  The sales price increase planned for 1994 will be 5% per bag.

Hint:  Assume Hungry Dog always gets the same number of bags per drum.  Thus, the price increase per drum will also be 5%.  The company expects to sell more bags of dog food in 1994 than in 1993.

3. Change the inventory worksheet to show the four planned purchases of 400 drums each in March, June, September, and December. Assume the quantity discount schedule does not go into effect. Check the inventory worksheet carefully to make sure the dates and formulas are appropriate. Save the inventory worksheet as **a:\proj8aws** and the pro forma income statement as **a:\proj8ais** and print them.

4. Change the inventory worksheet to show the two planned purchases of 800 drums each in March and September. Assume the quantity discount schedule goes into effect before the March purchase. Check the inventory worksheet carefully to make sure the dates and formulas are appropriate. Save the inventory worksheet as **a:\proj8bws** and the pro forma income statement as **a:\proj8bis** and print them.

5. (Optional) Type a note to Mr. Growl advising him which assumption (LIFO, FIFO, or AVCO) he should select. Also indicate whether he should include the cost of the labor to fill the five-pound bags, the cost of the bags, and other overhead costs in the total cost of sales amount.

# Assignment:

Prepare by hand the two inventory worksheets and two partial income statements required in the project.

# Chapter Eight Transmittal Sheet for Excel

A. Hand in this page to your instructor with the following items attached in the order requested:

1. Two project worksheets
2. Two project pro forma income statements
3. Hand-written assignment
4. Project step 5 note to Mr. Growl (optional)

B. How would you change the worksheets to better facilitate the transfer of information to the pro forma income statements?

# Chapter Nine

# Asset Depreciation

---

## Chapter Objectives:

A. Create macros to compute financial statement depreciation for various assets under the double-declining-balance (DDB) and the straight-line (STLN) methods assuming a mid-month convention.

B. Create macros to compute federal tax return depreciation under the Modified Accelerated Cost Recovery System (MACRS) rules that assume a mid-year convention.

## Tutorial:

Ms. T. L. Werthman, owner of Werthman High-Speed Printing, is considering the purchase of a 6-color printing press. The model she is looking at costs $6 million. By the time it is shipped from Europe to the United States, and is installed in her building, the expected cost of the press will jump to $10 million.

She plans to use the press for the next 10 years. Ms. Werthman is concerned, however, that technology changes may make the press obsolete before the end of that time period. Her feeling is that a schedule showing the double-declining-balance method of depreciation will be appropriate here. She also wants to see what the depreciation schedule will look like if the straight-line method is used instead. Assume a mid-month convention for the two methods.

Ms. Werthman also wants to see how the printing press will decrease in value from an original basis for tax purposes. Assume that you're not sure how the IRS classifies the life of a printing press, so you decide to use the MACRS percentages for 7-year property and 10-year property.

1. Do the following according to the instructions in the Introduction chapter:

Load **Microsoft® Excel** and run **Info Macro**

2. Create a schedule that is similar the one in Figure 9-A. Enter the numbers in cells G4 through G6 without commas. Then format them to show the commas.

> Hint: There is a quick way to enter years in cells B15 through B25. Enter the formula =b14+1 in cell B15. Copy cell B15 to cells B16 through B25 by dragging Edit to Fill Down.

## Figure 9-A: Single Asset Depreciation Schedule

| | B | C | D | E | F | G | H | I |
|---|---|---|---|---|---|---|---|---|
| 1 | Student Name | | | ASSET NAME: | | 6-COLOR PRINTING PRESS | | |
| 2 | 999-99-9999 | | | PURCHASE DATE: | | 14-May-93 | | |
| 3 | Acct150 | | MONTH OF PURCHASE (1-12): | | | 5 | | |
| 4 | Chapter 9 | | | CAPITAL VALUE: | | 10,000,000 | | |
| 5 | 15-Sep-93 | | RESIDUAL (OR SALVAGE) VALUE: | | | 1,000,000 | | |
| 6 | | | | TAX RETURN BASIS: | | 10,000,000 | | |
| 7 | | TAX RETURN DEPRECIATION METHOD: | | | | | | |
| 8 | FINANCIAL STATEMENT DEPRECIATION METHOD: | | | | | | | |
| 9 | | | | | | | | |
| 10 | YEAR | FINANCIAL STATEMENT DEPRECIATION | | | | TAX RETURN DEPRECIATION | | |
| 11 | | BOOK | PORTION | DEPRN EXP | | BASIS MINUS | DEPRN | DEPRN EXP |
| 12 | | VALUE | OF YEAR | FOR YEAR | | ACCUM DEPRN | PERCENT | FOR YEAR |
| 13 | | | | | | | | |
| 14 | 1993 | | | | | | | |
| 15 | 1994 | | | | | | | |
| 16 | 1995 | | | | | | | |
| 17 | 1996 | | | | | | | |
| 18 | 1997 | | | | | | | |
| 19 | 1998 | | | | | | | |
| 20 | 1999 | | | | | | | |
| 21 | 2000 | | | | | | | |
| 22 | 2001 | | | | | | | |
| 23 | 2002 | | | | | | | |
| 24 | 2003 | | | | | | | |
| 25 | 2004 | | | | | | | |

Note: The schedule in Figure 9-A is similar to one of two asset depreciation schedules that are often encountered in the workplace. The schedule not illustrated here, which is often called the annual schedule of assets, lists all of the depreciable assets in one report. It shows the depreciation expense for a particular year.

3. In the top portion of the schedule you just completed are some terms that may not be familiar to you. The term *capital value* is the cost of an asset plus any reasonable amounts paid to get that asset installed and ready for service. Assets acquired through an exchange (trade-in) may have different capital values.

The term *tax return basis* refers to the value of the asset for federal tax return purposes. It could be reduced by a Section 179 Election amount, but this subject is beyond the scope of this chapter. There could also be a state return basis, but this subject is also beyond the scope of this chapter.

The numbers that go in the Deprn Percent column come from IRS percentage tables that help business people cope with the elaborate set of rules for tax depreciation.

4. Put the following formulas in the Book Value column and format them:

> Type  =g4  in cell C14 and press <Enter>
> Type  =c14-e14  in cell C15 and press <Enter>
> Drag cell C15 to cell C25 and drag Edit to Fill Down
> Drag cell C14 to cell C25 and drag Format to Number
> Click on #,##0 and OK

5. Put formulas in the Basis Minus Accum Deprn column to show decreasing book value for tax purposes:

> Type  =g6  in cell G14 and press <Enter>
> Type  =g14-i14  in cell G15 and press <Enter>
>
> Drag cell G15 to cell G25 and drag Edit to Fill Down
> Drag cell G14 to cell G25
> Drag Format to Number and click on #,##0 and OK

6. Format cells E14 through E25 and I14 through I25 as you did column G in step 5. Continue the formatting by doing the following:

Drag cell **D14** to cell **D25**
Drag **Format** to **Number** and click on **0.00**

Move the icon until it appears to the right of **0.00** in the **Format box** and click the left-hand mouse button.

Add a **0** (zero) to the number that appears in the **Format Box** and click on **OK**
Drag cell **H14** to cell **H25**
Drag **Format** to **Number** and click on **0.00%** and **OK**

7. Now you will create your first MACRS macro:

Press **<Ctrl> <Home>** and drag **Macro** to **Record**
Type **MACRS7** and click on **OK**
Arrow to cell **G7**
Type **MACRS7** and press **<Enter>**
Press **<F5>** and type **h14** and press **<Enter>**

With **<Shift>** key pressed down,
Arrow to cell **I25**
Drag **Edit** to **Clear** and click on **OK**

Type **.1429** in cell **H14** and press **<Enter>**
Type **.2449** in cell **H15** and press **<Enter>**
Type **.1749** in cell **H16** and press **<Enter>**
Type **.1249** in cell **H17** and press **<Enter>**
Type **.0893** in cell **H18** and press **<Enter>**
Type **.0892** in cell **H19** and press **<Enter>**
Type **.0893** in cell **H20** and press **<Enter>**
Type **.0446** in cell **H21** and press **<Enter>**

8. Set up the formulas for the computation of the Tax Return Depreciation expense. These formulas have an IF function nested in a function that is new to you, the ROUND function. The ROUND function is important in schedules where numbers in one column are subtracted from numbers in another column. If you don't use the ROUND function, you will discover that certain mathematical answers may be off a dollar or so.

Type **=round($g$6*h14,0)** in cell **I14** and press **<Enter>**

The zero at the end of the formula indicates that your answer is being rounded to the nearest dollar. If the number *2* were there instead, your answer would be rounded to the nearest penny.

Drag cell **I14** to cell **I20** and drag **Edit** to **Fill Down**
Type  **=g21**  in cell **I21** and press **<Enter>**
Drag **Macro** to **Stop Recorder**

9.  To view the macro you just created do the following:

Drag **Window** to **Macro1** and drag **Format** to **Column Width**
Type  **18**  and press **<Enter>**

Arrow down column A slowly. Notice that Macro1 looks like any spreadsheet. Cell A1 contains the name of the Macro. Cell A2 shows your move to cell G7 (7th row, 7th column) of the worksheet. If you need to edit the Macro for any reason, use the regular edit commands discussed in the Introduction chapter.

Drag **Window** to **Sheet1**

10.  Create the macro for 10-year property:

Press  **<Ctrl> <Home>**  and drag **Macro** to **Record**
Type  **MACRS10**  and click on **OK**
Arrow to cell **G7**
Type  **MACRS10**  and press **<Enter>**
Press  **<F5>** and type  **h14**  and press **<Enter>**
With  **<Shift>**  key pressed down,
Arrow to cell **I25**
Drag **Edit** to **Clear** and click on **OK**

Type  **.1**  in cell **H14** and press **<Enter>**
Type  **.18**  in cell **H15** and press **<Enter>**
Type  **.144**  in cell **H16** and press **<Enter>**
Type  **.1152**  in cell **H17** and press **<Enter>**
Type  **.0922**  in cell **H18** and press **<Enter>**
Type  **.0737**  in cell **H19** and press **<Enter>**
Type  **.0655**  in cell **H20** and press **<Enter>**
Type  **.0655**  in cell **H21** and press **<Enter>**
Type  **.0656**  in cell **H22** and press **<Enter>**

Type  **.0655**  in cell **H23** and press  **<Enter>**
Type  **.0328**  in cell **H24** and press  **<Enter>**

Type  **=round($g$6*h14,0)**  in cell **I14** and press  **<Enter>**
Drag cell **I14** to cell **I23** and drag **Edit** to **Fill Down**
Type  **=g24**  in cell **I24** and press  **<Enter>**
Drag **Macro** to **Stop Recorder**

11.  As you recall from the beginning of this tutorial, Ms. Werthman expects to use the printing equipment for 10 years.  She is interested in seeing the results of both the straight-line and double-declining-balance methods for computing depreciation.  In this step you will be designing a macro for straight-line depreciation for assets with a 10-year life.

In your textbook there is probably a formula that would allow you to compute straight line depreciation as follows:

$$\frac{\text{Cost - Residual Value}}{\text{Years}} = \frac{10,000,000 - 1,000,000}{10} = 900,000$$

The $900,000 depreciation amount is the expense for one year of the asset's life.  There is a problem in applying the formula above in real life because the lives of assets rarely match fiscal years.  The formula really only works for assets that are purchased on "day one" of a company's fiscal year. Since most businesses have the calendar year as the fiscal year, all assets would have to be purchased on New Year's Day to comply with the formula.

Although the depreciation expense is $900,000 for the first year of the asset's life, only $562,500 (7.5/12) can be taken during the year ended 12/31/93.  When a mid-month convention is used, an asset purchased during a month is assumed to be purchased in the middle of that month.

12.  Set up the macro for straight-line depreciation for 10-year assets as follows:

Press  **<Ctrl> <Home>**  and drag **Macro** to **Record**
Type  **STLN10**  and click on **OK**

Arrow to cell **G8**, type  **STLN10**  and press  **<Enter>**
Press  **<F5>**  and type  **d14**  and press  **<Enter>**

With <Shift> key pressed down,
Arrow to cell **E25** and drag **Edit** to **Clear**
Click on **OK**

Even though the depreciation expense in this macro is computed for 10 years, that computation is actually included in a range of 11 years. You are recording just a portion of the asset's annual depreciation expense in the first and eleventh years.

Type  **=(12.5-g3)/12**  in cell **D14** and press **<Enter>**

---

**Since the fifth month is indicated in cell G3:**

**(12.5-g3) means there are 7.5 months between the middle of May and the end of December.**
**/12 means the 7.5-month period is divided by 12 to get the portion of the year expressed as a factor. You should see the factor, 0.625, in cell D14.**

---

Type  **1.000**  in cell **D15** and press **<Enter>**
Drag cell **D15** to cell **D23** and drag **Edit** to **Fill Down**
Type  **=(g3-.5)/12**  in cell **D24** and press **<Enter>**

Note: The factor 0.375 (representing 37.5% of a year) should appear on your computer screen in cell D24. There are 4.5 months between the beginning of the year and the middle of May (4.5 months / 12 months = .375).

Type  **=round(($g$4-$g$5)/10*d14,0)**  in cell **E14** and
       press **<Enter>**
Drag cell **E14** to cell **E23** and drag **Edit** to **Fill Down**
Type  **=c24-g5**  in cell **E24** and press **<Enter>**
Drag **Macro** to **Stop Recorder**

The Book Value column should show a decrease from 10,000,000 to 1,000,000 (no dollar signs should appear in the worksheet).

13.  Set up a macro for the double-declining-balance method of depreciation. The word *double* in this method means twice the straight-line

rate. If the straight-line rate is 10% per year, as it is for a 10-year asset, then the word *double* means 20% per year.

The term *declining balance* actually means declining-book-value balance (DBVB). It is because the DBVB goes down at a decreasing rate that you don't subtract the salvage value from the historical cost to find the amount subject to depreciation.

Before you set up the macro for DDB10, you need to be warned about the DDB Function in **Microsoft₀ Excel**:

> Arrow to cell **E14**
> Drag **Formula** to **Paste Function**
> Arrow to **DDB( )** and click on **Paste Arguments Box** (to put
>     an X in the box) and click on **OK**

If you look in the formula bar, that runs along the top of your computer screen, you should see:

> =**DDB(cost,salvage,life,period)**

This function works well if you are interested in finding the depreciation for one year of an asset's life. It does not work well when you want the depreciation for a company's fiscal year and the asset is purchased part-way through the year.

> Press **<Enter>** and drag **Edit** to **Clear**
> Click on **OK** and press **<Ctrl> <Home>**

It is time to set up the macro for DDB10:

> Drag **Macro** to **Record**
> Type  **DDB10**  and click on **OK**
> Arrow to cell **G8**, type  **DDB10**  and press **<Enter>**
> Press **<F5>** and type  **d14**  and press **<Enter>**
> With **<Shift>** key pressed down, arrow to cell **E25**
> Drag **Edit** to **Clear** and click on **OK**
> Type  **=(12.5-g3)/12**  in cell **D14** and press **<Enter>**
> Type  **1.000**  in cell **D15** and press **<Enter>**
> Drag cell **D15** to cell **D25** and drag **Edit** to **Fill Down**
> Type  **=round(c14*.2*d14,0)**  in cell **E14** and press **<Enter>**

Note: The .2 in the formula above is a factor that stands for "20% per year" as previously discussed. Notice the same .2 in the formula below.

The formula that goes into cell E15 is an IF function which is nested in another IF function which is nested in a ROUND function. An explanation of this complex formula appears in the box below.

Type
=round(if(c15-(c15*.2) > = $g$5,c15*.2,if(c15-$g$5 > -1,c15-$g$5,0)),0)
in cell **E15** and press **< Enter >**

---

**EXPLANATION OF FORMULA FOR
DOUBLE-DECLINING-BALANCE METHOD**

| | |
|---|---|
| **Question #1 (Argument):** | **Is the book value at the beginning of the year minus the depreciation expense for that year greater than or equal to the residual (or salvage) value?** |
| **If Yes (True):** | **Put the depreciation expense for that year in cell E15.** |
| **If No (False):** | **Ask Question #2.** |
| **Question #2 (Argument):** | **Is the book value at the beginning of the year minus the salvage value greater than −1 (minus one)?** |
| **If Yes (True):** | **Put the book value at the beginning of the year minus the salvage value in cell E15.** |
| **If No (False):** | **Put 0 (zero) in cell E15.** |

---

Drag cell **E15** to cell **E25**
Drag **Edit** to **Fill Down**
Drag **Macro** to **Stop Recorder**

14. To test, save, and print your work:

> Drag **Macro** to **Run** and click on **MACRS7** and **OK**
> Drag **Macro** to **Run** and click on **STLN10** and **OK**

Your worksheet should similar to the one in Figure 9-B. Save this worksheet as **a:\tut9a** and print it in a portrait orientation using compressed print.

## Figure 9-B: Worksheet with MACRS7 and STLN10

| Student Name | ASSET NAME: | 6-COLOR PRINTING PRESS |
| --- | --- | --- |
| 999-99-9999 | PURCHASE DATE: | 14-May-93 |
| Acct150 | MONTH OF PURCHASE (1-12): | 5 |
| Chapter 9 | CAPITAL VALUE: | 10,000,000 |
| 15-Sep-93 | RESIDUAL (OR SALVAGE) VALUE: | 1,000,000 |
| | TAX RETURN BASIS: | 10,000,000 |
| | TAX RETURN DEPRECIATION METHOD: | MACRS7 |
| | FINANCIAL STATEMENT DEPRECIATION METHOD: | STLN10 |

| YEAR | FINANCIAL STATEMENT DEPRECIATION | | | TAX RETURN DEPRECIATION | | |
| --- | --- | --- | --- | --- | --- | --- |
| | BOOK VALUE | PORTION OF YEAR | DEPRN EXP FOR YEAR | BASIS MINUS ACCUM DEPRN | DEPRN PERCENT | DEPRN EXP FOR YEAR |
| 1993 | 10,000,000 | 0.625 | 562,500 | 10,000,000 | 14.29% | 1,429,000 |
| 1994 | 9,437,500 | 1.000 | 900,000 | 8,571,000 | 24.49% | 2,449,000 |
| 1995 | 8,537,500 | 1.000 | 900,000 | 6,122,000 | 17.49% | 1,749,000 |
| 1996 | 7,637,500 | 1.000 | 900,000 | 4,373,000 | 12.49% | 1,249,000 |
| 1997 | 6,737,500 | 1.000 | 900,000 | 3,124,000 | 8.93% | 893,000 |
| 1998 | 5,837,500 | 1.000 | 900,000 | 2,231,000 | 8.92% | 892,000 |
| 1999 | 4,937,500 | 1.000 | 900,000 | 1,339,000 | 8.93% | 893,000 |
| 2000 | 4,037,500 | 1.000 | 900,000 | 446,000 | 4.46% | 446,000 |
| 2001 | 3,137,500 | 1.000 | 900,000 | 0 | | 0 |
| 2002 | 2,237,500 | 1.000 | 900,000 | 0 | | 0 |
| 2003 | 1,337,500 | 0.375 | 337,500 | 0 | | 0 |
| 2004 | 1,000,000 | | | 0 | | 0 |

> Drag **Macro** to **Run** and click on **MACRS10** and **OK**
> Drag **Macro** to **Run** and click on **DDB10** and **OK**

Your worksheet should look similar to the one in Figure 9-C. Save this worksheet as **a:\tut9b** and print it as above. Save your macro worksheet as **a:\deprn9a** and exit the program.

## Figure 9-C: Worksheet with MACRS10 and DDB10

```
Student Name                     ASSET NAME:   6-COLOR PRINTING PRESS
999-99-9999                     PURCHASE DATE:       14-May-93
Acct150              MONTH OF PURCHASE (1-12):           5
Chapter 9                       CAPITAL VALUE:       10,000,000
15-Sep-93        RESIDUAL (OR SALVAGE) VALUE:        1,000,000
                              TAX RETURN BASIS:       10,000,000
          TAX RETURN DEPRECIATION METHOD:   MACRS10
  FINANCIAL STATEMENT DEPRECIATION METHOD:   DDB10
```

| YEAR | FINANCIAL STATEMENT DEPRECIATION | | | TAX RETURN DEPRECIATION | | |
|------|------------|----------|----------|------------|---------|----------|
| | BOOK VALUE | PORTION OF YEAR | DEPRN EXP FOR YEAR | BASIS MINUS ACCUM DEPRN | DEPRN PERCENT | DEPRN EXP FOR YEAR |
| 1993 | 10,000,000 | 0.625 | 1,250,000 | 10,000,000 | 10.00% | 1,000,000 |
| 1994 | 8,750,000 | 1.000 | 1,750,000 | 9,000,000 | 18.00% | 1,800,000 |
| 1995 | 7,000,000 | 1.000 | 1,400,000 | 7,200,000 | 14.40% | 1,440,000 |
| 1996 | 5,600,000 | 1.000 | 1,120,000 | 5,760,000 | 11.52% | 1,152,000 |
| 1997 | 4,480,000 | 1.000 | 896,000 | 4,608,000 | 9.22% | 922,000 |
| 1998 | 3,584,000 | 1.000 | 716,800 | 3,686,000 | 7.37% | 737,000 |
| 1999 | 2,867,200 | 1.000 | 573,440 | 2,949,000 | 6.55% | 655,000 |
| 2000 | 2,293,760 | 1.000 | 458,752 | 2,294,000 | 6.55% | 655,000 |
| 2001 | 1,835,008 | 1.000 | 367,002 | 1,639,000 | 6.56% | 656,000 |
| 2002 | 1,468,006 | 1.000 | 293,601 | 983,000 | 6.55% | 655,000 |
| 2003 | 1,174,405 | 1.000 | 174,405 | 328,000 | 3.28% | 328,000 |
| 2004 | 1,000,000 | 1.000 | 0 | 0 | | 0 |

## Project:

The word from Ms. Werthman's CPA is the printing press is 7-year property for tax purposes. One of the CPA's tax manuals reads, "Property with a life of 10 to 16 years is 7-year property." Did you laugh at this little bit of nonsense? The 7-year category also includes office furniture. Most of the business assets owned by Werthman High-Speed Printing is 5-year property for tax purposes. This category includes: autos, trucks, typewriters, calculators, photocopy machines and computers.

1. Follow the instructions in the Introduction chapter to do the following:

Load **Microsoft**® **Excel** and open **a:\tut9a.xls**

2. Ms. Werthman asks you to make sure you have included among your Macros the MACRS percentage table for 5-year property:

| Recovery Year | 5-Year Property |
|:---:|:---:|
| 1 | 20.00% |
| 2 | 32.00% |
| 3 | 19.20% |
| 4 | 11.52% |
| 5 | 11.52% |
| 6 | 05.76% |

Create a MACRS5 macro for the federal tax return depreciation. Create a DDB6 Macro for the financial statement depreciation. The factor *.3333* is appropriate for your formulas here. Save your new macros as **a:\deprn9b**.

3. On June 21, 1993, Ms. Werthman buys a new delivery van. The listed price of the van is $18,085.11. She is able to get it for 6% less (including applicable taxes and license fees). She prefers that you enter the asset on the books at the full list price so that she can get a larger depreciation expense for tax purposes. You tell her that you will do what is right.

She has an accident on the way back to the company. The cost to repair the van is $530. She wants you to add the repair charge to the asset cost since it will not really be "ready for service" until the company logo is painted on the sides. You tell her that you will do what is right.

Create an asset depreciation schedule using the MACRS5 and DDB6 macros. Assume a 10% residual (or salvage) value of $1,700 for the financial statement depreciation. Save the depreciation schedule as **a:\proj9a** and print it.

4. A photocopy machine was purchased on April 13, 1990, for $3,217 (including sales tax). A salvage value of $217 was established at the time. Create an asset schedule showing the DDB6 method for financial statement

depreciation and MACRS5 for federal tax return depreciation. The year in cell B14 should be 1990. Save it as **a:\proj9b** and print it.

On August 10, 1994, the old machine is traded in on a new one that lists for $6,750 (including sales tax). A "generous" trade-in allowance of $500 is given on the old machine; the difference is financed with a note. Don't figure any depreciation expense in the trade year for the old machine.

Create an asset depreciation schedule for the new photocopy machine. Use a 10% residual (or salvage) value. Save it as **a:\proj9c** and print it.

5. (Optional) Type a memo to Ms. Werthman that suggests the journal entries showing the trade for the new machine and the year-end depreciation adjustment. Use the Figure 9-D as a guideline.

**Figure 9-D: Partial Illustration of a Memo**

```
                        MEMORANDUM


     Date:      Today's date


     To:        Ms. Werthman

     From:      Your name

     Subj:      The new photocopy machine
```

# Assignment:

Prepare by hand the depreciation expense schedules for the assets discussed in the project.

Student Name:_____

Date:_____

# Chapter Nine Transmittal Sheet for Excel

A. Hand in this page to your instructor with the following items attached in the order requested:

    1. Three project depreciation worksheets
    2. Hand-written assignment
    3. Project step 5 memo to Ms. Werthman (optional)

B. Show your computation for the capital value of the new delivery van in project step 3.

C. The amounts you computed for the capital value and the tax return basis on the new photocopy machine should be different. Show your computations below.

# Chapter Ten

# Notes Payable Comparison

---

## Chapter Objectives:

A. Create a schedule comparing a note showing a principle amount with an interest rate with a note showing a maturity value.

B. Create a chart showing the effects of interest and discount on two short-term notes.

## Tutorial:

Mr. Paul Bunyon, owner of Bunyon's Sporting Goods, needs to borrow some money for 90 days. He goes to the Uptown Bank, where he has his business checking account, and asks for the current interest rate. His loan officer tells him it is 12% on short-term notes with a principle amount of $100,000 or more. Since the interest rate is in the double digits, he decides to check out the deal at First City Bank, where he maintains his personal checking account.

The loan officer there indicates that their short-term notes show a maturity value on the face. Their current discount rate is 12% when $100,000 or more is borrowed.

Mr. Bunyon asks the First City Bank loan officer what the difference is between interest and discount. The loan officer explains that when an interest rate is used, he starts with the present value of a note (called *principle*). As time passes, he adds interest until the note balance reaches a maturity (or future) value on the due date of the note. When he uses a discount rate, he starts with the maturity value on the due date. He then backs up in time and deducts a discount amount until he has the present value balance (cash proceeds).

Mr. Bunyon says, "Yeah, right. . . ," and comes to you. He admits that he got confused by the explanation and forgot to ask the right question. He wants you to show him if the amount he could receive from a note with an interest rate of 12% is significantly different from the amount he could receive from a note with a discount rate of 12%. You decide (because this tutorial says so) that you are going to have the computer draw him a picture that shows the difference. The notes should have the same maturity value for a fair comparison.

1.    Load **Microsoft®** **Excel** and run the **Info Macro**.

2.  Set up a worksheet that looks similar to the one in Figure 10-A.

### Figure 10-A:  Tutorial Worksheet

| A | B | C | D | E |
|---|---|---|---|---|
| 1 | Student Name | BUNYON'S SPORTING GOODS | | |
| 2 | 999-99-9999 | NOTES PAYABLE COMPARISON | | |
| 3 | Acct150 | | | |
| 4 | Chapter 10 | PRINCIPLE | MATURITY VALUE | |
| 5 | 15-Sep-93 | PLUS INTEREST | LESS DISCOUNT | |
| 6 | | ------------------------- | ------------------------- | |
| 7 | DATE OF NOTE: | | | |
| 8 | DAYS TO MATURITY: | | | |
| 9 | DATE NOTE MATURES: | | | |
| 10 | INTEREST RATE: | | XXXXXXXXXXXX | |
| 11 | DISCOUNT RATE: | XXXXXXXXXXXX | | |
| 12 | PRINCIPLE AMOUNT: | | XXXXXXXXXXXX | |
| 13 | ADD INTEREST: | | XXXXXXXXXXXX | |
| 14 | MATURITY VALUE: | | | |
| 15 | LESS DISCOUNT: | XXXXXXXXXXXX | | |
| 16 | CASH PROCEEDS: | XXXXXXXXXXXX | | |
| 17 | | =============== | =============== | |
| 18 | | | | |
| 19 | DATES: | | | |
| 20 | NOTE WITH PRINCIPLE PLUS INTEREST: | | | |
| 21 | NOTE WITH MATURITY VALUE LESS DISCOUNT: | | | |
| 22 | | | | |

Hints:  The B column width should be 40.  The C and D column widths should be 15.  Press the <Spacebar> once before you type ---- as a dashed line under the column heading and before you type = = = = under the cash proceeds line.

3. Save the worksheet as **a:\tut10**. A good philosophy is to sa⟩ and save often.

4. Put the data in the appropriate cells:

> Type **7/1/93** in cell **C7** and press **<Enter>**
> Type **90** in cell **C8** and press **<Enter>**
> Type **=c7+c8** in cell **C9** and press **<Enter>**
> Drag cell **C7** to cell **D9** and drag **Edit** to **Fill Right**
> Drag cell **C7** to cell **D7** and drag **Format** to **Number**
> Arrow to **d-mmm-yy** and press **<Enter>**

Format the date in cells **C9** and **D9** the same way.

> Type **.12** in cells **C10** and **D11** and press **<Enter>**
> Drag cell **C10** to cell **D11** and drag **Format** to **Number**
> Arrow to **0.00%** and press **<Enter>**
> Type **100000** in cell **C12** and press **<Enter>**

Type the interest amount in cell C13 as a formula. You probably recall from your accounting class that the formula for interest is:

**I = P R T**

The P (or principle) is the amount in cell C12. The R (or rate) is the amount in cell C10. The T (or time) is the number of days in cell C8 divided by 365.

> Note: Your accounting textbook may use a 360-day year to keep the computations simple, but in the real world, a 365-day year is more common.

> Type **=round(c12*c10*c8/365,2)** in cell **C13** and press **<Enter>**
> Type **=c12+c13** in cell **C14** and press **<Enter>**
> Type **102958.90** in cell **D14** and press **<Enter>**

You will be typing the formula for the discount amount in cell D15. Some textbooks indicate the discount formula is:

**D = MV R T**

In this example the MV (or maturity value) is higher than the P (or principle) from the interest formula above. So if R (or rate) and T (or time) are identical, the discount amount will be larger than the interest amount. Notice that the money Mr. Bunyon can get from First City Bank (cash proceeds) is less than the money he can get from Uptown Bank (principle).

Type  **=round(d14\*d11\*d8/365,2)**  in cell **D15** and press **<Enter>**
Type  **=d14-d15**  in cell **D16** and press **<Enter>**

Drag cell **C12** to cell **D16**
Drag **Format** to **Number** and click on **#,##0.00** and **OK**

5.  Lastly, establish a range of information that will be used to create a chart.

Type  **=c7**  in cell **C19** and press **<Enter>**
Type  **=d9**  in cell **D19** and press **<Enter>**

Drag cell **C19** to cell **D19** and press **<Enter>**
Drag **Format** to **Number**
Arrow to **d-mmm-yy** and press **<Enter>**

Type  **=c12**  in cell **C20** and press **<Enter>**
Type  **=c14**  in cell **D20** and press **<Enter>**
Type  **=d16**  in cell **C21** and press **<Enter>**
Type  **=d14**  in cell **D21** and press **<Enter>**

Drag cell **C20** to cell **D21** and drag **Format** to **Number**
Click on **$#,##0 ;($#,##0)** and **OK**

Save the worksheet as  **a:\tut10**  and print it in a portrait orientation using a compressed type font.  Compare it with Figure 10-B.

You have probably noticed that you were asked to save your work often in the previous tutorials. Company managers often establish "comfort zones" when it comes to saving work. Some managers set a 4-hour policy. In other words, you should save (or back up) your work when you are done or every four hours, whichever is shorter.  When quick access to the work is critical, the policy may be to save (or back up) the work every 15 minutes.

## Figure 10-B: Interest versus Discount

```
Student Name                              BUNYON'S SPORTING GOODS
999-99-9999                               NOTES PAYABLE COMPARISON
Acct150
Chapter 10                                PRINCIPLE  MATURITY VALUE
15-Sep-93                                 PLUS INTEREST  LESS DISCOUNT
                                          ------------------  ------------------------
                      DATE OF NOTE:        1-Jul-93              1-Jul-93
                   DAYS TO MATURITY:             90                    90
                 DATE NOTE MATURES:      29-Sep-93             29-Sep-93
                     INTEREST RATE:         12.00%         XXXXXXXXXXXX
                     DISCOUNT RATE:  XXXXXXXXXXXX              12.00%
                   PRINCIPLE AMOUNT:     100,000.00       XXXXXXXXXXXX
                       ADD INTEREST:       2,958.90       XXXXXXXXXXXX
                    MATURITY VALUE:      102,958.90           102,958.90
                    LESS DISCOUNT:  XXXXXXXXXXXX              3,046.46
                    CASH PROCEEDS:  XXXXXXXXXXXX             99,912.44
                                          ===============  ===============

                           DATES:        1-Jul-93             29-Sep-93
     NOTE WITH PRINCIPLE PLUS INTEREST:    $100,000             $102,959
  NOTE WITH MATURITY VALUE LESS DISCOUNT:    $99,912             $102,959
```

6. Create a chart showing the difference between the two notes discussed in step 1 of this tutorial.

> Drag cell **C19** to cell **D21** and drag **File** to **New**
> Click on **Chart** and **OK**

A column chart should appear on your computer screen. Columns go up and down in this software program, and bars go left and right. A column chart is the wrong kind of chart for your purposes here.

> Drag **Gallery** to **Line** and click on **Chart 1** and **OK**

A line chart should replace the column chart on your screen. This chart has a horizontal axis which is a time line. The vertical axis shows dollars. This chart shows that there is a difference between the principle amount of one note and the cash proceeds of the other note, but the difference is small.

Drag **Chart** to **Attach Text** and click on **Chart Title** and **OK**
Type **NOTES PAYABLE COMPARISON** and press **<Enter>**
Drag **File** to **Page Setup** and click on **Full Page** and **OK**

7. Save the chart as **a:\tut10** and print it. Exit the program

Note: Your line chart may look a little different than the one in Figure 10-C. The chart was compressed to fit in this workbook.

**Figure 10-C: Line Chart**

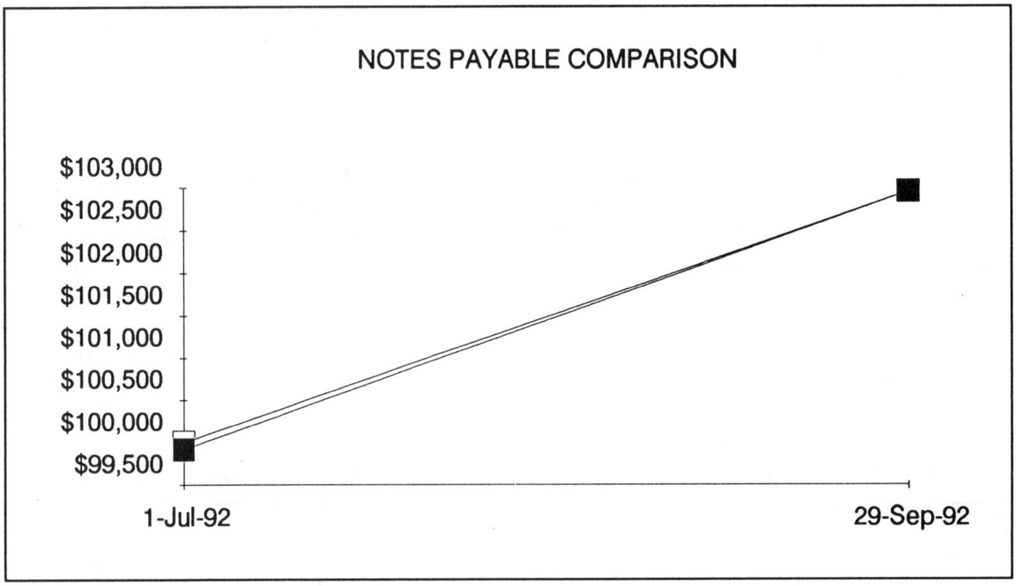

NOTES PAYABLE COMPARISON

## Project:

Paul Bunyon wants to take your notes payable comparison report and the chart to First City Bank to see if he can negotiate a lower and more competitive discount rate, but he needs more information.

1.  Load **Microsoft® Excel** and open **A:\TUT10.XLS.**

2. Figure the discount rate that brings the cash proceeds closest to the principle amount. Figure the discount rate to the nearest one-hundredth of

one percent. Save your worksheet as **a:\proj10a** and print it. Create a chart. Save it as **a:\proj10A** and print it. This information will help Paul Bunyon bargain for a better discount rate.

3. Assume that Mr. Bunyon finds he can get a 120-day note at an 11.75% interest rate through one of his suppliers, so he decides to finance his merchandise purchase through them. The date of the note is July 15, 1993. Assume the note is sold by the supplier at a discount rate of 14.25% on the same day. Save your revised worksheet as **a:\proj10b** and print it.

4. (Optional) If the supplier's operating cycle is 120 days and his gross profit is 30%, why is it worth it for the supplier to discount the note? Refer to the project 10b worksheet in step 3. Make the supplier's expected gross profit a part of your typed one-page answer.

5. Enter the appropriate information from the two notes that are illustrated on the following page. The discount rate on the second note is 13.25%. Save your worksheet as **a:\proj10c** and print it.

6. Create a chart to illustrate the two notes discussed in step 5. Save your chart as **a:\proj10c** and print it.

## Assignment:

Prepare by hand the notes payable comparison worksheets that illustrate the information in this chapter's project.

## Figure 10-D:  Note with Principle and Interest

_$_ 50,000.00         Denver, Colorado__February 22, 1994_

__Thirty Days_____after date___I__promise to pay to

the order of __Rocky Mountain Sporting Goods_____

__fifty thousand and no/100-------------------dollars

for value received with interest at __13.75%___

payable at __First City Bank__

                                    _____
                                        Paul Bunyon


## Figure 10-E:  Note Showing Maturity Value

_$_ 50,600.00         Denver, Colorado__February 22, 1994_

__Thirty Days_____after date___I__promise to pay to

the order of __Rocky Mountain Sporting Goods_____

__fifty thousand six hundred------------------dollars

for value received payable at _____First City Bank____

                                    _____
                                        Paul Bunyon

Student Name:_____

Date:_____

# Chapter Ten Transmittal Sheet for Excel

A. Hand in this page to your instructor with the following items attached in the order requested:

1. Three project notes payable comparison worksheets
2. Two project notes payable comparison charts
3. Hand-written assignment
4. Project step 4 report to your instructor (optional)

B. Use project steps 3 and 5 worksheets to answer the following questions:

1. How much does the supplier mentioned in step 3 lose by discounting the note? Show your computations.

2. Which note in step 5 is a better deal for Bunyon's Sporting Goods? Show your computations.

Notes:

# Chapter Eleven

# Payroll Analysis

---

## Chapter Objectives:

A.  Create databases for federal income tax withholding amounts for single and married persons.

B.  Create a database for an annual payroll register from which employee earnings records can be extracted.

C.  Create macros to determine federal income tax withheld according to gross pay amount, marital status, the number of allowances, and the payroll period length.

## Tutorial:

Raymond Evans is the owner and only employee of MINFORS Consulting Corp.  MINFORS is an acronym for "manufacturing information systems." He is a consultant to manufacturing companies that are too small to maintain a computer programming department.

Assume that he has come to you, his next door neighbor, to ask if you would design a simple payroll register for him.  He could design it himself, but he is not up on the current payroll tax laws.  You, with your characteristic enthusiasm, decide the project would be an interesting learning experience.

You go down to the local office of the Internal Revenue Service to pick up the Employer's Tax Guide, which is publication 15, Circular E (revised 2/92).  You find out that a 6.2% social security tax is to be computed on the first $55,500 of an employee's wages for 1992.  You also find out that a

11-1

1.45% medicare tax is to be computed on the first $130,200 of an employee's wages. MINFORS Consulting Corp. will incur expenses for the social security and medicare taxes that are equal to the deductions for each employee. The amounts will go into a Payroll Tax Expense account.

In addition, MINFORS will have an expense for federal unemployment tax. The tax is 6.2% of the first $7,000 of each employee's wages; however, a credit of 5.4% is given because your state has an unemployment tax system.

Next, you wander over to the state office building. Each state that has an income tax deduction system, has an annual guide similar to the federal payroll publication (Circular E). For the purpose of this chapter only, assume that the state income tax deduction for each employee is 30% of the federal income tax computed. Also assume that the state has a mandatory disability insurance program that requires a 1.2% deduction on the first $21,000 of each employee's wages. The program provides benefits to employees who get injured off the job and are not covered by worker's compensation.

The bureaucrats at the state office building won't give you the state unemployment tax percentage so you have to find that out from Mr. Evans. It is 2.5% according to the most recent quarterly tax return that he filed with the state.

1. Load **Microsoft₈ Excel** and run the **Info Macro**.

2. Create two databases for federal income tax withholding amounts, one for single employees and one for married employees, from Figure 11-A on the next page. You will be creating macros later in this tutorial and in the project that will use a VLOOKUP (Vertical Lookup) function to find the tax to withhold.

3. Create a payroll register database from Figures 11-B and 11-C. The payroll register is split into two figures because it is too long for this workbook. Cut and paste the student information block from cells B1 through B5 to cells K31 through F35. Transfer the company name and date by doing the following:

> Type = in cell **N31** and press **<Home>**
> Press **<PageUp>** and arrow to cell **E1** and press **<Enter>**
> Type = in cell **N34** and press **<Home>**
> Press **<PageUp>** and arrow to cell **E3** and press **<Enter>**

## Figure 11-A: FIT Withholding Tables

| | A | B | C | D | E | F | G | H | I |
|---|---|---|---|---|---|---|---|---|---|
| 1 | | Student Name | | | MINFORS CONSULTING CORP. | | | | |
| 2 | | 999-99-9999 | | | PAYROLL DATABASE | | | | |
| 3 | | Acct150 | | | DECEMBER 31, 1992 | | | | |
| 4 | | Chapter 11 | | | | | | | |
| 5 | | 15-Sep-93 | | | | | | | |
| 6 | | | | | | | | | |
| 7 | | | | | | | | | |
| 8 | | SINGLE PERSONS--MONTHLY PAYROLL PERIOD | | | | | | | |
| 9 | | | | | | | | | |
| 10 | | WAGES | | NUMBER OF WITHHOLDING | | | | | |
| 11 | | ARE AT | | ALLOWANCES CLAIMED IS: | | | | | |
| 12 | | LEAST | | 0 | 1 | 2 | 3 | | |
| 13 | | 4760 | | 1086 | 1027 | 967 | 908 | | |
| 14 | | 4800 | | 1098 | 1039 | 980 | 920 | | |
| 15 | | 4840 | | 1111 | 1051 | 992 | 933 | | |
| 16 | | 4880 | | 1123 | 1064 | 1004 | 945 | | |
| 17 | | 4920 | | 1136 | 1076 | 1017 | 957 | | |
| 18 | | | | | | | | | |
| 19 | | | | | | | | | |
| 20 | | MARRIED PERSONS--MONTHLY PAYROLL PERIOD | | | | | | | |
| 21 | | | | | | | | | |
| 22 | | WAGES | | NUMBER OF WITHHOLDING | | | | | |
| 23 | | ARE AT | | ALLOWANCES CLAIMED IS: | | | | | |
| 24 | | LEAST | | 0 | 1 | 2 | 3 | | |
| 25 | | 4760 | | 835 | 782 | 728 | 674 | | |
| 26 | | 4800 | | 847 | 793 | 739 | 686 | | |
| 27 | | 4840 | | 858 | 804 | 751 | 697 | | |
| 28 | | 4880 | | 880 | 827 | 773 | 719 | | |
| 29 | | 4920 | | 891 | 838 | 784 | 730 | | |
| 30 | | | | | | | | | |

Note: Be extra careful to enter the numbers in cells B13 through B17 and cells B25 through G29 as numbers and not as text. If the numbers are entered as text, they will fail to work in formulas in the payroll register.

## Figure 11-B:  Left Side of Payroll Register Database

| | K | L | M | N | O | P | Q | R | S |
|---|---|---|---|---|---|---|---|---|---|
| 31 | Student Name | | | | | | MINFORS CONSULTING CORP. | | |
| 32 | 999-99-9999 | | | | | | PAYROLL REGISTER | | |
| 33 | Acct150 | | | | | | FOR THE YEAR ENDED | | |
| 34 | Chapter 11 | | | | | | DECEMBER 31, 1992 | | |
| 35 | 15-Sep-93 | | | | | | | | |
| 36 | | | | | | | | | |
| 37 | LAST_NAME | FIRST_NAME | MI | SS_NMBR | M_STATUS | WH_ALLOW | ACCUM_EARN | GROSS_PAY | FIT_WH |
| 38 | Evans | Raymond | T | | | | | | |
| 39 | | | | | | | | | |
| 40 | | | | | | | | | |
| 41 | | | | | | | | | |
| 42 | | | | | | | | | |
| 43 | | | | | | | | | |
| 44 | | | | | | | | | |
| 45 | | | | | | | | | |
| 46 | | | | | | | | | |
| 47 | | | | | | | | | |
| 48 | | | | | | | | | |
| 49 | | | | | | | | | |
| 50 | | | | | | | | | |

A database looks like any another worksheet except it is organized into fields and records.  For example, the payroll register database (Figures 11-B and 11-C) has vertical fields and horizontal records.  At the top of each vertical field is a label like LAST_NAME or GROSS_PAY.  Two or more separate words in a label are connected together into a single string using the <Underline > key.  This database has 17 labels identifying 17 fields.

Each row in the payroll register database is a single record.  Each record in this data base has 17 field cells.  Each record can be accessed to retrieve certain information.  You will learn to sort database records.

4. It is time to complete the first record in the payroll register database. Enter Mr. Evans' social security number *333-22-4444* in cell N38.  Mr. Evans' M_STATUS (marital status) is single.  Type the word *Single* in cell O38 and right align it.  He has put one withholding allowance on his W-4 form.  Type the word *One* in cell P38 and right align it.

Since this is the first payroll check for 1992, his accumulated earnings from prior payment dates is entered as the number *0* in cell Q38.  Format the 0 to look like 0.00.  Enter *4770* as Mr. Evans' gross pay and format it to look like 4,770.00 without a dollar sign in cell R38.

**Figure 11-C: Right Side of Payroll Register Database**

| | T | U | V | W | X | Y | Z | AA |
|---|---|---|---|---|---|---|---|---|
| 31 | | | | | | | | |
| 32 | | | | | | | | |
| 33 | | | | | | | | |
| 34 | | | | | | | | |
| 35 | | | | | | | | |
| 36 | | | | | | | | |
| 37 | SST_WH | MCARE_WH | SIT_WH | DISAB_WH | NET_PAY | PE_DATE | PMT_DATE | CK_NMBR |
| 38 | | | | | | | | |
| 39 | | | | | | | | |
| 40 | | | | | | | | |
| 41 | | | | | | | | |
| 42 | | | | | | | | |
| 43 | | | | | | | | |
| 44 | | | | | | | | |
| 45 | | | | | | | | |
| 46 | | | | | | | | |
| 47 | | | | | | | | |
| 48 | | | | | | | | |
| 49 | | | | | | | | |
| 50 | | | | | | | | |

5. Create a macro to determine the federal income tax withheld. It takes into consideration the gross pay amount, marital status, number of allowances, and the payroll period length.

> Arrow to cell **S38** and drag **Macro** to **Record**
> Type **MSONE** and click on **OK**
> Type **=vlookup(** and press **<LeftArrow>**
> Type **,$b$13:$g$17,4)** and press **<Enter>**
> Drag **Macro** to **Stop Recorder**

6. Look at the Vertical Lookup Function that you just created within the MSONE (monthly, single, one) macro:

> Drag **Window** to **Macro1** and drag **Format** to **Column Width**
> Type **30** and press **<Enter>**

Your macro should look similar to the one in Figure 11-D. If it doesn't, drag File to Close and record the macro again.

**Figure 11-D: MSONE Macro**

| | A | B |
|---|---|---|
| 1 | MSONE | |
| 2 | =FORMULA("=VLOOKUP(RC[-1],R13C2:R17C7,4)") | |
| 3 | =RETURN() | |
| 4 | | |
| 5 | | |
| 6 | | |
| 7 | | |

In cell A1 is the macro name, MSONE. It stands for Monthly Table, Single Person, ONE Withholding Allowance. In cell B1 is the VLOOKUP (Vertical Lookup) function. It compares the gross pay in the cell to the left of the active cell (RC[-1]) with the wage amounts in the Monthly Single Persons Income Tax Withholding Table. The function selects a wage that is not greater than the gross pay. The dollar signs in $B$13:$G$17 establish the array in the withholding table as an absolute cell address range. Notice that this array appears as R13C2:R17C7 in the macro.

The number *4* that you see on the right side of cell B1 means you have selected the fourth column of the withholding table from which to draw the income tax to be withheld. The wages are in column 1. Column 2 is blank. Column 3 has the income tax amounts for a zero allowance. Column 4, for one allowance, is the one selected.

7. To test the macro you just created:

> Drag **Window** to **Sheet1** and make sure you are in cell **S38**
> Drag **Edit** to **Clear** and click on **OK**
> Drag **Macro** to **Run** and click on **MSONE** and **OK**

The amount *1027* should appear in cell S38. Format the number so that it looks like 1,027.00.

8. Compute the social security tax to be withheld in cell T38. A Nested IF function inside a Round function is required here.

> Type
> **=round(if(q38+r38<=55500,r38\*.062,if(55500-q38>0,(55500-q38)\*.062,0)),2)**
> in cell **T38** and press **<Enter>**

An explanation of the Nested IF function is in the shaded box.

---

### NESTED IF FUNCTION TEST
### FOR SOCIAL SECURITY TAX

**Upper Limit Test: Q38 + R38 < = 55500**
Is the sum of the accumulated earnings from prior payment dates plus the gross pay from this payment date less than or equal to $55,500?

**If the Answer Is Yes: R38*0.62**
The function multiplies the gross pay by 6.2% to get the social security tax to be withheld.

**If the Answer Is No:**
Conduct a lower limit test.

**Lower Limit Test: 55500-Q38 > 0**
Is $55,500 minus the accumulated earnings from prior payment dates greater than zero?

**If the Answer Is Yes: (55500-Q38)*0.062**
Subtract the accumulated earnings from $55,500 and multiply the result by 6.2% to get the social security tax to be withheld.

**If the Answer Is No: 0**
Put a 0 (zero) in cell T38.

---

Note: The number 2 at the end of the character string at the bottom of the previous page means the Round function will round the social security tax to two decimal places (cents).

9. The medicare tax to be withheld in cell U38 also requires a Nested IF function within a Round function.

Type   = round(if(q38 + r38 < = 130200,r38*.0145,
if(130200-q38 > 0,(130200-q38)*.0145,0)),2)
in cell **T38** and press **<Enter>**

Note: The character string shown above should be entered on one line.

## Figure 11-E: Left Side of Payroll Register Database

```
Student Name                                    MINFORS CONSULTING CORP.
999-99-9999                                     PAYROLL REGISTER
Acct150                                         FOR THE YEAR ENDED
Chapter 11                                      DECEMBER 31, 1992
15-Sep-93


LAST_NAME   FIRST_NAME  MI   SS_NMBR   M_STATUS  WH_ALLOW  ACCUM_EARN  GROSS_PAY  FIT_WH
Evans       Raymond     T    333-22-4444  Single    One          0.00   4,770.00 1,027.00
Evans       Raymond     T    333-22-4444  Single    One      4,770.00   4,800.00 1,039.00
```

10.  The state income tax to be withheld in cell V38 is assumed to be 30% of the federal income tax calculated in cell S38:

Type  **=round(s38*.3,2)**  and press  **<Enter>**

11.  The disability insurance withheld in cell W38 requires a Nested IF function within a Round function similar to the social security tax.  Assume it is 1.2% of the first $21,000 of an employee's wages.

Type
**=round(if(q38+r38<=21000,r38*.012,if(21000-q38>0,(21000-q38)*.012,0)),2)**
in cell **T38** and press  **<Enter>**

12.  The net pay in cell X38 is the gross pay minus the sum of the payroll deductions:

Type  **=r38-sum(s38:w38)**  in cell **X38** and press  **<Enter>**

**Figure 11-F:  Right Side of Payroll Register Database**

| SST_WH | MCARE_WH | SIT_WH | DISAB_WH | NET_PAY | PE_DATE | PMT_DATE | CK_NMBR |
|--------|----------|--------|----------|---------|---------|----------|---------|
| 295.74 | 69.17 | 308.10 | 57.24 | 3,012.75 | 12/31/91 | 1/2/92 | 12345 |
| 297.60 | 69.60 | 311.70 | 57.60 | 3,024.50 | 1/31/92 | 2/1/92 | 12346 |

13.  A period ending date, a payment date, and a check number have to be entered in the last three cells of this record (row):

> Type  **12/31/91**  in cell **Y39** and press **< Enter >**
> Type  **1/2/92**  in cell **Z38** and press **< Enter >**
> Drag cell **Y38** to cell **Z38** and drag **Format** to **Number**
>
> Click on the **DownArrow** in the **Format Number Box**
> Until **m/d/yy** appears
> Click on **m/d/yy** and **OK**
> Type  **12345**  in cell **AA38** and press **< Enter >**

14.  Assume that a month has passed by and you have to enter another record in the payroll register database.  This time Mr. Evans has earned $4,800.

> Drag cell **K38** to cell **P39** and drag **Edit** to **Fill Down**
> Type  **=**  in cell **Q39** and press **< UpArrow >**
> Type  **+**  and press **< UpArrow >** and press **< RightArrow >**
> Press **< Enter >**
> Type  **4800**  in cell **R39** and press **< Enter >**
> Run the **MSONE** macro in cell **S39**

11-9

Drag cell **T38** to cell **X39** and drag **Edit** to **Fill Down**
Format the dollar amounts in cells **Q39** through **X39**
Type  **1/31/92**  in cell **Y39** and press **<Enter>**
Type  **2/1/92**  in cell **Z39** and press **<Enter>**
Format the dates in cells **Y39** and **Z39**
Type  **12346**  in cell **AA39** and press **<Enter>**

Your tutorial should appear similar to Figures 11-E and 11-F.

15.  Save the macro as  **a:\pay11**  and save the worksheet as  **a:\tut11.**
Establish a print range in  **TUT11.XLS**  by doing the following:

Drag cell **J31** through cell **AA39**
Drag **Options** to **Set Print Area**

Print  **TUT11.XLS**  in a landscape orientation using a compressed font.
Exit the program.

# *Project:*

During the rest of the year a number of things happen to MINFORS
Consulting Corp. that affect the entries in the payroll register database.  Mr.
Evans gets married.  He also invites a close associate to join the firm.  The
business is still not big enough to invite a third person to invest in his
corporation. If it grows anymore, however, you'll get an invitation--if you'll
choose to accept it.

1.  Load **Microsoft®** **Excel** and open **A:\PAY11.XLM** and **A:\TUT11.XLS.**

2.  On March 1, 1992, Raymond Evans writes himself paycheck number
12347 in the amount of $3,050.  He asks you to figure the gross pay so that
his take home pay is the above amount.  You are delighted to figure this out
in exchange for dinner at his house prepared by his fiancee.

3.  Mr. Evans marries the love of his life during March and is back from
his honeymoon in time for his paycheck on April 1.  His gross pay is $4,900
for the period ended March 31, 1992.  His marital status has changed.  He
now wants two allowances.  Create a macro named MMTWO to compute
the federal income tax to be withheld.  Use check number 12348.

4. Use the same gross pay amount for the May 1 pay date. Use check number 12349. His net pay should be different because of the change in the disability insurance to be withheld. You're invited to his house for dinner again. Now that he is married, he will do the cooking.

5. Roberta J. Hummell joins the firm on May 1 as an equal partner (even though the firm is a corporation). Operationally, she is a partner. Legally, she is an employee of the firm. Her gross pay will be $4,900 per month. She is married and has declared three allowances on her W-4 form. Her social security number is 444-33-2222. Create a macro named MMTHREE to handle her situation. Use the next available paycheck number on June 1 (when she gets her first paycheck).

6. Also prepare a paycheck record for Mr. Evans for 6/1/92. An easy way to do this is as follows:

> Drag cell **K42** to cell **X42** and drag **Edit** to **Copy**
> Drag cell **K43** to cell **X43** and drag **Edit** to **Paste**
> Press **<Escape>** to turn the marquee off

Correct the accumulated earnings amount in cell Q43. It can be done by adding one cell location to another.

7. Prepare paycheck records for Mr. Evans and Mrs. Hummell for the next six payment dates (through December 1). Your last payroll record should be on row 56 and should include check number 12363. Type the word *Totals* in cell Q58. Total the Gross Pay, Deduction, and Net Pay columns in the register using SUM functions. The total net pay for the year should be 65,758.57.

8. Print the payroll register database. You don't want to print the whole worksheet, so you must establish the cell range to be printed:

> Drag cell **K31** to cell **AA58** and drag **Options** to **Set Print Area**

Print the payroll register database using a landscape orientation and a compressed font. Save your worksheet as **a:\proj11a** but do not leave the program.

9. Set up an employee earnings record for Mr. Evans. Copy the student information in cells K31 through K35 to cells K61 through K65.

Enter the following heading in cells Q61 through Q64:

> MINFORS CONSULTING CORP.
> EMPLOYEE EARNINGS RECORD
> FOR THE YEAR ENDED
> DECEMBER 31, 1992

Copy the field names in cells K37 through AA37 to cells K67 through AA67. Also, do the following:

> Type  **LAST_NAME**  in cell **G67** and press **<Enter>**
> Type  **="Evans"**  in cell **G68** and press **<Enter>**

10. Extract Mr. Evans' records from the payroll register database and put them in the employee earnings record. To do this, set the database range, the criteria range (his last name is the criteria), and the extract range (where the data is going).

> Drag cell **K37** to cell **AA56** and drag **Data** to **Set Database**
> Drag cell **G67** to cell **G68** and drag **Data** to **Set Criteria**
> Drag cell **K67** to cell **AA80**, drag **Data** to **Extract** and click on **OK**

11. Arrow up and down the FIT_WH and SST_WH fields. Notice that the formulas that were in the payroll register database cells are missing. Each cell in the extract range contains the value produced by a formula but not the formula itself. Enter the label *Totals* in cell Q81. Use the SUM function to get the totals for gross pay, deductions, and net pay.

12. Set the print area for cells K61 through AA81 and save the employee earnings record as **a:\proj11b** and print it using a landscape orientation and a compressed font.

13. Create an employee earnings record for Mrs. Hummell by doing the following:

> Type  **="Hummell"**  in cell **G68** and press **<Enter>**
> Drag cell **K67** to cell **AA80**, drag **Data** to **Extract** and click on **OK**

Save this record as  **a:\proj11c**  and print it.

14. (Optional) All databases can be sorted, but not all databases can be sorted with appropriate results. Typical sorted databases maintained by companies are customer lists or inventory schedules. Customer lists can be sorted by LAST_NAME/FIRST_NAME or STATE/CITY. Inventory schedules can be sorted by DESCRIPTION or ID_NMBR. This particular payroll register database, because of the way it is constructed, cannot be sorted with appropriate results.

You are going to sort it anyway. Do the following to sort the payroll register database by check number in descending order:

Drag cell **K38** through cell **AA56** and drag **Data** to **Sort**

Note: Rows is the default option by which you will sort since each record is by row.

Type **aa38** in the **1st Key** box and click on **Descending** and **OK**

Arrow through the payroll register database. Notice that certain cells have the phrase *#VALUE!* in them. Other cells may not have appropriate amounts in them. Type a one-page report indicating what a database MUST NOT HAVE to be suitable for sorting. Cite specific examples. You do not have to save or print this sorted database. Exit the program.

## *Assignment:*

Do the project payroll register by hand.

# Chapter Eleven Transmittal Sheet for Excel

A. Hand in this page to your instructor with the following items attached in the order requested:

1. Project payroll register database
2. Project Evans' employee earnings record
3. Project Hummell's employee earnings record
4. Hand-written assignment
5. Project step 14 report (optional)

B. The last paycheck for Raymond Evans should show a decrease in the social security tax withheld. Show below the computation for the amount.

C. Show the formula in cell X55 that computes the net pay.

# Chapter Twelve

# Partnership Profit and Loss Allocation

---

## Chapter Objectives:

A. Create schedules that show the allocation of partnership profit (net income) or loss using different methods that are determined by the articles of co-partnership.

B. Use what-if analysis at different levels of partnership net income (or loss) to determine each partner's share.

## Tutorial:

It has been said that business partnerships are a lot like marriages. They are easy to get into, just like marriages. In fact, they are easier to get into than marriages. You and a friend of yours can "put up some bucks," shake hands, and start a business partnership with an oral agreement.

Partnerships can be expensive to get out of, just like marriages. You may read about the high cost of divorce litigation in the news. Getting out of an acrimonious business partnership can be just as hard on the participants--both financially and emotionally.

If you ever think of forming a business partnership, take your ideas to a good attorney and a good accountant. The good attorney will probably advise you to start a corporation. The joint issues of "mutual agency" and "unlimited personal liability" make participation in general partnerships too risky. If you still insist on entering into a partnership, the attorney can draft a partnership agreement (articles of co-partnership) for you and your business partner.

Before you sign the agreement, take it to a good accountant. Your accountant can test the provisions of your agreement using different levels of net income (and loss). You are then in a position to make necessary changes to the partnership agreement before it is signed.

1. Assume for this tutorial that you are in a partnership with a friend (of your choosing) and that you, instead of your accountant, are preparing the worksheet illustrated in Figure 12-A. Create the worksheet after doing the following:

Load **Microsoft®** Excel and run **Info Macro**

## Figure 12-A: Tutorial Worksheet

| | A | B | C | D | E | F | G | H | I |
|---|---|---|---|---|---|---|---|---|---|
| 1 | | Student Name | | YOUR NAME & YOUR PARTNER'S NAME | | | | | |
| 2 | | 999-99-9999 | | PARTNERSHIP PROFIT & LOSS ALLOCATION | | | | | |
| 3 | | Acct150 | | DECEMBER 31, 1993 | | | | | |
| 4 | | Chapter 12 | | | | | | | |
| 5 | | 15-Sep-93 | | YOUR | | YOUR | | UNALLOCATED | |
| 6 | | | | NAME | | FRIEND'S | | NET INCOME | |
| 7 | | | | HERE | | NAME | | (NET LOSS) | |
| 8 | | | | | | | | | |
| 9 | | NET INCOME (LOSS) | | | | | | | |
| 10 | | First Allocation Based on | | | | | | | |
| 11 | | Average Capital Balances | | | | | | | |
| 12 | | Your Name | | | | | | | |
| 13 | | Your Friend's Name | | | | | | | |
| 14 | | TOTAL | | | | | | | |
| 15 | | | | | | | | | |
| 16 | | NET INCOME (LOSS) LEFT | | | | | | | |
| 17 | | FOR FURTHER ALLOCATION | | | | | | | |
| 18 | | Second Allocation Based on | | | | | | | |
| 19 | | Sharing of Service (Salary) | | | | | | | |
| 20 | | Your Name | | | | | | | |
| 21 | | Your Friend's Name | | | | | | | |
| 22 | | TOTAL | | | | | | | |
| 23 | | | | | | | | | |
| 24 | | NET INCOME (LOSS) LEFT | | | | | | | |
| 25 | | FOR FURTHER ALLOCATION | | | | | | | |
| 26 | | Third Allocation Based on | | | | | | | |
| 27 | | Sharing of Remaining | | | | | | | |
| 28 | | Net Income (Loss) | | | | | | | |
| 29 | | Your Name | | | | | | | |
| 30 | | Your Friend's Name | | | | | | | |
| 31 | | TOTAL | | | | | | | |
| 32 | | | | | | | | | |
| 33 | | NET INCOME (LOSS) LEFT | | | | | | | |
| 34 | | FOR FURTHER ALLOCATION | | | | | | | |
| 35 | | | | | | | | | |
| 36 | | TOTAL NET INCOME (LOSS) | | | | | | | |
| 37 | | ALLOCATED TO PARTNERS | | | | | | | |
| 38 | | | | | | | | | |
| 39 | | | | | | | | | |

2. Do the following:

> Set the row height to **3** for rows **35** and **38**
> Press **<Ctrl> <Home>** and save this worksheet as **a:\tut12**

3. Split the worksheet into two windows and enter some financial data:

> Click on **Control Menu Icon** (the minus sign at the left end of the
> document window title bar) and click on **Split**
> Click on the left edge of row **8** header
> Click on cell **B9** and arrow to cell **B39**

> Note: Don't remove the split now. You can remove it by moving your icon to the
> black bar between the two arrows on the right side of the split line. Your icon
> should change in shape to a white bar with two arrows. Drag the icon to the top
> of the vertical bar above the UpArrow.

Assume that you are projecting a net income of $90,000. Also assume that your average capital balance is $60,000 and that your partner's average capital balance is $40,000. Your partnership agreement calls for a 12% return on your average capital balances:

> Type **90000** in cell **H9** and press **<Enter>**
> Type **=60000\*.12** in cell **D12** and press **<Enter>**
> Type **=40000\*.12** in cell **F13** and press **<Enter>**
> Type **-(d12+f13)** in cell **H14** and press **<Enter>**

The minus sign at the beginning of the formula in cell H14 is there for a good reason. As you allocate dollars to the partners, you must subtract the amount you allocate from the Unallocated Net Income balance.

> Type **=h9+h14** in cell **H17** and press **<Enter>**

4. The second allocation, a Sharing of Service amount, is based on the time you put into the business. Your textbook may use the term *partners' salaries* for this allocation. Assume that you and your partner each put 100% of the time in the business (as defined by your articles of co-partnership). Your salary is $24,000 and your partner's salary is $18,000.

Notice that a Salary Expense account is not used here. A partner's salary is not an expense of the business. It is merely an allocation of the net income (or loss) that is produced by the business.

Type **24000** in cell **D20** and press **<Enter>**
Type **18000** in cell **F21** and press **<Enter>**
Type **−(d20+f21)** in cell **H22** and press **<Enter>**
Type **=h17+h22** in cell **H25** and press **<Enter>**

5. Your computer screen should show an Unallocated Net Income balance of 36000 in cell **H25**. This amount is to be divided equally:

Type **=h25/2** in cell **D29** and press **<Enter>**
Type **=h25/2** in cell **F30** and press **<Enter>**
Type **−(d29+f30)** in cell **H31** and press **<Enter>**
Type **+h25+h31** in cell **H34** and press **<Enter>**

Your answer in cell **H34** should be 0 (zero). It should always be zero! When you have allocated ALL of the net income, there is nothing left to allocate.

6. Use the SUM function to figure the total income allocated to each partner:

Type **=sum(d8:d34)** in cell **D37** and press **<Enter>**
Type **=sum(f8:f34)** in cell **F37** and press **<Enter>**
Type **=d37+f37** in cell **H37** and press **<Enter>**

The check figure in cell **H37** should be 90000. This number SHOULD ALWAYS BE EQUAL to the number in cell **H9**.

Go to cell **D9**
Drag cell **D9** to cell **H37** and drag **Format** to **Number**
Arrow to **$#,##0 ;($#,##0)**

DO NOT CLICK ON THE OK BOX OR PRESS THE <ENTER> KEY! (If you did, arrow to **$#,##0 ;($#,##0)** again.) Edit the number in the **Format Box** to take out the dollar signs since they are not necessary in worksheets:

Move the mouse until the **I-beam** icon appears between **$** and **#**
Click **Left-Hand** mouse button and press **<BackSpace>**
Remove the other dollar sign the same way and press **<Enter>**

Save the worksheet as **a:\tut12** and print it in a portrait orientation with regular-sized type. Exit the program.

**Figure 12-B: Tutorial Worksheet**

| | YOUR NAME HERE | YOUR FRIEND'S NAME | UNALLOCATED NET INCOME (NET LOSS) |
|---|---|---|---|
| Student Name<br>999-99-9999<br>Acct150<br>Chapter 12<br>15-Sep-93 | YOUR NAME & YOUR PARTNER'S NAME<br>PARTNERSHIP PROFIT & LOSS ALLOCATION<br>DECEMBER 31, 1993 | | |
| NET INCOME (LOSS) | | | 90,000 |
| First Allocation Based on | | | |
| Average Capital Balances | | | |
| Your Name | 7,200 | | |
| Your Friend's Name | | 4,800 | |
| TOTAL | | | (12,000) |
| NET INCOME (LOSS) LEFT | | | |
| FOR FURTHER ALLOCATION | | | 78,000 |
| Second Allocation Based on | | | |
| Sharing of Service (Salary) | | | |
| Your Name | 24,000 | | |
| Your Friend's Name | | 18,000 | |
| TOTAL | | | (42,000) |
| NET INCOME (LOSS) LEFT | | | |
| FOR FURTHER ALLOCATION | | | 36,000 |
| Third Allocation Based on | | | |
| Sharing of Remaining | | | |
| Net Income (Loss) | | | |
| Your Name | 18,000 | | |
| Your Friend's Name | | 18,000 | |
| TOTAL | | | (36,000) |
| NET INCOME (LOSS) LEFT | | | |
| FOR FURTHER ALLOCATION | | | 0 |
| TOTAL NET INCOME (LOSS) | | | |
| ALLOCATED TO PARTNERS | 49,200 | 40,800 | 90,000 |

# Project:

Assume that you are a gourmet chef and your friend is a nutritionist. The two of you have come up with a business plan that has the working name Lean City Deli. The new wrinkle to your plan is the following: When your potential customers FAX in their orders, they can specify a goal amount for the number of calories they want to eat for the next 24 hours.

Central to your business plan is a computer program that will suggest a diet plan that includes the food items your customers order within their calorie goal. It will print a 24-hour menu of meals and snacks that you will hand out to your customers when they come in to pick up their orders.

Your partner is excited about the computer part your new business plan because the customers, who follow the printed daily diet plan, will get the proper balance of carbohydrates, protein, fat, vitamins, and minerals. You are excited about the monetary part of the business plan because it includes revenue from "add-on" sales. Your "lunch bunch" may buy the dinner entre that is suggested on the 24-hour menu. Your "dinner crowd" might take home a frozen entre for the next day's lunch.

1. Do the following according to the instructions in the Introduction chapter:

Load **Microsoft**® **Excel** and open **A:\TUT12.XLS**

2. Assume that your accountant checks over your business plan and finds a critical thinking error. As a result, your expected net income for the first year of operations is only $9,000.

Type **9000** in cell **H9** and press **<Enter>**

Arrow down the H column. Notice that the "first allocation to partners" results in a $3,000 loss in cell H17. The allocation of partners' salaries increases the loss to $45,000 in cell H25.

The expected share of the $9,000 net income to you is $8,700. Your partner is unhappy with the $300 allocation he or she gets. Furthermore, your accountant is concerned that you did not budget enough advertising money to "prime the business pump." You will also need a stronger cash flow in order to survive.

Assume that your market study calls for radio spots and direct mail advertising to reach your target customers. Radio spots (commercials) cost five times the amount you budgeted during the time when your potential customers listen. Your accountant also suggests that you double the direct mail budget for the first month of operations.

When the new data are included in your business plan, you discover you will need an additional $80,000 cash before you open the doors.

3. Assume that you find a third partner with $80,000 to risk on your new venture. Change the worksheet to accommodate the additional person. This person will be a limited partner and will have no voice in the day-to-day operations of your business. Assume that he or she recognizes that the investment in your new business comes with greater risk than an investment in an existing business. Therefore, this person wants a 13.5% return on his or her capital investment and wants 40% of the net income (or loss) available for the third allocation.

Your friend, the nutritionist (partner number 2), has decided to work full time for the first half of the year and half time after that. Adjust the $18,000 annual salary accordingly. Remember, that in the third allocation, you and the nutritionist are splitting what's left after partner number 3 gets 40%.

After the changes above have been made to your worksheet, it should show that the $9,000 net income amount is allocated as follows:

| Partner | Amount |
|---|---|
| #1  You | $15,810 |
| #2  The nutritionist | $2,910 |
| #3  The new investor | $9,720 Loss |

4. Assume your accountant plays what-if and proposes a $67,000 loss for your first year of operations. Enter the loss and save your worksheet as **a:\proj12a**. Print the worksheet in a portrait orientation using a condensed-sized type.

5. Assume your accountant, who is still playing what-if, goes to the other extreme and proposes a $279,000 net income for the first operating year. Save this worksheet as **a:\proj12b** and print it showing each partner's share of the profit bonanza.

6. (Optional) As a result of the what-if exercises in steps 4 and 5, some changes are made to the partnership agreement. Your salary is increased to $32,000 plus a 15% bonus on all net income over a base of $100,000. Your friend, the nutritionist, gets a salary increase to $26,500 and gets the same bonus arrangement as yours. The nutritionist decides to work full time

throughout the year. The actual net income for the first year of operations is $124,504. Save your worksheet as **a:\proj12c** and print it.

Check the worksheet for rounding errors, if any. Write on the bottom of the worksheet how you can guarantee that no rounding errors will occur on future partnership profit and loss allocation worksheets. Exit the program.

## *Assignment:*

Prepare by hand the first two partnership profit and loss allocation worksheets discussed in the project. Enter the dollar amounts indicated in steps 4 and 5 of the project and compute the share of net income (or loss) allocated to each partner.

Student Name:_____

Date:_____

# *Chapter Twelve Transmittal Sheet for Excel*

A. Hand in this page to your instructor with the following items attached in the order requested:

1. PROJ12A partnership profit and loss allocation
2. PROJ12B partnership profit and loss allocation
3. Hand-written assignment
4. Project step 6 partnership profit and loss allocation (optional)

B. Assume that the new investor is unhappy with his or her share of the $67,000 loss in PROJ12A. What would the single best change to the partnership agreement be that could equalize the loss allocated to each partner?

C. What effect would the change you suggested, as an answer to question B, have on the PROJ12B allocation of $279,000?

Notes:

# Chapter Thirteen

# Stockholders' Equity

---

## Chapter Objectives:

A. Prepare a four-column worksheet suitable for comparative financial statements.

B. Prepare an automatic balance sheet that emphasizes the stockholders' equity section.

C. Prepare an automatic income statement and a statement of retained earnings.

## Tutorial:

Assume that you are the controller of a relatively new company called AmWest Alps Motel, Inc. Pretend that it was formed by a group of investors who love a particular part of the Colorado mountains. The company has just completed its second full year of operations.

One of your duties is to come up with preliminary financial statements for the management team. Auditors from a CPA firm will be testing your transactions and adjusting entries to render an opinion on your financial statements and your system of internal control.

In Chapter 3 you learned how to put together a six-column worksheet for a service business. In this chapter you will be using a similar worksheet that is more suitable for comparative financial statements.

1. Do the following according to the instructions in the Introduction chapter:

Load **Microsoft®** **Excel** and run the **Info Macro**

## Figure 13-A:  Four-Column Worksheet

| | A | B | C | D | E | F | G | H | I |
|---|---|---|---|---|---|---|---|---|---|
| | | | | | | | | | |
| 1 | | Student Name | | | | | AMWEST ALPS MOTEL, INC. | | |
| 2 | | 999-99-9999 | | | | | WORKSHEET | | |
| 3 | | Acct150 | | | | | DECEMBER 31, 1993 | | |
| 4 | | Chapter 13 | | | | | | | |
| 5 | | 15-Sep-93 | | | | | | | |
| 6 | | | | | | ----------CURRENT YEAR---------- | | | PRIOR YEAR |
| 7 | | ACCOUNT | | | TRIAL BAL | ADJUSTMENTS | | ADJ TBAL | ADJ TBAL |
| 8 | | NUMBER | | ACCOUNT NAME | DR (CR) | DR (CR) | | DR (CR) | DR (CR) |
| 9 | | | | | | | | | |
| 10 | | 1010 | | House Funds | 20,000 | | | | 10,000 |
| 11 | | 1030 | | Cash in Bank--Checking | 155,869 | | | | 80,151 |
| 12 | | 1210 | | Accts Rec--Guests | 43,841 | | | | 22,509 |
| 13 | | 1250 | | Stock Subscriptions Rec | | | | | 20,000 |
| 14 | | 1450 | | Operating Supplies | 10,176 | | | | 9,450 |
| 15 | | 1510 | | Prepaid Insurance | 26,822 | | | | 24,516 |
| 16 | | 1710 | | Land | 1,150,000 | | | | 1,150,000 |
| 17 | | 1720 | | Buildings | 1,925,000 | | | | 1,925,000 |
| 18 | | 1760 | | Fixtures & Equipment | 410,000 | | | | 410,000 |
| 19 | | 1880 | | Accum Depreciation | (163,500) | | | | (163,500) |
| 20 | | 1920 | | Preopening Costs | 10,500 | | | | 10,500 |
| 21 | | 2010 | | Accounts Payable | (29,228) | | | | (28,932) |
| 22 | | 2360 | | Occupancy Taxes Payable | (35,460) | | | | (32,000) |
| 23 | | 2410 | | Corp Income Taxes Pay | (36,000) | | | | (30,000) |
| 24 | | 2550 | | Advance Deposits | (38,446) | | | | (35,709) |
| 25 | | 2700 | | Cur Port--LT Debt | | | | | (1,846) |
| 26 | | 2750 | | Mortgage Payable | (746,154) | | | | (748,000) |
| 27 | | 2751 | | Less Cur Port--LT Debt | | | | | 1,846 |
| 28 | | 2820 | | Common Stock | (650,000) | | | | (620,000) |
| 29 | | 2830 | | Common Stock Subscribed | | | | | (30,000) |
| 30 | | 2860 | | Paid-in Capital | (1,215,000) | | | | (1,215,000) |
| 31 | | 2890 | | Retained Earnings | (758,985) | | | | (111,396) |
| 32 | | 2910 | | Cash Dividends Paid | 400,000 | | | | |
| 33 | | 3010 | | Transient Room Revenue | (2,087,020) | | | | (2,476,134) |
| 34 | | 5100 | | Salaries and Wages Exp | 284,160 | | | | 256,000 |
| 35 | | 5500 | | Payroll Taxes Exp | 31,258 | | | | 28,160 |
| 36 | | 5600 | | Employee Benefits Exp | 14,208 | | | | 12,800 |
| 37 | | 6000 | | Operating Supplies Exp | 17,081 | | | | 15,388 |
| 38 | | 6300 | | Data Processing Exp | 24,130 | | | | 21,739 |
| 39 | | 6600 | | Marketing Exp | 123,038 | | | | 110,845 |
| 40 | | 6700 | | Property Operation Exp | 51,976 | | | | 46,825 |
| 41 | | 6800 | | Energy Expense | 36,049 | | | | 32,477 |
| 42 | | 6900 | | Guest Transport Exp | 20,437 | | | | 18,412 |
| 43 | | 7210 | | Real Estate Tax Exp | 58,025 | | | | 52,275 |
| 44 | | 7300 | | Insurance Expense | 38,013 | | | | 34,246 |
| 45 | | 7400 | | Interest Expense | 739,210 | | | | 740,000 |
| 46 | | 7510 | | Depreciation Expense | | | | | 109,000 |
| 47 | | 7580 | | Amortization Expense | | | | | 2,000 |
| 48 | | 7900 | | Corp Income Tax Exp | 170,000 | | | | 348,378 |
| 49 | | | | | | | | | |
| 50 | | | | TOTALS | | | | | |

The worksheet illustrated in Figure 13-A has three current year columns and one prior year column. Notice that the debits and credits are shown within each column. The credits are shown as negative numbers (in brackets). The debits equal the credits when the column totals are zero.

When a lot of accounts are on a worksheet, it is common to include account numbers beside them. These particular account names and numbers are based upon a sample chart of accounts provided by the Educational Institute of the American Hotel & Motel Association. Certain account names are unique to that industry.

House funds represent cash on hand. Account number 1210 is the control account for a subsidiary ledger called the *guest ledger*. The account record cards in the guest ledger are called *folios*. Each folio contains the amounts receivable from a guest while he or she is staying at the hotel. Organization costs are in an account called *Preopening Costs* and are classified as Other Assets.

The *Occupancy Taxes Payable* account is like Sales Taxes Payable, except it is based upon daily room rents. Account 2550 is a control account for a subsidiary ledger called the *advance ledger*. It contains the deposits that future guests send to a hotel or motel for the first night's lodging. The Operating Expense accounts on this worksheet are really categories of expenses. They can be broken down into much more detailed accounts.

2. Create a four-column worksheet similar to the one in Figure 13-A. The formula in cell H10 should be  =e10+g10  and should be copied to cells H11 through H48. Column total cells should contain the SUM function.

3. Make the following adjusting entries for the year ended December 31, 1993:

        a. The depreciation expense adjustment is $109,000.
        b. The amortization expense adjustment is $2,000.
        c. The current portion of long-term debt is $2,075.
        d. The corp income tax expense needs to be increased
            by an additional $20,000.

You should list the adjusting entry explanations in cells D52 through D55. You should also indicate the net income for each year in cells H53 and I53.

4. Save your worksheet as **a:\tut13** and compare it with Figure 13-B. Print it in a portrait orientation using a compressed font. Exit the program.

## Figure 13-B: Tutorial Worksheet Without Explanations

Student Name
999-99-9999
Acct150
Chapter 13
15-Sep-93

AMWEST ALPS MOTEL, INC.
WORKSHEET
DECEMBER 31, 1993

| ACCOUNT NUMBER | ACCOUNT NAME | CURRENT YEAR TRIAL BAL DR (CR) | ADJUSTMENTS DR (CR) | | ADJ TBAL DR (CR) | PRIOR YEAR ADJ TBAL DR (CR) |
|---|---|---|---|---|---|---|
| 1010 | House Funds | 20,000 | | | 20,000 | 10,000 |
| 1030 | Cash in Bank--Checking | 155,869 | | | 155,869 | 80,151 |
| 1210 | Accts Rec--Guests | 43,841 | | | 43,841 | 22,509 |
| 1250 | Stock Subscriptions Rec | | | | 0 | 20,000 |
| 1450 | Operating Supplies | 10,176 | | | 10,176 | 9,450 |
| 1510 | Prepaid Insurance | 26,822 | | | 26,822 | 24,516 |
| 1710 | Land | 1,150,000 | | | 1,150,000 | 1,150,000 |
| 1720 | Buildings | 1,925,000 | | | 1,925,000 | 1,925,000 |
| 1760 | Fixtures & Equipment | 410,000 | | | 410,000 | 410,000 |
| 1880 | Accum Depreciation | (163,500) | (a) | (109,000) | (272,500) | (163,500) |
| 1920 | Preopening Costs | 10,500 | (b) | (2,000) | 8,500 | 10,500 |
| 2010 | Accounts Payable | (29,228) | | | (29,228) | (28,932) |
| 2360 | Occupancy Taxes Payable | (35,460) | | | (35,460) | (32,000) |
| 2410 | Corp Income Taxes Pay | (36,000) | (d) | (20,000) | (56,000) | (30,000) |
| 2550 | Advance Deposits | (38,446) | | | (38,446) | (35,709) |
| 2700 | Cur Port--LT Debt | | (c) | (2,075) | (2,075) | (1,846) |
| 2750 | Mortgage Payable | (746,154) | | | (746,154) | (748,000) |
| 2751 | Less Cur Port--LT Debt | | (c) | 2,075 | 2,075 | 1,846 |
| 2820 | Common Stock | (650,000) | | | (650,000) | (620,000) |
| 2830 | Common Stock Subscribed | | | | 0 | (30,000) |
| 2860 | Paid-in Capital | (1,215,000) | | | (1,215,000) | (1,215,000) |
| 2890 | Retained Earnings | (758,985) | | | (758,985) | (111,396) |
| 2910 | Cash Dividends Paid | 400,000 | | | 400,000 | |
| 3010 | Transient Room Revenue | (2,087,020) | | | (2,087,020) | (2,476,134) |
| 5100 | Salaries and Wages Exp | 284,160 | | | 284,160 | 256,000 |
| 5500 | Payroll Taxes Exp | 31,258 | | | 31,258 | 28,160 |
| 5600 | Employee Benefits Exp | 14,208 | | | 14,208 | 12,800 |
| 6000 | Operating Supplies Exp | 17,081 | | | 17,081 | 15,388 |
| 6300 | Data Processing Exp | 24,130 | | | 24,130 | 21,739 |
| 6600 | Marketing Exp | 123,038 | | | 123,038 | 110,845 |
| 6700 | Property Operation Exp | 51,976 | | | 51,976 | 46,825 |
| 6800 | Energy Expense | 36,049 | | | 36,049 | 32,477 |
| 6900 | Guest Transport Exp | 20,437 | | | 20,437 | 18,412 |
| 7210 | Real Estate Tax Exp | 58,025 | | | 58,025 | 52,275 |
| 7300 | Insurance Expense | 38,013 | | | 38,013 | 34,246 |
| 7400 | Interest Expense | 739,210 | | | 739,210 | 740,000 |
| 7510 | Depreciation Expense | | (a) | 109,000 | 109,000 | 109,000 |
| 7580 | Amortization Expense | | (b) | 2,000 | 2,000 | 2,000 |
| 7900 | Corp Income Tax Exp | 170,000 | (d) | 20,000 | 190,000 | 348,378 |
| | TOTALS | 0 | 0 | | 0 | 0 |

# *Project:*

You will be preparing automatic financial statements as you did in Chapters 4 and 5, except these will have two monetary columns. The current year information should always be in the left-hand monetary column. The prior year information should be in the right-hand column. Most accounting principles textbooks have financial statements of actual corporations to use as models.

1. Do the following according to the instructions in the Introduction chapter:

> Load **Microsoft**® **Excel** and open  **a:\tut13.xls**
> **Drag Window** to **Arrange All**

2. Prepare an automatic balance sheet in the Sheet1 window that emphasizes the Stockholders' Equity section. Figure 13-C gives you an idea about column widths and the placement of information.

**Figure 13-C:  Partial Balance Sheet**

| | A | B | C | D | E | F | G | H | I | J | K | L |
|---|---|---|---|---|---|---|---|---|---|---|---|---|
| 1 | | Student Name | | | | AMWEST ALPS MOTEL, INC. | | | | | | |
| 2 | | 999-99-9999 | | | | BALANCE SHEET | | | | | | |
| 3 | | Acct150 | | | | | | | | | | |
| 4 | | Chapter 13 | | | | | | | | | | |
| 5 | | 15-Sep-93 | | | | | | | | | | |
| 6 | | | | | | | | | | | | |
| 7 | | | | DECEMBER 31 | | | | 1993 | | | 1992 | |
| 8 | | | | ------------------------------------------------------------- | | | | | | | | |
| 9 | | | | | | | | | | | | |
| 10 | | | | ASSETS | | | | | | | | |
| 11 | | | | | | | | | | | | |
| 12 | | | | CURRENT ASSETS: | | | | | | | | |
| 13 | | | | House Funds | | | $ | 20,000 | | $ | 10,000 | |
| 14 | | | | Cash in Bank--Checking | | | | 155,869 | | | 80,151 | |
| 15 | | | | Accts Rec--Guests | | | | 43,841 | | | 22,509 | |
| 16 | | | | Stock Subscriptions Rec | | | | 0 | | | 20,000 | |
| 17 | | | | Operating Supplies | | | | 10,176 | | | 9,450 | |
| 18 | | | | Prepaid Insurance | | | | 26,822 | | | 24,516 | |
| 19 | | | | | | | | | | | | |
| 20 | | | | TOTAL CURRENT ASSETS | | | $ | 256,708 | | $ | 166,626 | |
| 21 | | | | | | | | | | | | |
| 22 | | | | PROPERTY, PLANT & EQUIPMENT | | | | | | | | |

Note: Specific instructions for transferring account names and dollar amounts start at step 6 on page 4-3. Be careful. The Accounts Payable balances appear as negative numbers on the worksheet, but must appear as positive numbers on the balance sheet. The combination  =- (the equal key followed by the minus key) changes a negative number from a worksheet cell to a positive number in an income statement cell.

The Preopening Costs account should be classified as an Other Asset. The liabilities should be either Current Liabilities or Long-Term Debt.

Refer to the chapters in your accounting principles textbook that discuss corporations to format the stockholders' equity section. The following information is relevant:

a. The balance in the Stock Subscriptions Receivable account at the end of 1992 was received in early 1993 before any cash dividends were declared or paid. The common stock subscribed at the end of 1992 amounted to 3,000 shares.

b. The common stock is $10 par, 100,000 shares authorized. The number of shares outstanding at the end of 1992 was 62,000. The shares outstanding at the end of 1993 increased to 65,000.

c. The balance in the Paid-in Capital account is all excess over par on the common stock.

Hint: Your accounting principles textbook probably has an appendix that shows comparative financial statements for a major corporation. Look there for formatting ideas (or ask your instructor).

3. Save your balance sheet as **a:\proj13bs** and print it (without gridlines) in a portrait orientation using condensed type. Make sure the financial statement is properly positioned on the page.

4. Prepare an automatic income statement showing two monetary columns--current year earnings and prior year earnings. Use the same format for this statement as you did for the balance sheet.

## Figure 13-D: Partial Income Statement

| Student Name<br>999-99-9999<br>Acct150<br>Chapter 13<br>15-Sep-93 | AMWEST ALPS MOTEL, INC.<br>INCOME STATEMENT | | |
|---|---|---|---|
| FOR THE YEARS ENDED DECEMBER 31 | | 1993 | 1992 |
| REVENUE | | | |
| Transient Room Revenue | | $ 2,087,020 | $ 2,476,134 |
| TOTAL REVENUE | | $ 2,087,020 | $ 2,476,134 |
| OPERATING EXPENSES | | | |
| Salaries and Wages Exp | | $ 284,160 | $ 256,000 |
| Payroll Taxes Exp | | 31,258 | 28,160 |

Include the Depreciation Expense and Amortization Expense accounts in the Operating Expense section. The Corporate Income Tax Expense account balances should be deducted from the Operating Income amounts to arrive at the Net Income amounts. Include at the bottom of the income statement the earnings-per-share information for each of the years.

5. Save the income statement as  **a:\proj13is**  and print it in a portrait orientation using condensed type.

6. Prepare an automatic statement of retained earnings showing both years. Your textbook should show an appropriate example of this statement. Cash dividends were paid for the first time during the current year.

7. Save the statement of retained earnings as  **a:\proj13re**  and print it in a portrait orientation using condensed type.

8. (Optional)  The income statement prepared in this project is for continuing operations only. Why is it important to include information about "discontinued operations" and "extraordinary items" on income statements when they occur? Limit your answer to one typed page.

# *Assignment:*

Prepare by hand the tutorial worksheet and the project financial statements.

# Chapter Thirteen Transmittal Sheet for Excel

A. Hand in this page to your instructor with the following items attached in the order requested:

1. PROJ13BS automatic balance sheet
2. PROJ13IS automatic income statement
3. PROJ13RE automatic statement of retained earnings
4. Hand-written assignment
5. Project step 8 report (optional)

B. On the balance sheet should be a 12/31/93 balance in the Operating Supplies account in the amount of $10,176. What is the formula that transferred this number from the worksheet?

C. On the income statement should be a 12/31/92 balance in the Payroll Taxes Expense account in the amount of $28,160. What is the formula that transferred this number from the worksheet?

D. On the statement of retained earnings should be a Cash Dividends negative amount for 1993. What is the formula that transferred this number from the worksheet?

# Chapter Fourteen

# Bond Amortization Table

## Chapter Objectives:

A. Prepare a flexible bond amortization table for 5-year bonds that can show either discount or premium amounts using the effective interest method.

B. Modify the bond amortization table so that it can be used for 10-year bonds.

C. Use the bond amortization table as a what-if analysis tool to estimate bond issue proceeds at different market interest rates.

## Tutorial:

Assume that you are the newest number cruncher in a company called NewAge SolarTronic Corporation (NASTROC), a company devoted to harnessing the sun's energy for use in vehicles with electric motors.

The NASTROC board of directors is considering the financing of a small capital project with a $1,000,000 bond issue. The board has asked the treasurer to provide some figures showing estimated cash proceeds. The treasurer has passed the job down to you.

1. Do the following in accordance with the instructions in the Introduction chapter:

**Load Microsoft® Excel and run the Info Macro**

2. Create a bond amortization table that is similar to the one in Figure 14-A:

### Figure 14-A: Partially Completed Bond Amortization Table

| | A | B | C | D | E | F | G | H |
|---|---|---|---|---|---|---|---|---|
| 1 | | Student Name | | NEWAGE SOLARTRONIC CORP. | | | | |
| 2 | | 999-99-9999 | | BOND AMORTIZATION TABLE | | | | |
| 3 | | Acct150 | | | | | | |
| 4 | | Chapter 14 | | BOND DATA: | | | | |
| 5 | | 15-Sep-93 | | Maturity Value: | | | 1,000,000 | |
| 6 | | | | Contract Interest Rate: | | | 9.00% | |
| 7 | | | | Expected Market Interest Rate: | | | 10.00% | |
| 8 | | | | Expected Cash Proceeds: | | | 961,391 | |
| 9 | | | | Projected Bond Issue Date: | | | 1-Oct-93 | |
| 10 | | | | | | | | |
| 11 | | INTEREST | | | PREMIUM | PREMIUM | BOND | |
| 12 | | PAYMENT | INTEREST | INTEREST | (DISCOUNT) | (DISCOUNT) | CARRYING | |
| 13 | | DATE | PAYMENT | EXPENSE | AMORTIZATION | A/C BALANCE | VALUE | |
| 14 | | | | | | | | |
| 15 | | 1-Oct-93 | | | | | | |
| 16 | | 1-Apr-93 | | | | | | |
| 17 | | 1-Oct-93 | | | | | | |
| 18 | | 1-Apr-94 | | | | | | |
| 19 | | 1-Oct-94 | | | | | | |
| 20 | | 1-Apr-95 | | | | | | |
| 21 | | 1-Oct-95 | | | | | | |
| 22 | | 1-Apr-96 | | | | | | |
| 23 | | 1-Oct-96 | | | | | | |
| 24 | | 1-Apr-97 | | | | | | |
| 25 | | 1-Oct-97 | | | | | | |

Hints: Be careful with the numbers in cells G5 through G8. Remember that the first number should be entered as 1000000 and formatted to look like 1,000,000. The first percent should be entered as .09 and formatted to look like 9.00%.

Your accounting principles textbook should have definitions of the various terms used in the table. Since you are doing what-if analysis, the market interest rate and cash proceeds are *expected* instead of *guaranteed*.

3. If the bonds are issued at a discount, the cash proceeds will be less than the maturity value. This occurs when the contract interest rate is lower than the market interest rate. Note that Figure 14-B shows discount amounts

as negative numbers (with brackets around them) rather than as positive numbers. Enter the following to produce a negative value in cell F15:

Type   =g8-g5  in cell **F15** and press < **Enter** >

4. The bond carrying value as of the bond issue date should be the same as the bond issue proceeds:

Type   =g8  in cell **G15** and press < **Enter** >

5. Record the first semiannual interest payment in cell C16. Note the dollar signs which make G5 and G6 absolute cell references. This formula will be copied to lower cells in another step. The interest payments should not change over the five-year period.

Type   =$g$5*$g$6/2  in cell **C16** and press < **Enter** >

6. The interest expense amounts in column D depend upon a bond carrying value that changes every six months and the market interest rate that is fixed on the bond issue date. You need a relative cell reference to pick up the change in carrying values and an absolute cell reference to fix the market interest rate. Note that the interest expense is rounded to the nearest dollar.

Type   =round(g15*$g$7/2,0)  in cell **D16** and press < **Enter** >

7. With a table such as this, you don't want to change formulas every time you use it. You will be entering a formula that will show discount amortization amounts as a negative numbers. The same formula will show premium amortization amounts as a positive numbers.

Type   =c16-d16  in cell **E16** and press < **Enter** >

8. On each interest payment date, some of the discount balance in column F is transferred to interest expense. Cell F16 should, therefore, show a smaller negative number than cell F15.

Type   =f15-e16  in cell **F16** and press < **Enter** >

9. As some of the discount balance is transferred to interest expense, the carrying value of the bond issue should increase.

Type  =g15-e16  in cell **G16** and press **< Enter >**

10. Complete the rest of the table by doing the following:

Drag cell **C16** to cell **G25** and drag **Edit** to **Fill Down**

11. Format the numbers by doing the following:

Drag cell **C15** to cell **G25** and drag **Format** to **Number**
Click on  **$#,##0 ;($#,##0)**  and move the icon inside
the **Format** box
Click the left-hand mouse button and edit out (remove)
the dollar signs
Click on **OK**

Your bond amortization table should look similar to the one illustrated in Figure 14-B:

### Figure 14-B:  Bond Discount Illustrated

```
Student Name          NEWAGE SOLARTRONIC CORP.
999-99-9999           BOND AMORTIZATION TABLE
Acct150
Chapter 14            BOND DATA:
15-Sep-93             Maturity Value:                        1,000,000
                      Contract Interest Rate:                    9.00%
                      Expected Market Interest Rate:            10.00%
                      Expected Cash Proceeds:                   961,391
                      Projected Bond Issue Date:               1-Oct-93
```

| INTEREST PAYMENT DATE | INTEREST PAYMENT | INTEREST EXPENSE | PREMIUM (DISCOUNT) AMORTIZATION | PREMIUM (DISCOUNT) A/C BALANCE | BOND CARRYING VALUE |
|---|---|---|---|---|---|
| 1-Oct-93 | | | | (38,609) | 961,391 |
| 1-Apr-93 | 45,000 | 48,070 | (3,070) | (35,539) | 964,461 |
| 1-Oct-93 | 45,000 | 48,223 | (3,223) | (32,316) | 967,684 |
| 1-Apr-94 | 45,000 | 48,384 | (3,384) | (28,932) | 971,068 |
| 1-Oct-94 | 45,000 | 48,553 | (3,553) | (25,379) | 974,621 |
| 1-Apr-95 | 45,000 | 48,731 | (3,731) | (21,648) | 978,352 |
| 1-Oct-95 | 45,000 | 48,918 | (3,918) | (17,730) | 982,270 |
| 1-Apr-96 | 45,000 | 49,114 | (4,114) | (13,616) | 986,384 |
| 1-Oct-96 | 45,000 | 49,319 | (4,319) | (9,297) | 990,703 |
| 1-Apr-97 | 45,000 | 49,535 | (4,535) | (4,762) | 995,238 |
| 1-Oct-97 | 45,000 | 49,762 | (4,762) | 0 | 1,000,000 |

12.  Save the bond amortization table as **a:\tut14a** and print it in a portrait orientation.

13.  Change the market interest rate in cell G7 to 8.00% and change the bond issued proceeds in cell G8 to 1,040,556. Your table should look like the on in Figure 14-C.

### Figure 14-C:  Bond Premium Illustrated

| Student Name | NEWAGE SOLARTRONIC CORP. | | | | |
|---|---|---|---|---|---|
| 999-99-9999 | BOND AMORTIZATION TABLE | | | | |
| Acct150 | | | | | |
| Chapter 14 | BOND DATA: | | | | |
| 15-Sep-93 | Maturity Value: | | | | 1,000,000 |
| | Contract Interest Rate: | | | | 9.00% |
| | Expected Market Interest Rate: | | | | 8.00% |
| | Expected Cash Proceeds: | | | | 1,040,556 |
| | Projected Bond Issue Date: | | | | 1-Oct-93 |

| INTEREST PAYMENT DATE | INTEREST PAYMENT | INTEREST EXPENSE | PREMIUM (DISCOUNT) AMORTIZATION | PREMIUM (DISCOUNT) A/C BALANCE | BOND CARRYING VALUE |
|---|---|---|---|---|---|
| 1-Oct-93 | | | | 40,556 | 1,040,556 |
| 1-Apr-93 | 45,000 | 41,622 | 3,378 | 37,178 | 1,037,178 |
| 1-Oct-93 | 45,000 | 41,487 | 3,513 | 33,665 | 1,033,665 |
| 1-Apr-94 | 45,000 | 41,347 | 3,653 | 30,012 | 1,030,012 |
| 1-Oct-94 | 45,000 | 41,200 | 3,800 | 26,212 | 1,026,212 |
| 1-Apr-95 | 45,000 | 41,048 | 3,952 | 22,260 | 1,022,260 |
| 1-Oct-95 | 45,000 | 40,890 | 4,110 | 18,150 | 1,018,150 |
| 1-Apr-96 | 45,000 | 40,726 | 4,274 | 13,876 | 1,013,876 |
| 1-Oct-96 | 45,000 | 40,555 | 4,445 | 9,431 | 1,009,431 |
| 1-Apr-97 | 45,000 | 40,377 | 4,623 | 4,808 | 1,004,808 |
| 1-Oct-97 | 45,000 | 40,192 | 4,808 | 0 | 1,000,000 |

14.  Save your amortization table showing bond premium as **a:\tut14b** and print it as above. Exit the program.

## *Project:*

Assume that the NASTROC treasurer was just testing you with the tutorial to see if you could come up with the right information on the bond amortization tables. The board of directors really plans to issue $45,000,000 in 10-year debenture bonds at 9 7/8%.

The board members realize that the market rate on new bond issues fluctuates. They have been told that it could be as much as 1/4% higher or lower than the contract rate of the bonds. They want two tables from your department. One will show the cash proceeds if the market interest rate is lower than the contract rate. The other table will show the proceeds if the market interest rate is higher.

1.    Do the following in accordance with the instructions in the Introduction chapter:

Load **Microsoft**® **Excel** and open  **a:\tut14a.xls**

2.  Add 10 interest payment dates.  The last payment date (in cell B35) should be 1-Oct-03.  Fill down the formulas in columns C through G.  You may have to adjust your column widths because you will be displaying larger numbers.

3.  Enter the $45,000,000 amount in cell G5.  The new contract interest rate should be entered as .09875.  The market interest rate should be entered at 1/4% lower.  Format the contract and market interest rates to three decimal places (for example, the contract interest rate should appear as 9.875%).

4.  Change the cash proceeds amount until the carrying value in cell G35 equals the maturity value in cell G5.

> Hint:  The cash proceeds are more than the maturity value but less than $46,000,000.  You can put the formula that is in cell G35 in a temporary location (such as cell F8).  This will save your having to go back and forth between cells G5 and G35.  Clear the temporary cell information before you print the schedule.

Save the bond amortization table as  **a:\proj14a**  and print it in a portrait orientation.

5.  Change the market interest rate to 1/4% above the contract interest rate.  Adjust the cash proceeds until the carrying value in cell G35 is equal to the maturity value in cell G5.  Save this table as  **a:\proj14b**  and print it as above.

6. (Optional) One of the members of the NASTROC board of directors believes that the market interest rate could be lowered by at least 0.5% if a bond sinking fund were established. Type a one-page report that supports or opposes the board member's view. Defend your opinion.

## *Assignment:*

(Optional) If you have access to present value tables or an appropriate calculator, create the bond amortization tables in the project by hand.

Student Name:_____

Date:_____

# Chapter Fourteen Transmittal Sheet for Excel

A. Hand in this page to your instructor with the following items attached in the order requested:

    1. PROJ14A bond amortization table showing a premium
    2. PROJ14B bond amortization table showing a discount
    3. Hand-written assignment (optional)
    4. Project step 6 report (optional)

B. On April 1, 2002, your PROJ14A schedule should show interest expense in the amount of $2,175,266. What is the formula that produces that number?

C. Your PROJ14B schedule should show a 10/1/03 interest payment in the amount of $2,221,875 and interest expense in the amount of $2,275,415. Record this information as a compound journal entry in the general journal below:

|  |  |  |  |
|--|--|--|--|
|  |  |  |  |
|  |  |  |  |
|  |  |  |  |
|  |  |  |  |

*Chapter Fifteen*

# Consolidated Balance Sheet Worksheet

## *Chapter Objectives:*

A. Prepare a worksheet that shows the consolidated balance sheet information for a parent company with a subsidiary.

B. Show the elimination of intercompany items on the worksheet.

C. Show the effect of a minority interest when the parent company does not own 100% of the subsidiary.

## *Tutorial:*

When a company owns more than 50% of the voting stock in another company, it is said to have a controlling interest in that company. The investor is called the *parent company* and the investee is called the *subsidiary*. The two companies must be combined for accounting purposes because they stand as a single economic entity. A way to show this is through the use of consolidated financial statements.

This chapter's tutorial demonstrates the type of worksheet used to create the balance sheet. On this worksheet, the use of intercompany eliminations is shown. You will also see how to treat a minority interest when the parent company does not own 100% of the voting stock.

1. Do the following in accordance with the instructions in the Introduction chapter:

**Load Microsoft® Excel and run the Info Macro**

2. Create a worksheet that is similar to the one in Figure 15-A.

## Figure 15-A: Worksheet for a Consolidated Balance Sheet

| | B | C | D | E | F | G | H |
|---|---|---|---|---|---|---|---|
| | A | | | | | | |
| 1 | Student Name | RAGS CORPORATION & CONSOLIDATED SUBSIDIARY | | | | | |
| 2 | 999-99-9999 | WORKSHEET | | | | | |
| 3 | Acct150 | DECEMBER 31, 1993 | | | | | |
| 4 | Chapter 15 | | | | | | |
| 5 | 15-Sep-93 | | | | | | |
| 6 | | PARENT | SUBSIDIARY | ELIMINATIONS | | CONSOLIDATED | |
| 7 | | COMPANY | COMPANY | DR (CR) | | AMOUNTS | |
| 8 | ASSETS | | | | | | |
| 9 | Cash and cash equivalents | 345,000 | 175,000 | | | | |
| 10 | Notes receivable | | 125,000 | | | | |
| 11 | Accounts receivable, net | 539,000 | 365,000 | | | | |
| 12 | Inventory | 919,000 | 437,000 | | | | |
| 13 | Investment in subsidiary | 1,088,000 | | | | | |
| 14 | Plant and equipment, net | 2,250,000 | 1,195,000 | | | | |
| 15 | | | | | | | |
| 16 | TOTAL ASSETS | | | | | | |
| 17 | | | | | | | |
| 18 | LIAB & STKHLDRS' EQUITY | | | | | | |
| 19 | Accounts payable | 912,000 | 455,000 | | | | |
| 20 | Notes payable | 325,000 | 210,000 | | | | |
| 21 | Common stock | 1,150,000 | 600,000 | | | | |
| 22 | Paid-in capital | 1,261,000 | 450,000 | | | | |
| 23 | Retained earnings | 1,493,000 | 582,000 | | | | |
| 24 | Minority interest | | | | | | |
| 25 | | | | | | | |
| 26 | TOTAL LIAB & S. EQUITY | | | | | | |
| 27 | | | | | | | |
| 28 | | | | | | | |

Note: Set the row height to 3 for rows 15, 17, 25 and 27.

3. An analysis of the parent company general ledger shows that a $125,000 note is payable to the subsidiary. The subsidiary records show the offsetting note receivable. To eliminate the intercompany note, do the following:

Type  (a)  in cell **E10** and press <Enter>
Type  -125000  in cell **F10** and press <Enter>
Type  (a)  in cell **E20** and press <Enter>

Type  **125000**  in cell **F20** and press <Enter>
Type  **(a) Elimination of intercompany note**  in cell **B29**
        and press <Enter>

4. The parent company owns two-thirds of the voting stock outstanding. The following entry eliminates the investment in the subsidiary and sets up the minority interest for an individual who owns the remaining third of the subsidiary voting stock.

Enter **(b)** in cells **E13, E21, E22, E23,** and **E24**
Type **-1088000** in cell **F13** and press **<Enter>**
Type **600000** in cell **F21** and press **<Enter>**
Type **450000** in cell **F22** and press **<Enter>**

Type **582000** in cell **F23** and press **<Enter>**
Type **-544000** in cell **F24** and press **<Enter>**
Type **(b) Investment elimination** in cell **B30**
           and press **<Enter>**

5. In the Consolidated Amounts column a formula is needed to take into account the asset balances from the two balance sheets and any entries in the Eliminations column. The assets balances are added together then are changed by any debits or credit eliminations. Debits increase asset balances and credits decrease them.

Type **+c9+d9+f9** in cell **G9** and press **<Enter>**
Drag cell **G9** to cell **G14** and drag **Edit** to **Fill Down**
Enter the SUM function in cells **C16, D16,** and **G16**

6. The formula in the Consolidated Amounts column has to be changed for balances in the Liability and Stockholders' Equity accounts. Credits increase balances in this part of the balance sheet and debits decrease balances.

Type **+c19+d19-f19** in cell **G19** and press **<Enter>**
Drag cell **G19** to cell **G24** and drag **Edit** to **Fill Down**
Enter the SUM function in cells **C26, D26, F26,** and **G26**

Note: Be careful with the SUM function in cell F26. This column total should always be zero.

7. Your worksheet should look similar to the one in Figure 15-B on the next page. Save your worksheet as **a:\tut15** and print it in a portrait orientation using a compressed type font. Exit the program.

## Figure 15-B: Completed Worksheet

```
Student Name              RAGS CORPORATION & CONSOLIDATED SUBSIDIARY
999-99-9999               WORKSHEET
Acct150                   DECEMBER 31, 1993
Chapter 15
15-Sep-93
```

|  | PARENT COMPANY | SUBSIDIARY COMPANY | ELIMINATIONS DR (CR) | | CONSOLIDATED AMOUNTS |
|---|---|---|---|---|---|
| **ASSETS** | | | | | |
| Cash and cash equivalents | 345,000 | 175,000 | | | 520,000 |
| Notes receivable | | 125,000 | (a) | (125,000) | 0 |
| Accounts receivable, net | 539,000 | 365,000 | | | 904,000 |
| Inventory | 919,000 | 437,000 | | | 1,356,000 |
| Investment in subsidiary | 1,088,000 | | (b) | (1,088,000) | 0 |
| Plant and equipment, net | 2,250,000 | 1,195,000 | | | 3,445,000 |
| TOTAL ASSETS | 5,141,000 | 2,297,000 | | | 6,225,000 |
| **LIAB & STKHLDRS' EQUITY** | | | | | |
| Accounts payable | 912,000 | 455,000 | | | 1,367,000 |
| Notes payable | 325,000 | 210,000 | (a) | 125,000 | 410,000 |
| Common stock | 1,150,000 | 600,000 | (b) | 600,000 | 1,150,000 |
| Paid-in capital | 1,261,000 | 450,000 | (b) | 450,000 | 1,261,000 |
| Retained earnings | 1,493,000 | 582,000 | (b) | 582,000 | 1,493,000 |
| Minority interest | | | (b) | (544,000) | 544,000 |
| TOTAL LIAB & S. EQUITY | 5,141,000 | 2,297,000 | | 0 | 6,225,000 |

(a) Elimination of intercompany note
(b) Investment elimination

# Project:

Assume that you are the outside accountant for a regional distributor of rubber foam products used to make mattresses, pillows, and seat cushions. The board of directors of this corporation decides to embark upon a "vertical integration" acquisition policy. They purchase the voting stock of their major customer, Nautical Cushions Corp.

1. Do the following:

Load **Microsoft® Excel** and open **A:\TUT15.XLS**

2. Modify the worksheet you created in the tutorial to take into account the information from the balance sheets illustrated on the following pages.

15-4

## Figure 15-C: Foam Distributors, Inc. (Parent)

---

BALANCE SHEET

June 30, 1993
_____

ASSETS
Current
| | | |
|---|---|---|
| Cash................................................................... | $ | 5,656 |
| Receivables........................................................ | | 542,759 |
| Inventories......................................................... | | 410,680 |
| Prepaid expenses, deposits, and other assets | | 26,986 |
| | | |
| Total current assets.................................... | $ | 986,081 |
| Long-term notes and receivables............................. | | 28,510 |
| Investments and intangible assets............................ | | 86,658 |
| Goodwill net of amortization................................... | | 437,714 |
| Property, plant, and equipment, net......................... | | 964,645 |
| | | |
| Total................................................................ | $ | 2,503,608 |

LIABILITIES AND SHAREHOLDERS' EQUITY
Current
| | | |
|---|---|---|
| Short-term debt................................................. | $ | 225,252 |
| Accounts payable and accrued liabilities.................... | | 502,098 |
| Federal and state income taxes payable..................... | | 20,389 |
| | | |
| Total current liabilities................................... | $ | 747,739 |
| Long-term debt.................................................... | | 447,825 |
| Long-term liabilities.............................................. | | 199,789 |
| Deferred income taxes........................................... | | 135,793 |
| Shareholders' equity.............................................. | | 972,462 |
| | | |
| Total................................................................ | $ | 2,503,608 |

---

3. Insert a new row above *Shareholders' equity* and label it *Minority equity in subsidiary*. The minority shareholders have a 25% equity interest in the subsidiary. Designate the first elimination entry as: (a) Investment elimination.

4. The parent company, Foam Distributors, Inc., has an Accounts Receivable balance in the amount of $12,746 from Nautical Cushions Corp. Designate this elimination entry as: (b) A/R elimination.

5. Nautical Cushions Corp. has a Long-Term Note Receivable balance from the parent company in the amount of $10,000. (Debit Long-Term Liabilities.) Designate this elimination entry as: (c) N/R elimination.

## Figure 15-D: Subsidiary Balance Sheet

```
                            BALANCE SHEET

June 30, 1993
_____

ASSETS
Current
    Cash...................................................................... $        1,886
    Receivables.............................................................        176,806
    Inventories...............................................................      153,351
    Prepaid expenses, deposits, and other assets..................          8,995

        Total current assets..........................................  $      341,038

Long-term notes and receivables.........................................        19,504
Investments and intangible assets.......................................        16,544
Property, plant, and equipment, net....................................       237,587

        Total........................................................... $      614,673

LIABILITIES AND SHAREHOLDERS' EQUITY
Current
    Short-term debt......................................................  $       58,627
    Accounts payable and accrued liabilities.........................       179,710
    Federal and state income taxes payable..........................          6,796

        Total current liabilities........................................ $      245,133

Long-term debt...............................................................      198,306
Long-term liabilities..........................................................       63,264
Deferred income taxes......................................................       58,598
Shareholders' equity........................................................       49,372

        Total........................................................... $      614,673
```

6.   Save your worksheet as   **a:\proj15**   and print it in a portrait orientation with a compressed type font.

7. (Optional)  If you eliminate the investment in the subsidiary company as you did on your worksheet, how can you be sure that the value of the investment in the subsidiary is on the consolidated balance sheet?  Type the answer in a letter to your instructor.

## *Assignment:*

Do the project worksheet by hand.

Student Name:_____

Date:_____

# *Chapter Fifteen Transmittal Sheet for Excel*

A. Hand in this page to your instructor with the following items attached in the order requested:

  1. Project worksheet for consolidated balance sheet
  2. Hand-written assignment
  3. Project step 7 letter (optional)

B. According to your project worksheet, what are the parent and subsidiary company names?

C. What is the formula that produces the consolidated balance for Investments and Intangible Assets?

D. What is the formula that produces the consolidated balance for Shareholders' Equity?

Notes:

# Chapter Sixteen

# Cash Flows Worksheet

---

## Chapter Objectives:

A.  Prepare a worksheet that shows cash flows classified by operating, investing, and financing activities using the indirect method.

B.  Prepare the statement of cash flows from the information provided by the worksheet.

C.  Explain the usefulness of the statement of cash flows.

## Tutorial:

Many of your fellow students believe that the chapter on cash flows in your accounting principles textbook is one of the hardest to digest.  The purpose of a statement of cash flows is easy enough to understand.  It is to provide information about the cash receipts and cash payments of a business between two balance sheet dates.  The difficult part is trying to decide which of the three cash flow activities (operating, investing, or financing) is affected by certain major transactions.

The worksheet in this tutorial should help you understand these cash flow activities and how accountants assemble the information for the statement of cash flows.  It shows a worksheet style that is similar to those used by many CPA firms.

1.  Do the following:

### Load **Microsoft**® **Excel** and run the **Info Macro**

2. Create a worksheet that is similar to the one in Figure 16-A.

## Figure 16-A: Cash Flows Worksheet

| | A | B | C | D | E | F | G | H | I |
|---|---|---|---|---|---|---|---|---|---|
| 1 | | Student Name | NO FRILLS SERVICE CORPORATION | | | | | | |
| 2 | | 999-99-9999 | CASH FLOWS WORKSHEET | | | | | | |
| 3 | | Acct150 | DECEMBER 31, 1993 | | | | | | |
| 4 | | Chapter 16 | | | | | | | |
| 5 | | 15-Sep-93 | | | | | | | |
| 6 | | | BALANCE | | | | | BALANCE | |
| 7 | | | SHEET | - - -RECONCILING ITEMS- - - | | | | SHEET | |
| 8 | | BALANCE SHEET ACCOUNTS | 12/31/92 | | DEBIT | | CREDIT | 12/31/93 | |
| 9 | | | | | | | | | |
| 10 | | Cash | | | | | | | |
| 11 | | Accounts Receivable | | | | | | | |
| 12 | | Prepaid Expenses | | | | | | | |
| 13 | | Furniture and Equipment | | | | | | | |
| 14 | | Accum Deprn--F & E | | | | | | | |
| 15 | | Accounts Payable | | | | | | | |
| 16 | | Notes Payable | | | | | | | |
| 17 | | Common Stock | | | | | | | |
| 18 | | Retained Earnings | | | | | | | |
| 19 | | | | | | | | | |
| 20 | | TOTALS | | | | | | | |
| 21 | | | | | | | | | |
| 22 | | | | | | | | | |
| 23 | | STATEMENT OF CASH FLOWS EFFECTS | | | | | | | |
| 24 | | | | | | | | | |
| 25 | | OPERATING ACTIVITIES | | | | | | | |
| 26 | | Net Income | | | | | | | |
| 27 | | Decrease in Accounts Receivable | | | | | | | |
| 28 | | Increase in Prepaid Expenses | | | | | | | |
| 29 | | Depreciation Expense--F & E | | | | | | | |
| 30 | | Increase in Accounts Payable | | | | | | | |
| 31 | | | | | | | | | |
| 32 | | INVESTING ACTIVITIES | | | | | | | |
| 33 | | Purchase of Furniture & Equipment | | | | | | | |
| 34 | | | | | | | | | |
| 35 | | FINANCING ACTIVITIES | | | | | | | |
| 36 | | Principle Payments on Long-Term Borrowings | | | | | | | |
| 37 | | Dividends Paid | | | | | | | |
| 38 | | | | | | | | | |
| 39 | | SUBTOTALS | | | | | | | |
| 40 | | Increase in Cash | | | | | | | |
| 41 | | | | | | | | | |
| 42 | | TOTALS | | | | | | | |
| 43 | | | | | | | | | |
| 44 | | | | | | | | | |

3.  Enter only the <u>12/31/92 account totals</u> from the comparative balance sheet illustrated in Figure 16-B.  They should be entered as debit and credit balances.  Enter the SUM function in cell C20.  Your total should equal zero.

## Figure 16-B:  Comparative Financial Statement

```
NO FRILLS SERVICE CORPORATION
BALANCE SHEET
DECEMBER 31, 1993 & 1992


                                    1993            1992

         ASSETS
         Cash                  $    53,000    $    32,000
         Accounts Receivable        107,000        120,000
         Prepaid Expenses            37,000         28,000
         Furniture & Equipment       78,000         66,000
         Accum Deprn--F & E         (13,000)        (6,000)

            TOTALS            $    262,000    $   240,000

         LIABILITIES & EQUITY
         Accounts Payable     $     78,000    $    70,000
         Notes Payable              68,000         60,000
         Common Stock               60,000         60,000
         Retained Earnings          56,000         50,000

            TOTALS            $    262,000    $   240,000
```

Note:  The columns showing account balances on the worksheet are in a different order than the columns on the balance sheet.  On the worksheet the 12/31/92 account balances are to the left of the 12/31/93 account balances.  On the comparative balance sheet, the reverse is true.

4.  You can tell from the comparative balance sheet that the Cash account balance increased $21,000 from 12/31/92 to 12/31/93.  Show this on the worksheet by doing the following:

Type  **(a)**  in cell **D10** and press  **<Enter>**
Type  **21000**  in cell **E10** and press  **<Enter>**
Type  **=c10+e10-g10**  in cell **H10** and press  **<Enter>**

The amount *53,000* should appear in cell H10.  Notice that this same amount appears on your comparative balance sheet.  Copy the formula in cell H10 to cells H11 through H18.

5. Enter 21,000 in cell G40 as a credit. Enter (a) in cell F40. This credit represents a net change in all of the other general ledger accounts that produced the debit increase in the cash account. The total of the debits must equal the total of the credits.

6. The debit balance in Accounts Receivable dropped from $120,000 on 12/31/92 to $107,000 on 12/31/93. The net effect of all the entries to the Accounts Receivable account over the year between the two balance sheet dates is a credit of $13,000. The Accounts Receivable balances in this example are created by the billing of services. Providing services is an Operating Activity for this corporation. Therefore, the corresponding debit should go in the operating activities section.

> Type **(b)** in cell **F11** and press **<Enter>**
> Type **13000** in cell **G11** and press **<Enter>**
> Type **(b)** in cell **D26** and press **<Enter>**
> Type **13000** in cell **E26** and press **<Enter>**

7. The change in the prepaid expense account balance would also have to be described in the Operating Activities section. Prepaid expenses are operating costs that have not yet been matched against revenues. Enter the reconciling debit and credit as illustrated in Figure 16-C on page 16-6.

8. The Furniture and Equipment balance increased by $12,000. In real life you would have to look at that account in the general ledger to find out why the account balance changed. Assume that you did look at the account and you found out that the company bought some new furniture and equipment as illustrated by the following transaction:

| Furniture & Equipment | 12,000 | |
|---|---|---|
| Notes Payable | | 10,000 |
| Cash | | 2,000 |

Purchasing and selling long-term assets are investing activities. In the transaction above, however, the corporation didn't pay all cash. A portion of the purchase was financed with a note. Enter the reconciling debits and credits as illustrated in Figure 16-C on page 16-6.

Note: This reconciling item shows that only the down payment came out of the checking account. The cash outflow for this investing activity was $2,000.

9. Changes in the Accumulated Depreciation account could be related to either operating activities or investing activities depending upon the reason for the change. Writing off some depreciation to expense is considered an operating activity. Depreciation expense is one of the expenses that are deducted from revenue to arrive at net income from operations. On the other hand, if a long-term asset is sold, cash could be generated by that investing activity. The change in accumulated depreciation is due to operations during 1993. Enter reconciling items (e) according to the illustration in Figure 16-C on the next page.

10. The Accounts Payable account balance increased from $70,000 to $78,000 during 1993. This is a service business so the Accounts Payable account is used for unpaid operating costs. In an actual situation you would analyze the account and related journals to identify financing costs that flowed through the Accounts Payable account during 1993. Enter reconciling items (f) according to the illustration in Figure 16-C.

11. The Notes Payable account balance went up by $10,000 during 1993 because of the furniture and equipment purchase. It also went down because of principle. Principle payments are financing activities. Enter the reconciling debit and credit (g) as shown in Figure 16-C.

> Note: The related interest payments are operating activities, but are already part of the net income. They don't need to be shown separately when the indirect method is used.

12. An analysis of the Retained Earnings account shows that the credit balance increased $36,000 because of net income from operations. It also decreased $30,000 because of dividends paid. Enter the reconciling items (h) and (i) according to the illustration in Figure 16-C.

13. What you end up with, then, are the numbers and the descriptions needed for the statement of cash flows. The $36,000 net income in the Operating Activities section is the result of both cash and noncash activities. The reconciling items represent the noncash adjustments to net income so that you can see the net amount of cash increase generated by operating activities.

You can tell by looking at the financing activities section that management decided the company didn't need $30,000 for future operating and investing activities--they paid it out in the form of dividends.

# Figure 16-C:  Cash Flows Worksheet

```
Student Name                    NO FRILLS SERVICE CORPORATION
999-99-9999                     CASH FLOWS WORKSHEET
Acct150                         DECEMBER 31, 1993
Chapter 16
15-Sep-93
```

| BALANCE SHEET ACCOUNTS | BALANCE SHEET 12/31/92 | | ---RECONCILING ITEMS--- DEBIT | | CREDIT | BALANCE SHEET 12/31/93 |
|---|---|---|---|---|---|---|
| Cash | 32,000 | (a) | 21,000 | | | 53,000 |
| Accounts Receivable | 120,000 | | | (b) | 13,000 | 107,000 |
| Prepaid Expenses | 28,000 | (c) | 9,000 | | | 37,000 |
| Furniture & Equipment | 66,000 | (d) | 12,000 | | | 78,000 |
| Accum Deprn--F & E | (6,000) | | | (e) | 7,000 | (13,000) |
| Accounts Payable | (70,000) | | | (f) | 8,000 | (78,000) |
| Notes Payable | (60,000) | (g) | 2,000 | (d) | 10,000 | (68,000) |
| Common Stock | (60,000) | | | | | (60,000) |
| Retained Earnings | (50,000) | (h) | 30,000 | (i) | 36,000 | (56,000) |
| TOTALS | 0 | | | | | 0 |

## STATEMENT OF CASH FLOWS EFFECTS

### OPERATING ACTIVITIES

| | | | | | |
|---|---|---|---|---|---|
| Net Income | (i) | 36,000 | | | |
| Decrease in Accounts Receivable | (b) | 13,000 | | | |
| Increase in Prepaid Expenses | | | (c) | 9,000 | |
| Depreciation Expense--F & E | (e) | 7,000 | | | |
| Increase in Accounts Payable | (f) | 8,000 | | | |

### INVESTING ACTIVITIES

| | | | | |
|---|---|---|---|---|
| Purchase of Furniture & Equipment | | | (d) | 2,000 |

### FINANCING ACTIVITIES

| | | | | |
|---|---|---|---|---|
| Principle Payments on Long-Term Borrowings | | | (g) | 2,000 |
| Dividends Paid | | | (h) | 30,000 |
| SUBTOTALS | | 138,000 | | 117,000 |
| Increase in cash | | | (a) | 21,000 |
| TOTALS | | 138,000 | | 138,000 |

16-6

14. Complete your worksheet so that it looks similar to the illustration in Figure 16-C. Save your worksheet as **a:\tut16** and print it in a portrait orientation using regular sized type. Exit the program.

# *Project:*

Maggie Williams did it right. She wanted to open up a women's fashion accessories store, so she got an assistant manager position in another store in the same business. The store owner taught her two rules for fashion merchandising success.

First, location is everything. Most successful apparel and accessories stores are in upscale malls with excellent foot traffic. They are also in highly visible locations within the malls.

Second, pricing the merchandise must be flexible. Her boss marked the accessories up three times over cost. Certain customers were willing to pay the relatively high prices for the newest fashion merchandise. Then, her boss would advertise "30% off" sales after the merchandise had been in the store for a while. This attracted the customers who loved to shop the sales. After the end of a certain selling season, her boss would advertise "60% off" close-out prices, which attracted the buyers with a "flea market" or "swap meet" mentality.

So, Maggie was prepared when she decided to open her own fashion accessories store in a nearby town. She set up a corporation called Williams, Inc. dba Fashion's Latest. Assume that you are the accountant who has prepared the balance sheet showing the financial position of the corporation at the end of the first two years. You are to prepare a cash flows worksheet and a statement of cash flows using the indirect method. You may also have to prepare a letter to Ms. Williams that explains the statement of cash flows and points out its usefulness to her.

1. Do the following in accordance with the instructions in the Introduction chapter:

**Load Microsoft® Excel and run the Info Macro**

2. Prepare a cash flows worksheet using the information on the comparative balance sheet illustrated in Figure 16-D on the following page.

## Figure 16-D: Comparative Financial Statement

```
WILLIAMS, INC. DBA FASHION'S LATEST
BALANCE SHEET
DECEMBER 31, 1993 & 1992


                                    1993            1992


ASSETS
Cash                          $    49,500    $    36,000
Inventory                         155,000        140,000
Prepaid Expenses                   27,000         21,000
Store Fixtures & Equipment        120,000        110,000
Leasehold Improvements             80,000         80,000
Accumulated Depreciation          (27,000)       (13,000)
Security Deposits                   4,000          4,000
Organization Costs                  1,500          2,000
   TOTALS                     $   410,000    $   380,000

LIABILITIES & EQUITY
Accounts Payable                   90,000    $    85,000
Notes Payable                      85,000         70,000
Common Stock                      160,000        160,000
Retained Earnings                  75,000         65,000
   TOTALS                     $   410,000    $   380,000
```

The change in the Prepaid Expenses account was because of the purchase of a higher priced insurance policy. The change in the Store Fixtures and Equipment account was based upon a cash purchase of shelving and equipment from a store that was going out of business. Organization Costs were amortized.

The accounts payable are to vendors who sell merchandise to the store. The notes payable at the end of 1992 were paid off during 1993. The notes payable at the end of 1993 will be paid off in 1994. All interest due on the notes was paid on December 31 of each year. A $40,000 cash dividend was paid during 1993.

3. Save the worksheet as **a:\proj16a** and print it as you did the tutorial.

4. Prepare an automatic statement of cash flows following a format illustrated in an accounting principles textbook. Transfer the information from one window to another as you did in Chapter 4. Save the cash flows statement as **a:\proj16b** and print it.

5. (Optional) Type a letter to Ms. Williams that explains the statement of cash flows and points out its usefulness to her.

# Assignment:

Prepare the project worksheet and statement of cash flows by hand.

# Chapter Sixteen Transmittal Sheet for Excel

A.  Hand in this page in to your instructor with the following items attached in the order requested:

1.  PROJ16A cash flows worksheet
2.  PROJ16B statement of cash flows
3.  Hand-written assignment
4.  Project step 5 letter (optional)

B.  The following questions relate to PROJ16B statement of cash flows:

1. The net cash inflow from operating activities should be $48,500. What items (besides net income) contribute to this amount?

2.  The Cash Flows from Investing Activities section of your statement should show a $10,000 cash outflow for the purchase of shelving and equipment.  What formula is responsible for placing this number on your statement?

# Chapter Seventeen

# Financial Statement Analysis

## Chapter Objectives:

A. Prepare an independent worksheet containing the adjusted trial balances used for comparative financial statements.

B. Prepare a dependent financial ratios report including a comparison between key income statement percentages and the percentages for companies of similar size in the same industry.

C. Express an opinion about what is happening to Wood Furniture Corporation.

## Tutorial:

P. J. Wood, chairman of the board of Wood Furniture Corporation, is disappointed with the net income for the year ended December 31, 1993. The percentage change in net income is about the same as the percentage change due to inflation. In Mr. Wood's opinion, the company is treading water.

Assume you are the company controller. Mr. Wood asks you to take a closer look at the figures to see what's what. The adjusted trial balances used to prepare the comparative financial statements are illustrated in the abbreviated worksheet in Figure 17-A on the next page.

1. Do the following:

Load **Microsoft**® **Excel** and run the **Info Macro**

# Figure 17-A: Independent Worksheet

| | A | B | C | D | E | F |
|---|---|---|---|---|---|---|
| 1 | | Student Name | WOOD FURNITURE CORPORATION | | | |
| 2 | | 999-99-9999 | WORKSHEET (ABBREVIATED) | | | |
| 3 | | Acct150 | DECEMBER 31, 1993 & 1992 | | | |
| 4 | | Chapter 17 | | | | |
| 5 | | 15-Sep-93 | ADJUSTED | | ADJUSTED | |
| 6 | | | TRIAL BAL | | TRIAL BAL | |
| 7 | | In thousands of dollars (000 omitted) | 12/31/93 | | 12/31/92 | |
| 8 | | | | | | |
| 9 | | Cash | 146.0 | | 161.0 | |
| 10 | | Receivables | 550.0 | | 582.0 | |
| 11 | | Inventories | 872.6 | | 818.0 | |
| 12 | | Other current assets | 57.8 | | 55.0 | |
| 13 | | Property, plant, and equipment | 560.6 | | 560.6 | |
| 14 | | Accumulated depreciation | (408.8) | | (306.6) | |
| 15 | | Accounts payable--trade | (625.8) | | (596.0) | |
| 16 | | Accrued liabilities | (251.0) | | (239.0) | |
| 17 | | Current portion of long-term debt | (33.0) | | (38.0) | |
| 18 | | Long-term debt, less current portion | (198.3) | | (263.0) | |
| 19 | | Deferred income taxes | (12.0) | | (14.0) | |
| 20 | | Common stock | (500.0) | | (500.0) | |
| 21 | | Retained earnings | (220.0) | | (214.0) | |
| 22 | | Cash dividends | 210.0 | | 130.0 | |
| 23 | | Net sales revenue | (5,960.0) | | (5,675.0) | |
| 24 | | Cost of goods sold | 3,910.7 | | 3,816.0 | |
| 25 | | Compensation of officers | 408.6 | | 298.6 | |
| 26 | | Advertising expense | 43.5 | | 39.5 | |
| 27 | | Bad debts expense | 17.9 | | 17.0 | |
| 28 | | Depreciation expense | 102.2 | | 102.2 | |
| 29 | | Pensions expense | 83.4 | | 79.5 | |
| 30 | | Rent expense | 47.7 | | 45.4 | |
| 31 | | Repairs expense | 23.8 | | 22.7 | |
| 32 | | Taxes expense | 155.0 | | 147.6 | |
| 33 | | Other expenses | 895.9 | | 862.6 | |
| 34 | | Interest Expense | 63.6 | | 51.1 | |
| 35 | | Provision for income taxes | 59.6 | | 56.8 | |
| 36 | | | | | | |
| 37 | | TOTALS | 0.0 | | 0.0 | |
| 39 | | | | | | |
| 40 | | ASSETS - LIABILITIES | 658.1 | | 720.0 | |
| 41 | | STOCKHOLDERS' EQUITY | (658.1) | | (720.0) | |
| 42 | | | | | | |

2. Prepare an independent worksheet that is similar to the one illustrated in Figure 17-A. The numbers in cells C37, C40, C42, E37, E40, and E42 should be the result of SUM functions. The revenue and expense account balances should be included in Stockholders' Equity. Save your independent worksheet as **a:\proj17i** and print it.

3. Open a new worksheet and set up a dependent report that looks similar to the one in Figure 17-B. Save your report as **a:\tut17d** but do not print it at this time.

## Figure 17-B: Financial Ratios Report

| | J | K | L | M | N | O | P | Q |
|---|---|---|---|---|---|---|---|---|
| 101 | | Student Name | WOOD FURNITURE CORPORATION | | | | | |
| 102 | | 999-99-9999 | FINANCIAL RATIOS REPORT | | | | | |
| 103 | | Acct150 | DECEMBER 31. 1993 & 1992 | | | | | |
| 104 | | Chapter 17 | | | | | | |
| 105 | | 15-Sep-93 | | | | | INDUSTRY | |
| 106 | | | | 1993 | 1992 | | AVERAGES | |
| 107 | | | | | | | | |
| 108 | | ABILITY TO PAY CURRENT LIABILITIES: | | | | | | |
| 109 | | | | | | | | |
| 110 | | Current ratio................................................. | | | | | 2.0 | |
| 111 | | Quick (acid-test) ratio............................................ | | | | | 1.0 | |
| 112 | | | | | | | | |
| 113 | | SALEABILITY OF INVENTORY: | | | | | | |
| 114 | | | | | | | | |
| 115 | | Inventory turnover................................................. | | | | | | |
| 116 | | | | | | | | |
| 117 | | COLLECTIBILITY OF RECEIVABLES: | | | | | | |
| 118 | | | | | | | | |
| 119 | | Accounts receivable turnover................................. | | | | | | |
| 120 | | Days' sales in receivables................................. | | | | | | |
| 121 | | | | | | | | |
| 122 | | ABILITY TO PAY LONG-TERM DEBT: | | | | | | |
| 123 | | | | | | | | |
| 124 | | Debt ratio................................................. | | | | | 51.8% | |
| 125 | | Times-interest-earned ratio................................. | | | | | 5.6 | |
| 126 | | | | | | | | |
| 127 | | PROFITABILITY: | | | | | | |
| 128 | | | | | | | | |
| 129 | | Rate of return on net sales................................. | | | | | | |
| 130 | | Rate of return on total assets................................. | | | | | 12.2% | |
| 131 | | Rate of return on common | | | | | | |
| 132 | | stockholders' equity............................................ | | | | | 16.0% | |
| 133 | | Earnings per share of common stock.................... | | | | | | |
| 134 | | | | | | | | |
| 135 | | COMMON STOCK AS AN INVESTMENT: | | | | | | |
| 136 | | | | | | | | |
| 137 | | Price/earnings ratio................................................. | | | | | | |
| 138 | | Dividend yield................................................. | | | | | | |
| 139 | | Book value per share of common stock................. | | | | | | |
| 140 | | | | | | | | |
| 141 | | KEY INCOME STATEMENT PERCENTAGES: | | | | | | |
| 142 | | | | | | | | |
| 143 | | Cost of goods sold................................................. | | | | | 68.3% | |
| 144 | | Compensation of officers....................................... | | | | | 3.5% | |
| 145 | | Advertising expense................................................. | | | | | 1.4% | |
| 146 | | | | | | | | |

4. The textbook formula for the current ratio is current assets divided by current liabilities. This formula, which you will put into cell C10 of the dependent report, is expressed in terms of cell locations found in the independent worksheet. You will be working from an adjusted trial balance, here, as you would in an actual situation. In this worksheet, the debits are positive numbers and the credits are negative numbers. The formula for the current ratio is, then, the sum of the current asset cell locations divided by minus the sum of the current liability cell locations.

> Arrow to cell **B10** of the dependent **report** then arrow to cell **C10**
> Type  **=sum(**  and click on the independent **worksheet**
> Arrow to cell **B12** to display the current asset account names
>
> Arrow to cell **C12** and drag cell **C9** to cell **C12**
> Type  **)/-sum(**  and click on the independent worksheet
> Arrow to cell **B17** to display the current liability account names
>
> Arrow to cell **C17** and drag cell **C15** to cell **C17**
> Type  **)**  and press **<Enter>**

5. Format the number in cell C10 by doing the following:

> Drag **Format** to **Number** and arrow to  **0.00**
>      (note that the number appears in the format box below)
> Position your icon to the right of the  **0.00**  in the format box
> Click the left-hand button on your mouse
> Press **<Backspace>** to remove one of the zeros and click on **Ok**

Your current ratio for 1993 should be 1.8. Follow the same procedure to get a current ratio of 1.9 for 1992.

7. Save your partially completed dependent report as  **a:\tut17d**  and print it in a portrait orientation without the row and column headings. Exit the program.

## Project:

In this project you will complete a dependent financial ratios report. Your accounting principles textbook has the formulas for the ratios called for in Figure 17-B on the previous page.

Because debits are positive numbers and credit are negative numbers, be careful with the automatic formulas you develop. You will be using minus signs to make negative cell locations positive.

Notice the ratios and percentages in the industry averages column. These are actual numbers obtained from <u>Almanac of Business and Industrial Financial Ratios, 1991 Edition</u>, by Leo Troy, published by Prentice Hall.

1. Do the following:

> Load **Microsoft**₈ **Excel** and drag **File** to **Close**
> Open files **a:\proj17i.xls** and **a:\tut17d.xls**
> Save **a:\tut17d.xls** as **a:\proj17d.xls**

2. Enter cell-location based formulas for each ratio for each year:

> a. Current ratio: This was done in the tutorial for 1993. Just a reminder--the sum of the current asset cell locations is divided by minus the sum of the current liability cell locations.
>
> b. Quick ratio: Only the cash and receivables cell locations are used in the numerator. Format as for the current ratio.
>
> c. Inventory turnover: Assume that the 12/31/91 inventory is $777,000. Remember that in the worksheet, three zeros are omitted.
>
> d. Accounts receivable turnover: Assume that there are no cash sales. The 12/31/91 receivables balance is $490,800.
>
> e. Days' sales in receivables: Parentheses should enclose the cell location for net sales revenue divided by 365. For example the denominator should be −(proj17i.xls!$c$23/365) for 1993. Format your answer to the nearest day.
>
> f. Debt ratio: Remember that credits are minus numbers. The formula is minus the sum of the liability cell locations divided by the sum of the asset (and contra-asset) cell locations. Format your answer to the nearest one-tenth of one percent.

g.  Times-interest-earned (or coverage) ratio:  The numerator should not contain interest expense or provision for income taxes.

h.  Rate of return on net sales:  Use the SUM function in the numerator for all revenue and expense accounts (including the provision for income taxes).  Format your answer to the nearest one-tenth of one percent.

i.  Rate of return on total assets:  Don't forget the minus sign in front of the SUM function in the numerator.  The total assets on 12/31/91 are $1,776,000.  Format your answer to the nearest one-tenth of one percent.

j.  Rate of return on common stockholders' equity:  The common stockholders' equity information for 1991 is:

| | |
|---|---|
| Common stock (100,000 shares outstanding) | $500,000 |
| Retained earnings at beginning of year | $204,000 |
| Cash dividends paid during year | $120,000 |
| Net income for 1991 | $130,000 |

k.  Earnings per share of common stock:  There are 100,000 shares of common stock issued and outstanding for both years.  Format your answer to the nearest penny.

l.  Price/earnings ratio:  The market price for this over-the-counter stock is 10 1/4 for 1993 and 9 1/4 for 1992.

m.  Dividend yield:  Use cell locations for cash dividends paid.

n.  Book value per share of common stock:  This is not a ratio. Format your answers to the nearest penny.

3.  Save your report as  **a:\proj17d**  and print it.

4.  (Optional)  Type a report to Mr. Wood that gives your opinion of what is happening in the company.  Use the information on the financial ratios report to back up your opinion.

# Assignment:

Do by hand the financial ratios and percentages found in the tutorial and project based upon the numbers in the adjusted trial balances in the worksheet in Figure 17-A.

Student Name:_____

Date:_____

# Chapter Seventeen Transmittal Sheet for Excel

A. Hand in this page to your instructor with the following items attached in the order requested:

1. PROJ17A independent worksheet
2. PROJ17B dependent financial ratios report
3. Hand-written assignment
4. Project step 4 report (optional)

B. The following questions relate to PROJ16B financial ratios report.

1. The rate of return on common stockholders' equity was better than the industry average in 1992 and much better in 1993. Why?

2. What is the cell-location based formula that yields the price/earnings ratio of 6.9 for 1993?

3. What is the cell-location based formula that yields the cost of goods sold percentage (67.2%) for 1992?

# Chapter Eighteen

# The Master Budget

---

## Chapter Objectives:

A. Prepare a master budget which contains the following:

    1. Data input area
    2. Sales and merchandise purchases budgets
    3. Operating expenses budget
    5. Cash receipts and payments budgets
    6. Budgeted income statement and balance sheet

B. Use what-if analysis to determine the budget with the best net income and financial position for one full year.

## Tutorial:

Assume that you have been hired as controller of Phone Sales Corp. dba 1-800-GADGETS. Your first responsibility is to prepare a master budget for the coming year. The budget you will be preparing in this tutorial has a data entry area where you are allowed to change numbers as you do some what-if analysis. If you can appreciate the fact that accounting is the art of communicating financial information, you'll enjoy the symmetry of the rows and columns, and the relationships among the numbers in this budget.

1. Do the following:

      Load **Microsoft**® **Excel** and run the **Info Macro**

2. Set the B column width to 29 and columns C through G to 9. Enter the text and numbers in the rows and columns indicated in Figure 18-A. Do not enter your numbers as text. Format them so that they look like the numbers in the illustration. The dashed line under "percent of annual sales" is entered by pressing <SpaceBar> twice, then pressing – (the minus key) several times and then pressing <Enter>.

## Figure 18-A: Data Input Area

| | B | C | D | E | F | G | |
|---|---|---|---|---|---|---|---|
| 1 | Student Name | PHONE SALES CORP. DBA 1-800-GADGETS | | | | | |
| 2 | 999-99-9999 | ANNUAL MASTER BUDGET | | | | | |
| 3 | Acct150 | FOR THE YEAR ENDING | | | | | |
| 4 | Chapter 18 | DECEMBER 31, 1994 | | | | | |
| 5 | 15-Sep-93 | | | | | | |
| 6 | | | | | | | |
| 7 | Cost of sales percentage......................................... | | 68% | PERCENT OF ANNUAL SALES | | | |
| 8 | Sales forecast for this year..................................... | | 920,000 | - - - - - - - - - - - - - - - - - - - - - - - - - - | | | |
| 9 | Sales forcast for Jan, next year.............................. | | 48,000 | | BANK | ON | |
| 10 | Cash in bank, Dec 31, last year............................. | | 22,000 | MONTH | CARD | ACCOUNT | |
| 11 | Minimum bal required in cash account................... | | 10,000 | - - - - - - - | - - - - - - - | - - - - - - - | |
| 12 | Accounts receivable, Dec 31,last year................... | | 44,000 | JAN | 3.00% | 2.00% | |
| 13 | Inventory, Dec 31, last year.................................... | | 42,000 | FEB | 4.00% | 3.00% | |
| 14 | Property & equipment, Dec 31,last year.............. | | 60,000 | MARCH | 5.00% | 3.00% | |
| 15 | Planned equipment purchase, this year................. | | 20,000 | APRIL | 6.00% | 3.00% | |
| 16 | Accum depreciation, Dec 31, last year................. | | 36,000 | MAY | 6.00% | 3.00% | |
| 17 | Accounts payable, Dec 31, last year...................... | | 20,000 | JUNE | 5.00% | 3.00% | |
| 18 | Accrued advertising, Dec 31, last year.................. | | 6,000 | JULY | 4.00% | 2.00% | |
| 19 | Accrued payroll, Dec 31, last year......................... | | 3,400 | AUG | 4.00% | 3.00% | |
| 20 | Capital stock, Dec 31, last year............................. | | 50,000 | SEPT | 3.00% | 2.00% | |
| 21 | Retained earnings, Dec 31, last year..................... | | 52,600 | OCT | 6.00% | 5.00% | |
| 22 | Planned cash dividend, Dec, this year................... | | 6,000 | NOV | 8.00% | 6.00% | |
| 23 | Depreciation, this year............................................ | | 9,000 | DEC | 6.00% | 5.00% | |
| 24 | Insurance, this year, monthly payment................... | | 225 | | | | |
| 25 | Payroll expense, this year....................................... | | 84,000 | | | | |
| 26 | Rent, office & warehouse, this year........................ | | 27,000 | | | | |
| 27 | Utilities, this year, monthly payment...................... | | 275 | | | | |
| 28 | Provision for corp income tax, this year................. | | 3600 | | | | |
| 29 | | | | | | | |

3. The next part of the budget consists of Schedules A through E as illustrated in Figure 18-B. Enter and center the months in cells C31 through G31. Enter the text in column B starting with row 32. DO NOT ENTER THE NUMBERS. All of the numbers in the schedules, with the exception of certain zero amounts, are the result of functions or formulas. As you change the numbers in the Data Input Area of this worksheet, the numbers in these schedules will automatically change.

# Figure 18-B: Budget Schedules

| | B | C | D | E | F | G |
|---|---|---|---|---|---|---|
| 30 | SALES BUDGET--SCHED A | JAN | FEB | MARCH | APRIL | MAY |
| 31 | Sales--bank card............................... | 27,600 | 36,800 | 46,000 | 55,200 | 55,200 |
| 32 | Sales on account.............................. | 18,400 | 27,600 | 27,600 | 27,600 | 27,600 |
| 33 | | ------- | ------- | ------- | ------- | ------- |
| 34 | Net sales........................................ | 46,000 | 64,400 | 73,600 | 82,800 | 82,800 |
| 35 | | ======= | ======= | ======= | ======= | ======= |
| 36 | PURCHASES BUDGET--SCHED B | JAN | FEB | MARCH | APRIL | MAY |
| 37 | Cost of goods sold........................... | 31,280 | 43,792 | 50,048 | 56,304 | 56,304 |
| 38 | Add ending inventory........................ | 51,034 | 56,038 | 61,043 | 61,043 | |
| 39 | Less beginning inventory.................. | (42,000) | (51,034) | (56,038) | (61,043) | |
| 40 | | ------- | ------- | ------- | ------- | ------- |
| 41 | Purchases on account....................... | 40,314 | 48,797 | 55,053 | 56,304 | |
| 42 | | ======= | ======= | ======= | ======= | ======= |
| 43 | EXPENSES BUDGET--SCHED C | JAN | FEB | MARCH | APRIL | |
| 44 | Advertising expense.......................... | 5,520 | 7,728 | 8,832 | 9,936 | |
| 45 | Depreciation expense........................ | 750 | 750 | 750 | 750 | |
| 46 | Insurance expense............................ | 225 | 225 | 225 | 225 | |
| 47 | Payroll expense................................ | 7,000 | 7,000 | 7,000 | 7,000 | |
| 48 | Rent expense................................... | 2,250 | 2,250 | 2,250 | 2,250 | |
| 49 | Telephone expense........................... | 1,380 | 1,932 | 2,208 | 2,484 | |
| 50 | Utilities expense............................... | 275 | 275 | 275 | 275 | |
| 51 | | ------- | ------- | ------- | ------- | ------- |
| 52 | Total operating expenses................... | 17,400 | 20,160 | 21,540 | 22,920 | |
| 53 | | ======= | ======= | ======= | ======= | ======= |
| 54 | CASH RECEIPTS BUDGET--SCHED D | JAN | FEB | MARCH | APRIL | |
| 55 | This month's sales--bank card.................. | 27,600 | 36,800 | 46,000 | 55,200 | |
| 56 | Last month's sales on account.................. | 44,000 | 18,400 | 27,600 | 27,600 | |
| 57 | | ------- | ------- | ------- | ------- | ------- |
| 58 | Total cash receipts........................... | 71,600 | 55,200 | 73,600 | 82,800 | |
| 59 | | ======= | ======= | ======= | ======= | ======= |
| 60 | CASH PAYMENTS BUDGET--SCHED E | JAN | FEB | MARCH | APRIL | |
| 61 | 50% of last month's purchases.................... | 20,000 | 20,157 | 24,398 | 27,526 | |
| 62 | 50% of this month's purchases.................... | 20,157 | 24,398 | 27,526 | 28,152 | |
| 63 | Last month's advertising.............................. | 6,000 | 5,520 | 7,728 | 8,832 | |
| 64 | This month's insurance............................. | 225 | 225 | 225 | 225 | |
| 65 | 50% of last month's payroll........................ | 3,400 | 3,500 | 3,500 | 3,500 | |
| 66 | 50% of this month's payroll........................ | 3,500 | 3,500 | 3,500 | 3,500 | |
| 67 | This month's rent.................................... | 2,250 | 2,250 | 2,250 | 2,250 | |
| 68 | This month's telephone........................... | 1,380 | 1,932 | 2,208 | 2,484 | |
| 69 | This month's utilities............................... | 275 | 275 | 275 | 275 | |
| 70 | Quarterly corp. income taxes...................... | 0 | 0 | 0 | 900 | |
| 71 | Credit line principle payment..................... | 0 | 0 | 144 | 0 | |
| 72 | Credit line interest payment........................ | 0 | 0 | 1 | 0 | |
| 73 | | ------- | ------- | ------- | ------- | ------- |
| 74 | Total cash payments........................... | 57,187 | 61,757 | 71,756 | 77,644 | |
| 75 | | ======= | ======= | ======= | ======= | ======= |

4. Since the people at Phone Sales Corp. do not have walk-in customers, they must sell all of their merchandise on account (for commercial customers only) or on bank credit cards. The Percent of Annual Sales table in the Data Input Area of this worksheet indicates the actual percentages from the previous year for each type of sale. Those percentages show that this is a seasonal business. The best sales come at the end of the year during the holiday selling season.

The $27,600 you see in cell C31 of the Sales Budget (Schedule A) is the result of a formula that shows cell locations. It is the result of the annual sales amount in cell D8 and the percentage in cell F12:

> Type = in cell **C31** and arrow to cell **D8**
> Type * and arrow to cell **F12** and press **< Enter >**

Follow a similar procedure for cells D31 through G31 and C32 through G32. The dashes in cell C33 can be gotten by pressing <Spacebar> first, then pressing – (the minus key), and then pressing <Enter>.

The $46,000 Net Sales account total in cell C34 is result of two cell locations added together. Assume that there are no sales returns.

> Type = in cell **C34** and arrow to cell **C31**
> Type + and arrow to cell **C32** and press **< Enter >**
> Drag cell **C34** to cell **G34** and drag **Edit** to **Fill Right**

5. To find the purchases amount in the Purchases Budget (Schedule B), you must first find the Cost of Goods Sold. Then add the expected Ending Inventory and subtract the Beginning Inventory.

The Cost of Goods Sold in cell C37 is equal to the Net Sales balance in cell C34 times the cost-of-sales percentage in cell D7.

> Type =c34*$d$7 in cell **C37** and press **< Enter >**
> Drag cell **C37** to cell **G37** and drag **Edit** to **Fill Right**

The Ending Inventory in cell C38 is equal to a base amount plus 80% of the expected Cost of Goods Sold for the next month.

> Type =16000+d37*.8 in cell **C38** and press **< Enter >**
> Drag cell **C38** to cell **F38** and drag **Edit** to **Fill Right**

The Beginning Inventory in cell C39 is the physical inventory taken on December 31 (last year). Notice the minus sign:

> Type  = –  in cell **C39**
> Arrow to cell **B13**  (to identify the 12/31 Inventory row)
> Arrow to cell **D13** and press **<Enter>**

The Beginning Inventory in cell D39 is the expected Ending Inventory from the previous month:

> Type  = –  in cell **D39** and arrow to cell **C38** and press **<Enter>**
> Drag cell **D39** to cell **F39** and drag **Edit** to **Fill Right**

The budgeted purchases-on-account amount in cell C41 is equal to the sum of the numbers in cells C37 through C39:

> Type  = sum(c37:c39)  in cell **C41** and press **<Enter>**
> Drag cell **C41** to cell **F41** and drag **Edit** to **Fill Right**

6. The Expenses Budget (Schedule C) contains some expenses that vary with the change in sales and some that remain fixed from month to month. The first one, Advertising Expense, varies with the Net Sales amount:

> Type  = c34*.12  in cell **C44** and press **<Enter>**
> Drag cell **C44** to cell **F44** and drag **Edit** to **Fill Right**

Depreciation Expense is 1/12 of the estimated annual depreciation in cell D23. You have to make cell D23 an absolute cell reference in your formula:

> Type  = $d$23/12  in cell **C45** and press **<Enter>**
> Drag cell **C45** to cell **F45** and drag **Edit** to **Fill Right**

Insurance premiums are paid monthly by the company. Cell D24 has to be an absolute cell reference in your formula:

> Type  + $d$24  in cell **C46** and press **<Enter>**
> Drag cell **C46** to cell **F46** and drag **Edit** to **Fill Right**

You can tell from the size of the annual payroll that Phone Sales Corp. has very few employees. The company president wears the marketing manager's hat. She even mans the phones (...or is it *persons* the phones?)

during the holiday selling season. The bookkeeper ships the gadgets and helps out on the phones.

> Type  =$d$25/12  in cell C47 and press <Enter>
> Drag cell C47 to cell F47 and drag Edit to Fill Right

The company rents a warehouse with office space near the entrance:

> Type  =$d$26/12  in cell C48 and press <Enter>
> Drag cell C48 to cell F48 and drag Edit to Fill Right

The Telephone Expense amounts vary with Net Sales activity:

> Type  =c34*.03  in cell C49 and press <Enter>
> Drag cell C49 to cell F49 and drag Edit to Fill Right

The company has an agreement with the Gas & Electric Company to pay a fixed monthly fee at the beginning of each month. This fee is updated once each year.

> Type  =$d$27  in cell C50 and press <Enter>
> Drag cell C50 to cell F50 and drag Edit to Fill Right

Total Operating Expenses for January is the sum of the amounts in cells C44 through C50:

> Type  =sum(c44:c50) in cell C52 and press <Enter>
> Drag cell C52 to cell F52 and drag Edit to Fill Right

7.  The Cash Receipts Budget (Schedule D) consists of the current month's credit card sales and the previous month's sales on account:

> Type  =c31  in cell C55 and press <Enter>
> Drag cell C55 to cell F55 and drag Edit to Fill Right

The previous month's sales on account in cell C56 is the 12/31 Accounts Receivable balance located in the Data Input Area:

> Type  =  in cell C56
> Arrow to cell D12 and press <Enter>

The previous month's sales on account in cell D56 comes from the Sales Budget (Schedule A):

> Type  =  in cell **D56**
> Arrow to cell **C32** and press **<Enter>**
> Drag cell **D56** to cell **F56** and drag **Edit** to **Fill Right**

The January cash receipts in cell C58 is the amount in cell C55 plus the amount in cell C56.

> Type  **=c55+c56**  in cell **C58** and press **<Enter>**
> Drag cell **C58** to cell **F58** and drag **Edit** to **Fill Right**

8. The descriptions in the Cash Payments Budget (Schedule E) indicate which formulas you should use here. To start with, the amount in cell C61 is the 12/31 Accounts Payable balance located in the Data Input Area.

> Type  =  in cell **C61**
> Arrow to cell **D12** and press **<Enter>**

The February amount in cell D61 is one-half of the January purchases on account from the Purchases Budget (Schedule B). You may notice that the company is using a net price method of recording purchases and is taking advantage of all purchase discounts.

> Type  **=c41*.5** in cell **D61** and press **<Enter>**
> Drag cell **D61** to cell **F61** and drag **Edit** to **Fill Right**

The amount in cell C62 is one-half of the purchases on account in cell C41. These payments on account take advantage of purchase discounts.

> Type  **=c41*.5**  in cell **C62** and press **<Enter>**
> Drag cell **C62** to cell **F62** and drag **Edit** to **Fill Right**

Last month's advertising in cell C63 is the 12/31 Accrued Advertising balance in the Data Input Area.

> Type  **=d18**  in cell **C63** and press **<Enter>**

The February payment for advertising is January's Advertising Expense balance.

> Type  =c44  in cell **D63** and press **<Enter>**
> Drag cell **D63** to cell **F63** and drag **Edit** to **Fill Right**

The insurance premium in cell C64 comes from cell C46 because it is paid at the beginning of the month.

> Type  =c46  in cell **C64** and press **<Enter>**
> Drag cell **C64** to cell **F64** and drag **Edit** to **Fill Right**

The payroll (including payroll taxes) is paid twice each month a few days after the close of the payroll period.  The amount in cell C65 is the 12/31 Accrued Payroll balance in the Data Input Area.

> Type  =d19  in cell **C65** and press  **<Enter>**

The amount in cell D65 is one-half of the January Payroll Expense balance in cell C47.

> Type  =c47/2  in cell **D65** and press  **<Enter>**
> Drag cell **D65** to cell **F65** and drag **Edit** to **Fill Right**

The amount in cell C66 is also one-half of the amount in cell C47.

> Type  =c47/2  in cell **C66** and press  **<Enter>**
> Drag cell **C66** to cell **F66** and drag **Edit** to **Fill Right**

The rent is paid on the first day of the month.  The telephone and utility bills are paid on the last day of the month.

> Type  =c48  in cell **C67** and press **<Enter>**
> Type  =c49  in cell **C68** and press **<Enter>**
> Type  =c50  in cell **C69** and press **<Enter>**
> Drag cell **C67** to cell **F69** and drag **Edit** to **Fill Right**

Put zeros in cells C70 through E70 since a payment for corporate income taxes is not made until April.  Do the following:

> Type  =d28*3/12  in cell **F70** and press  **<Enter>**

Since it is unlikely that the company will need to borrow money on its credit line, there will be no principle and interest payments in January. Enter zeros in cells C71 and C72. If short-term money has to be borrowed in January, it will be paid back in February at an annual interest rate of 12%.

Type  **= c90**  in cell **D71** and press **<Enter>**
Type  **= c90*.01**  in cell **D72** and press **<Enter>**
Drag cell **D71** to cell **F72** and drag **Edit** to **Fill Right**

The total cash payments in cell C74 is equal to the sum of the amounts in cells C61 through C72.

Type  **= sum(c61:c72)**  in cell **C74** and press **<Enter>**
Drag cell **C74** to cell **F74** and drag **Edit** to **Fill Right**

The total in cell E74 should not agree with the amount in Figure 18-B at this time. The amount will change as you complete the Receipts and Payments Analysis.

9. Enter the text illustrated in Figure 18-C, but DO NOT ENTER THE NUMBERS:

### Figure 18-C: Receipts and Payments Analysis

| | A | B | C | D | E | F | G | H |
|---|---|---|---|---|---|---|---|---|
| 76 | | RECEIPTS & PAYMENTS ANALYSIS | JAN | FEB | MARCH | APRIL | | |
| 77 | | Beginning cash balance............................ | 22,000 | 16,413 | 10,000 | 11,844 | | |
| 78 | | Cash receipts from sched d...................... | 71,600 | 55,200 | 73,600 | 82,800 | | |
| 79 | | | ------- | ------- | ------- | ------- | | |
| 80 | | Cash available for payments.................... | 93,600 | 71,613 | 83,600 | 94,644 | | |
| 81 | | | ------- | ------- | ------- | ------- | | |
| 82 | | Cash payments from sched e.................. | 57,187 | 61,757 | 71,756 | 77,644 | | |
| 83 | | Planned purchase of new assets.............. | 20,000 | 0 | 0 | 0 | | |
| 84 | | Planned cash dividend............................ | 0 | 0 | 0 | 0 | | |
| 85 | | Minimum cash balance............................ | 10,000 | 10,000 | 10,000 | 10,000 | | |
| 86 | | | ------- | ------- | ------- | ------- | | |
| 87 | | This month's cash requirement................. | 87,187 | 71,757 | 81,756 | 87,644 | | |
| 88 | | | ------- | ------- | ------- | ------- | | |
| 89 | | Cash excess (deficiency)........................ | 6,413 | (144) | 1,844 | 6,999 | | |
| 90 | | Add credit line borrowing........................ | 0 | 144 | 0 | 0 | | |
| 91 | | | ------- | ------- | ------- | ------- | | |
| 92 | | Ending cash balance............................... | 16,413 | 10,000 | 11,844 | 16,999 | | |
| 93 | | | ======= | ======= | ======= | ======= | | |

10. As you have done in the schedules above, you should enter appropriate formulas in the Cash Receipts and Payments Analysis based upon the information given.

The beginning cash balance for January in cell C77 is the 12/31 Cash in Bank balance in the Data Input Area. The beginning cash balance for February in cell D77 is the ending cash balance for January in cell C92.

> Drag cell **D77** to cell **F77** and drag **Edit** to **Fill Right**

The cash receipts total in cell C78 is the amount in cell C58.

> Drag cell **C78** to cell **F78** and drag **Edit** to **Fill Right**

The cash available for payments in cell C80 is the sum of the amounts in cells C77 and C78.

> Drag cell **C80** to cell **F80** and drag **Edit** to **Fill Right**

The total cash payments for January in cell C82 comes from cell C74.

> Drag cell **C82** to cell **F82** and drag **Edit** to **Fill Right**

The cash payments amount for new equipment in cell C83 is located in cell D15 in the Data Input Area. Put zeros in cells D83 through F83.

No cash dividend is planned until the end of the year. Enter zeros in cells C84 through F84.

The president of Phone Sales Corp. takes pride in the fact that the company has never bounced a check. The reason for success in this area is the fact that she insists upon a high minimum cash balance relative to the disbursements per month.

> Type  =$d$11  in cell **C85** and press **<Enter>**
> Drag cell **C85** to cell **F85** and drag **Edit** to **Fill Right**

The cash requirement for January in cell C87 is the sum of the amounts in cells C82 through C85.

> Drag cell **C87** to cell **F87** and drag **Edit** to **Fill Right**

The cash excess in cell C89 is the difference between the amounts in cell C80 and cell C87.

> Type **=c80−c87** in cell **C89** and press **<Enter>**
> Drag cell **C89** to cell **F89** and drag **Edit** to **Fill Right**

You will be entering an IF function in cell C90. This function tests the amount in cell C89. If it is less than zero (a negative number), a positive number is put in cell C90. If the amount in cell C89 is zero or more, a zero is put in cell C90.

> Type **=if(c89<0,-c89,0)** in cell **C90** and press **<Enter>**
> Drag cell **C90** to cell **F90** and drag **Edit** to **Fill Right**

> Note: The amount in cell D89 is a minus $144. The IF function put a plus $144 in cell D90. This will cause an automatic principle payment the following month in cell E71 accompanied by an interest payment in cell E72. The interest percentage is one percent per month.

The ending cash balance is not as straight forward as you might think. You will be picking the amounts in certain cell locations to arrive at the correct balance:

> Type **=c80-c82-c83-c84+c90** in cell **C92** and press **<Enter>**
> Drag cell **C92** to cell **F92** and drag **Edit** to **Fill Right**

11. Enter the text illustrated in Figure 18-D, but DO NOT ENTER THE NUMBERS.

### Figure 18-D: Budgeted Income Statement

| | A | B | C | D | E | F | G | H |
|---|---|---|---|---|---|---|---|---|
| 94 | | BUDGETED INCOME STATEMENT | JAN | FEB | MARCH | APRIL | | |
| 95 | | Net sales from schedule a.................... | 46,000 | 64,400 | 73,600 | 82,800 | | |
| 96 | | CGS from sched b.............................. | 31,280 | 43,792 | 50,048 | 56,304 | | |
| 97 | | | ------- | ------- | ------- | ------- | | |
| 98 | | Gross profit....................................... | 14,720 | 20,608 | 23,552 | 26,496 | | |
| 99 | | Operating exp from sched c................ | 17,400 | 20,160 | 21,540 | 22,920 | | |
| 100 | | | ------- | ------- | ------- | ------- | | |
| 101 | | Operating income (loss)...................... | (2,680) | 448 | 2,012 | 3,576 | | |
| 102 | | Interest expense................................ | 0 | 0 | 1 | 0 | | |
| 103 | | Prov. for corp. income taxes................ | 300 | 300 | 300 | 300 | | |
| 104 | | | ------- | ------- | ------- | ------- | | |
| 105 | | Net income (loss)............................... | (2,980) | 148 | 1,711 | 3,276 | | |
| 106 | | | ======= | ======= | ======= | ======= | | |

Even though the Budgeted Income Statement is a pro forma statement (prepared from projections rather than transactions) it can still be prepared with the *revenue* (or realization) *principle* and the *matching principle* in mind. (Check your accounting textbook for definitions.)

Notice that the Interest Expense account is separated from the other Operating Expense accounts. It is considered a financing expense. The Provision for Corporate Income Taxes is not related to monthly taxable income. It is merely the annual estimate found in the Data Input Area divided by 12.

The January Net Sales amount comes from the Sales Budget:

> Type  =c34  in cell **C95** and press **<Enter>**
> Drag cell **C95** to cell **F95** and drag **Edit** to **Fill Right**

The January Cost of Goods Sold comes from the Purchases Budget:

> Type  =c37  in cell **C96** and press **<Enter>**
> Drag cell **C96** to cell **F96** and drag **Edit** to **Fill Right**

The Gross Profit for January is the Net Sales minus the Cost of Goods Sold:

> Type  =c95-c96  in cell **C98** and press **<Enter>**
> Drag cell **C98** to cell **F98** and drag **Edit** to **Fill Right**

Since there is an operating expense schedule (Schedule C), it is not necessary to put the individual expense accounts in the Budgeted Income Statement.

> Type  =c52  in cell **C99** and press **<Enter>**
> Drag cell **C99** to cell **F99** and drag **Edit** to **Fill Right**

Many retail businesses do not make an operating profit every month. An expected loss appears in cell C101:

> Type  =c98-c99  in cell **C101** and press **<Enter>**
> Drag cell **C101** to cell **F101** and drag **Edit** to **Fill Right**

Assume that the Interest Expense for each month will be paid at the end of the month:

> Type  =c72  in cell C102 and press <Enter>
> Drag cell C102 to cell F102 and drag Edit to Fill Right

You must have an absolute cell reference in the formula in cell C103:

> Type  =$d$28/12  in cell C103 and press <Enter>
> Drag cell C103 to cell F103 and drag Edit to Fill Right

The expected Net Income (or Loss) for January is computed as follows:

> Type  =c101-c102-c103  in cell C105 and press <Enter>
> Drag cell C105 to cell F105 and drag Edit to Fill Right

12. Enter the text illustrated in Figure 18-E, but DO NOT ENTER THE NUMBERS. The Budgeted Balance Sheet represents the projected financial position of the company at the end of each month.

### Figure 18-E:  Budgeted Balance Sheet

| | A | B | C | D | E | F | G | H |
|---|---|---|---|---|---|---|---|---|
| 107 | | BUDGETED BALANCE SHEET | JAN | FEB | MARCH | APRIL | | |
| 108 | | Assets: | | | | | | |
| 109 | | Cash................................. | 16,413 | 10,000 | 11,844 | 16,999 | | |
| 110 | | Accounts receivable........................... | 18,400 | 27,600 | 27,600 | 27,600 | | |
| 111 | | Inventory............................... | 51,034 | 56,038 | 61,043 | 61,043 | | |
| 112 | | Plant & equipment........................... | 80,000 | 80,000 | 80,000 | 80,000 | | |
| 113 | | Accumulated depreciation.................. | (36,750) | (37,500) | (38,250) | (39,000) | | |
| 114 | | | ------- | ------- | ------- | ------- | | |
| 115 | | Total assets........................... | 129,097 | 136,138 | 142,237 | 146,643 | | |
| 116 | | | ======= | ======= | ======= | ======= | | |
| 117 | | Liabilities & stockholders' equity: | | | | | | |
| 118 | | Note payable--credit line.................... | 0 | 144 | 0 | 0 | | |
| 119 | | Accounts payable--trade................... | 20,157 | 24,398 | 27,526 | 28,152 | | |
| 120 | | Accrued advertising......................... | 5,520 | 7,728 | 8,832 | 9,936 | | |
| 121 | | Accrued payroll.............................. | 3,500 | 3,500 | 3,500 | 3,500 | | |
| 122 | | Accrued corp income taxes................ | 300 | 600 | 900 | 300 | | |
| 123 | | Capital stock............................... | 50,000 | 50,000 | 50,000 | 50,000 | | |
| 124 | | Cash dividends.............................. | 0 | 0 | 0 | 0 | | |
| 125 | | Retained earnings........................... | 52,600 | 52,600 | 52,600 | 52,600 | | |
| 126 | | YTD net income (loss)....................... | (2,980) | (2,832) | (1,121) | 2,155 | | |
| 127 | | | ------- | ------- | ------- | ------- | | |
| 128 | | Total liab & stkhldrs equity................. | 129,097 | 136,138 | 142,237 | 146,643 | | |
| 129 | | | ======= | ======= | ======= | ======= | | |
| 130 | | ASSETS - (LIAB + EQUITY) = | 0 | 0 | 0 | 0 | | |

The January cash balance in cell C109 comes from the ending cash balance in the Receipts and Payments Analysis:

Type  **=c92**  in cell **C109** and press **<Enter>**
Drag cell **C109** to cell **F109** and drag **Edit** to **Fill Right**

The Accounts Receivable balance for January is the sales-on-account amount from the Sales Budget:

Type  **=c32**  in cell **C110** and press **<Enter>**
Drag cell **C110** to cell **F110** and drag **Edit** to **Fill Right**

The Inventory account balance in cell C111 is the target inventory amount in the Purchases Budget:

Type  **=c38**  in cell **C111** and press **<Enter>**
Drag cell **C111** to cell **F111** and drag **Edit** to **Fill Right**

The Plant and Equipment account balance in cell C112 is the 12/31 balance in the Data Input Area plus any January purchases.  The February balance is the January balance plus any February purchases.

Type  **=d14+c83**  in cell **C112** and press **<Enter>**
Type  **=c112+d83**  in cell **D112** and press **<Enter>**
Drag cell **D112** to cell **F112** and drag **Edit** to **Fill Right**

The contra-asset account, Accumulated Depreciation, increases in a negative direction by the amount of depreciation expense each successive month.  Watch for the minus keys:

Type  **=-d16-c45** in cell **C113** and press **<Enter>**
Type  **=c113-d34**  in cell **D113** and press **<Enter>**
Drag cell **D113** to cell **F113** and drag **Edit** to **Fill Right**

Total Assets for January is the sum of the amounts in cell C109 through cell C113:

Type  **=sum(c109:c113)**  in cell **C115** and press **<Enter>**
Drag cell **C115** to cell **F115** and drag **Edit** to **Fill Right**

The Notes Payable account balance in cell C118 comes from the row labeled *Add Credit Line Borrowing* in the Receipts and Payments Analysis:

> Type  =c90  in cell **C118** and press **<Enter>**
> Drag cell **C118** to cell **F118** and drag **Edit** to **Fill Right**

For the Accounts Payable--Trade balance in cell C119, assume that all merchandise purchases on account are recorded using the net price method and that all purchase discounts are taken. Because of the purchase discount terms from the vendors, no more than one-half of the January purchases will be obligations at month end.

> Type  =c41/2  in cell **C119** and press **<Enter>**
> Drag cell **C119** to cell **F119** and drag **Edit** to **Fill Right**

All advertising costs incurred during one month are not paid until the following month when the statements arrive from the cable television network.

> Type  =c44  in cell **C120** and press **<Enter>**
> Drag cell **C120** to cell **F120** and drag **Edit** to **Fill Right**

The payroll for the second half of January is not paid until February:

> Type  =c47/2  in cell **C121** and press **<Enter>**
> Drag cell **C121** to cell **F121** and drag **Edit** to **Fill Right**

The January Accrual for Corporate Income Taxes in C122 is the Provision for Income Taxes in the Budgeted Income Statement. It is increased in successive months until it is paid in April.

> Type  =c103  in cell **C122** and press **<Enter>**
> Type  =c122+d103  in cell **D122** and press **<Enter>**
> Drag cell **D122** to cell **E122** and drag **Edit** to **Fill Right**
> Type  =e122+f103-f70  in cell **F122** and press **<Enter>**

An absolute cell reference is needed in cell C123 because this balance does not change from month to month:

> Type  =$d$20  in cell **C123** and press **<Enter>**
> Drag cell **C123** to cell **F123** and drag **Edit** to **Fill Right**

Cash dividends are not budgeted for the first four months, so place zeros in cells C124 through F124.

The Retained Earnings account balance in cell C125 is the 12/31 balance from the Data Input Area. Notice the absolute cell reference:

> Type  =$d$21  in cell **C125** and press <Enter>
> Drag cell **C125** to cell **F125** and drag **Edit** to **Fill Right**

The year-to-date net loss in cell C126 comes from the Budgeted Income Statement. This amount is changed each successive month by the net income or loss for that month.

> Type  =c105  in cell **C126** and press <Enter>
> Type  =c126+d105  in cell **D126** and press <Enter>
> Drag cell **D126** to cell **F126** and drag **Edit** to **Fill Right**

The balance in cell C128 is the sum of the amounts in cells C118 through C126:

> Type  =sum(c118:c126)  in cell **C128** and press <Enter>
> Drag cell **C128** to cell **F128** and drag **Edit** to **Fill Right**

The cells of row 130 contain check figures based upon the a variation of the accounting equation. If you have no input errors, assets − (liabilities + stockholders' equity) should always equal zero.

> Type  =c115-c128  in cell **C130** and press <Enter>
> Drag cell **C130** to cell **F130** and drag **Edit** to **Fill Right**

Save your tutorial as  **a:\tut18**  and print it in a portrait orientation using regular-sized type. Exit the program.

## *Project:*

The first paragraph of the tutorial indicates that you were going to prepare an annual master budget. So far you have been guided through the first four months of the year. In the project you are going to complete the remaining months in the master budget.

1.  Do the following in accordance with the instructions in the Introduction chapter:

Load **Microsoft**₈ **Excel** and open the file **a:\tut18.xls**

2.  Set the widths of columns H through O to 9. Enter and center the months June through December where appropriate (use abbreviations). The word Total is entered in column O where appropriate.

3.  Complete the Sales Budget (Schedule A). The column heading in cell O30 is the word Total. Your check figures are:

Total sales--bank card  =  $552,000
Total sales on account  =  $368,000

4.  The next schedule to be completed is the Purchases Budget. The total Cost of Goods Sold in cell O37 should be $625,600.

> Hint: The formula in cell N38 contains information from cell D9. Cell O38 should contain a double underline. Cells O39 and O40 should be blank. The check figure for cell O41 is $625,712.

5.  Complete the remaining schedules. Certain check figures are:

Cell O52  =  $264,000
Cell O58  =  $918,000
Cell O74  =  $887,173

Additional quarterly income tax payments are in June, September, and December. They are equal to the April payment.

6.  The Receipts and Payments Analysis contains a planned cash dividend in cell N84 that comes from cell D22. Cells O76 through O93 are blank.

7.  Check figures for the Budgeted Income Statement are as follows:

Gross Profit in cell O98  =  $294,400
Net Income in cell O105  =  $26,710

8.  There is no Total column for the Budgeted Balance Sheet. Cells O107 through O129 should be blank. Be careful on row 122. Your formulas should produce zero amounts in cells H122, K122, and N122. Total Assets

on December 31, 1994, should be $158,892. Your check figures on row 130 should all be zero.

9. Save your project as **a:\proj18** and print it in a landscape format with compressed print as follows:

| | |
|---|---|
| page 1 | Data input area (rows 1-29) |
| page 2 | Schedules A through E (rows 30-75) |
| page 3 | Receipts and Payments Analysis and Budgeted Income Statement (rows 76-106) |
| page 4 | Budgeted Balance Sheet and check figures (rows 107-130) |

For example: To select the data input area to be printed:

Drag cell **A1** to cell **G29**
Drag **Options** to **Set Print Area**

10. (Optional) The $920,000 sales forecast for 1994 is in the middle of a range of likely total Net Sales amounts for the year. The lower end of the range is $860,000. The upper end of the range is $980,000. Make no other changes in the Data Input Area. Type a report to the company president that indicates the impact on cash flows, net income (loss), and financial position for all three forecasted amounts.

# Assignment:

Prepare by hand schedules A through E, the Receipts and Payments Analysis, and the financial statements in the project assuming a total sales projection of $920,000.

Student Name:_____ _____

Date:_____

# *Chapter Eighteen Transmittal Sheet for Excel*

A. Hand in this page to your instructor with the following items attached in the order requested:

    1. PROJ18 pages 1 through 4
    2. Hand-written assignment
    3. Project step 10 report (optional)

B. The number in cell D8 should be formatted to look like 920,000. How was it entered?

C. The amount in cell O31 (552,000) represents the expected bank card sales for the year. What is the cell-location based formula or function that produces that number?

D. The last credit line principle payment for the year should appear in cell M71. From what cell does that amount come?

E. Cells O107 through O130 should be blank. Why?

Notes:

## Chapter Nineteen

# Cost-Volume-Profit Relationships

---

## Chapter Objectives:

A.  Prepare a cost-volume-profit worksheet which contains a data input area and information for a chart.

B.  Create and label a cost-volume-profit chart.

C.  Use what-if analysis to determine the impact of changes in unit selling price, unit cost, and fixed cost on profit.

## Tutorial:

Assume that you work in the Accounting Department at Sam's Souvenirs, Inc.  Your boss tells you that she has to make the usual "fearless forecast" to the board of directors.  This month, however, she wants to surprise them.  When they suggest the usual data changes, she wants to show them the effects of their suggestions instantly.

Since their eyes seem to glaze over when they see rows and columns of numbers, she wants to show them a chart instead.  Your boss asks you to design such a chart that can be projected up on a screen.

1.   Do the following in accordance with the instructions in the Introduction chapter:

**Load Microsoft® Excel and run the Info Macro**

2.  Create a cost-volume-profit worksheet similar to the one illustrated in Figure 19-A.  Notice that the worksheet has a Data for Relevant Range section where changes can be made for what-if analysis purposes.

**Figure 19-A:  CVP Worksheet**

| | A | B | C | D | E | F | G | H |
|---|---|---|---|---|---|---|---|---|
| 1 | | Student Name | | | | | | |
| 2 | | 999-99-9999 | | SAM'S SOUVENIRS, INC. | | | | |
| 3 | | Acct150 | | CVP WORKSHEET | | | | |
| 4 | | Chapter 19 | | FOR THE MONTH ENDED | | | | |
| 5 | | 15-Sep-93 | | MAY 31, 1993 | | | | |
| 6 | | | | | | | | |
| 7 | | | | | | | | |
| 8 | | | | | | | | |
| 9 | | DATA FOR RELEVANT RANGE: | | | | | | |
| 10 | | | | | | | | |
| 11 | | Selling Price per Unit: | | 7.50 | | | | |
| 12 | | Variable Cost per Unit: | | 2.50 | | | | |
| 13 | | Total Fixed Cost: | | 20,000 | | | | |
| 14 | | | | | | | | |
| 15 | | INFORMATION FOR CVP CHART: | | | | | | |
| 16 | | | | | | | | |
| 17 | | No. Of | Units Entered | Fixed | Total | Total | Profit | |
| 18 | | Units | As Text | Costs | Costs | Sales | (Loss) | |
| 19 | | -------- | --------------- | --------- | --------- | --------- | ---------- | |
| 20 | | | | | | | | |

The date in cell D5 should be typed as the text string  ="May 31, 1993".  In the INFORMATION FOR CVP GRAPH section, the headings for columns B and C are right-aligned and the headings for columns D through G are centered.  The dashed lines are entered by pressing the <SpaceBar> first, then by pressing the  –  (the minus key) several times, and then by pressing <Enter>.

3.  There is a quick way to enter numbers in the Number of Units column.  Use a formula to make your work easier:

Type  **0**  (the number zero) in cell **B20** and press **<Enter>**
Type  **=b20+1000**  in cell **B21** and press **<Enter>**
Drag cell **B21** to cell **B30** and drag **Edit** to **Fill Down**

Format the numbers in column B as in figure 19-B on page 19-4.

4. Another column is needed where the same numbers are entered as text. The numbers will be needed in this column when you create a graph. Notice in particular how the number *0* has to be entered as text:

> Type  = "0"  in cell **C20** and press < **Enter** >
> Type  **1K**  in cell **C21** and press < **Enter** >

The "K" in "1K" stands for the word *thousand*. Enter the remaining numbers as text for cells C22 through C30 as you did in cell C21. Make sure these text items are right aligned.

5. The fixed-cost formula in cell D20 must have an absolute cell reference. When you copy the formula to cells D21 through D30, you don't want the formula to change.

> Type  = **$d$13** in cell **D20** and press < **Enter** >
> Drag cell **D20** to cell **D30** and drag **Edit** to **Fill Down**

6. Cell E20 contains a total-cost formula that has both absolute and relative cell references:

> Type  = **$d$12\*b20+d20**  in cell **E20** and press < **Enter** >

Copy the formula above to cells E21 through E30 as you did in step 5.

7. The same situation applies to the total-sales formula in cell F20. You have an absolute cell reference with the dollar signs and a relative cell reference without them:

> Type  = **$d$11\*b20**  in cell **F20** and press < **Enter** >

Copy the formula to cells F21 through F30.

8. The formula in cell G20 follows the equation:

> **Total Sales - Total Costs = Profit (Loss)**

The equation is expressed in terms of relative cell references when you enter the following:

> Type  = **f20−e20**  in cell **G20** and press < **Enter** >

Copy the formula to cells G21 through G30.

9. Format the numbers in columns D through G by doing the following:

Drag cell **D20** through cell **G30** and drag **Format** to **Number**
Click on **$#,##0 ;($#,##0)** and **OK**

10. Compare your worksheet with the one in Figure 19-B. Make any necessary corrections. Save it as **a:\tut19** and print it in a portrait orientation using a regular-sized type font.

### Figure 19-B: Completed CVP Worksheet

| Student Name | | | | | |
|---|---|---|---|---|---|
| 999-99-9999 | | SAM'S SOUVENIRS, INC. | | | |
| Acct150 | | CVP WORKSHEET | | | |
| Chapter 19 | | FOR THE MONTH ENDED | | | |
| 15-Sep-93 | | MAY 31, 1993 | | | |

DATA FOR RELEVANT RANGE:

| | | |
|---|---|---|
| Selling Price per Unit: | 7.50 | |
| Variable Cost per Unit: | 2.50 | |
| Total Fixed Cost: | 20,000 | |

INFORMATION FOR CVP CHART:

| No. Of Units | Units Entered As Text | Fixed Costs | Total Costs | Total Sales | Profit (Loss) |
|---|---|---|---|---|---|
| 0 | 0 | $20,000 | $20,000 | $0 | ($20,000) |
| 1,000 | 1K | $20,000 | $22,500 | $7,500 | ($15,000) |
| 2,000 | 2K | $20,000 | $25,000 | $15,000 | ($10,000) |
| 3,000 | 3K | $20,000 | $27,500 | $22,500 | ($5,000) |
| 4,000 | 4K | $20,000 | $30,000 | $30,000 | $0 |
| 5,000 | 5K | $20,000 | $32,500 | $37,500 | $5,000 |
| 6,000 | 6K | $20,000 | $35,000 | $45,000 | $10,000 |
| 7,000 | 7K | $20,000 | $37,500 | $52,500 | $15,000 |
| 8,000 | 8K | $20,000 | $40,000 | $60,000 | $20,000 |
| 9,000 | 9K | $20,000 | $42,500 | $67,500 | $25,000 |
| 10,000 | 10K | $20,000 | $45,000 | $75,000 | $30,000 |

11. Create a chart reflecting the information in columns C through G:

Drag cell **C20** to cell **G30** and drag **File** to **New**
Click on **Chart** and **OK**
Drag **Gallery** to **Line** and click on **#2** and **OK**

12. Create a title for the chart in the following manner:

Drag **Chart** to **Attach Text** and click on **Chart Title** and **OK**
Type **THIS MONTH'S CVP FORECAST** and press **<Enter>**

**Figure 19-C:  Line Chart**

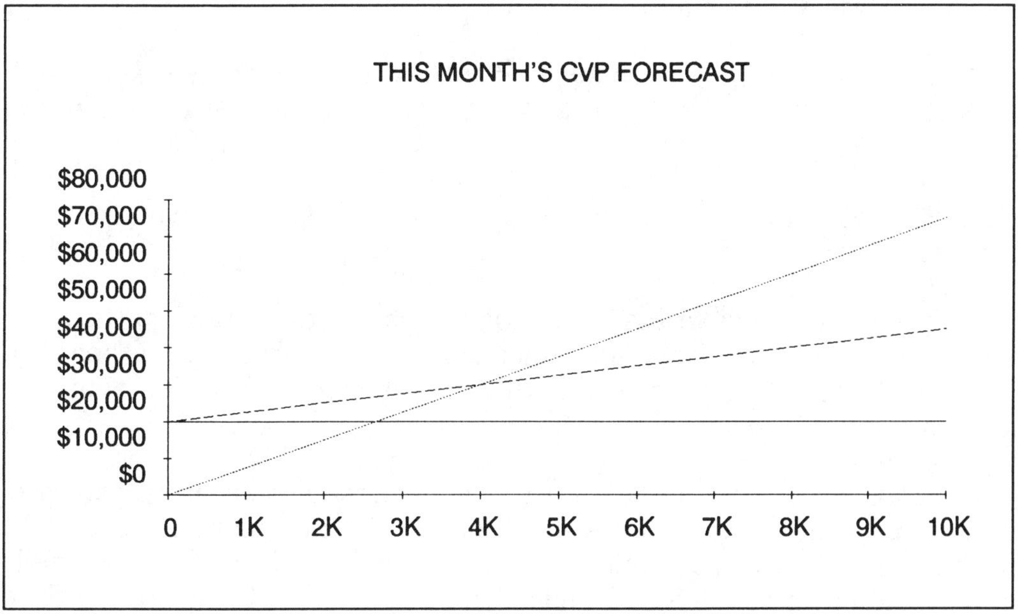

THIS MONTH'S CVP FORECAST

13. Save the chart as  **a:\tut19**  and print it.  Exit the program.

## *Project:*

Assume that you take your CVP worksheet and chart to your boss.  She takes one look at your work and pumps up your ego by exclaiming, "outstanding job!!!"  Then she starts to pick it apart.  You go back to your computer and make certain changes that you consider unnecessary, but she's the boss.

1. Do the following in accordance with the instructions in the Introduction chapter:

Load **Microsoft®** **Excel** and drag **File** to **Close**

Open your worksheet which was saved as, **a:\tut19.xls**.

2. Rearrange columns D through F so that Total Sales are in D, Fixed Costs are in E, and Total Costs are in F. Make sure the formulas in column G reflect these changes. Create a new chart.

Drag **Window** to **Arrange All**

3. Change the selling price per unit to $8 and the variable cost per unit to $3. Change the fixed cost to $24,000. Notice that each change brings about a change in the chart.

4. Save your worksheet as **a:\proj19a** and print it. Save your chart as **a:\proj19a** and print it.

5. Your boss needs to have you label, in pencil, the various parts of the chart so that she won't act like a tongue-tied fool in front of the board of directors. Be sure to name the various lines. Show the break-even point, the net loss area and the net income area.

6. Assume that the board of directors is concerned about running so close to capacity of about 9,000 units per month. So, the board members are planning to make changes to the plant so that they can increase the monthly output to a maximum of 20,000 units. These changes will increase the fixed cost to $40,000, but will decrease the variable cost per unit to $2.25.

Create a CVP worksheet and a chart that will reflect these changes. Save the worksheet as **a:\proj19b** and print it. Save the chart as **a:\proj19b** and print it.

7. (Optional) Type a memo for your boss to present to the board of directors. The memo should contrast the sales, cost, and profit at 9,000 units before and after the changes to the plant. The memo should also indicate the volume level required after the planned changes to produce the same

profit that a level of 9,000 units produced before the changes. The two project worksheets and charts should be used to back up your memo.

## Assignment:

Do by hand the CVP worksheets and charts required by the project.

# Chapter Nineteen Transmittal Sheet for Excel

A. Hand in this page to your instructor with the following items attached in the order requested:

1. PROJ19A worksheet
2. PROJ19A chart
3. PROJ19B worksheet
4. PROJ19B chart
5. Hand-written assignment
6. Project step 7 memo with worksheets and charts (optional)

B. The following questions concern the PROJ19B worksheet and chart.

1. The profit (loss) line crosses the horizontal (or X) axis near what quantity? Your answer should be to the nearest 1,000 units.

2. The break-even point is a little lower than what dollar amount in total sales? Your answer should be to the nearest $1,000.

3. To the nearest $1,000, what is the total variable cost at the break-even point?

4. In order to achieve a break-even point at 5,000 units, to what should the selling price per unit be changed?

# Chapter Twenty

# Activity-Based Costing Worksheet

## Chapter Objectives:

A.  Prepare an activity-based costing (ABC) worksheet which uses different cost drivers.

B.  Use what-if analysis to determine how financial decisions affect the unit cost of two different products.

## Tutorial:

Assume that you do some of the accounting work for Star Handbags, Inc., a manufacturing company that produces high-quality, name-brand handbags. Your company currently uses a simple cost accounting system with a single cost driver, direct labor hours, which worked well while the company produced one product.

This year, however, the company decided to venture into manufacturing private-label handbags. Company management expected that adding the second line of handbags would reduce the per-unit cost of the name-brand handbags. Quite the reverse happened. You are being asked to come up with a better costing system.

1.  Do the following:

    Load **Microsoft® Excel** and run the **Info Macro**

2.  Enter the text and numbers shown in Figures 20-A and 20-B.

# Figure 20-A:  Upper Portion of ABC Worksheet

|  | A | B | C | D | E | F | G | H | I | J | K | L | M | N | O | P |
|---|---|---|---|---|---|---|---|---|---|---|---|---|---|---|---|---|
| 1 | | Student Name | | | | | | | | | | | | | | |
| 2 | | 999-99-9999 | | | | | | | | | | | | | | |
| 3 | | Acct150 | STAR HANDBAGS, INC. | | | | | | | | | | | | | |
| 4 | | Chapter 20 | ABC WORKSHEET | | | | | | | | | | | | | |
| 5 | | 15-Sep-93 | FOR THE MONTH ENDED | | | | | | | | | | | | | |
| 6 | | | APRIL 30, 1993 | | | | | | | | | | | | | |
| 7 | | NOTE: ENTER NUMBERS BETWEEN THE > < (ARROWS). | NAME-BRAND HANDBAGS | | | | | | PRIVATE-LABEL HANDBAGS | | | | | | TOTALS | |
| 8 | | ALL OTHER NUMBERS COME FROM | | | | | | | | | | | | | THIS | |
| 9 | | FUNCTIONS AND FORMULAS. | | DETAIL | | TOTAL | | | DETAIL | | | TOTAL | | | MONTH | |
| 10 | | | | | | | | | | | | | | | | |
| 11 | | GENERAL DATA INPUT: | | | | | | | | | | | | | | |
| 12 | | Batches This Month............ | > | 60 | < | | | > | 100 | < | | | | | | |
| 13 | | Handbags per Batch............ | > | 144 | < | | | > | 24 | < | | | =========== | | =========== | |
| 14 | | Handbags This Month........... | | | | | | | | | | | | | =========== | |
| 15 | | | | ========= | | ========= | | | ========= | | | ========= | | | | |
| 16 | | RAW MATERIALS: | | | | | | | | | | | | | | |
| 17 | | Leather, Cost Per Yard............ | > | 16.00 | < | | | > | 16.00 | < | | | | | | |
| 18 | | Leather, Yards Per Batch.......... | > | 144.00 | > | | | > | 12.00 | < | | | | | | |
| 19 | | Leather, Cost Per Batch........... | | | | | | | | | | | | | | |
| 20 | | Leather, Total Cost This Month... | | | | | | | | | | | | | | |
| 21 | | Synthetic, Cost Per Yard........... | > | 0.00 | < | | | > | 6.00 | < | | | | | | |
| 22 | | Synthetic, Yards Per Batch......... | > | 0.00 | > | | | > | 12.00 | < | | | | | | |
| 23 | | Synthetic, Cost Per Batch......... | | | | | | | | | | | | | | |
| 24 | | Synthetic, Total Cost This Month... | | | | | | | | | | | | | | |
| 25 | | Fabric, Cost Per Yard............. | > | 4.50 | < | | | > | 4.50 | < | | | | | | |
| 26 | | Fabric, Yards Per Batch........... | > | 144.00 | < | | | > | 24.00 | < | | | | | | |
| 27 | | Fabric, Cost Per Batch............ | | | | | | | | | | | | | | |
| 28 | | Fabric, Total Cost This Month..... | | | | | | | | | | | | | | |
| 29 | | Buckles & Snaps, Cost Per Set.... | > | 2.00 | < | | | > | 2.00 | < | | | | | | |
| 30 | | Buckles & Snaps, Sets Per Batch.. | > | 144.00 | < | | | > | 24.00 | < | | | | | | |
| 31 | | Buckles & Snaps, Cost Per Batch.. | | | | | | | | | | | | | | |
| 32 | | Buckles & Snaps, Total Cost This Month.. | | | | | | | | | | | | | | |
| 33 | | DIRECT LABOR: | | | | | | | | | | | | | | |
| 34 | | Direct Labor, Cost Per Hour...... | > | 14.00 | < | | | > | 14.00 | < | | | | | | |
| 35 | | Direct Labor, Hours Per Batch.... | > | 80.00 | < | | | > | 8.00 | < | | | | | | |
| 36 | | Direct Labor, Cost Per Batch..... | | | | | | | | | | | | | | |
| 37 | | Direct Labor, Total Cost This Month.. | | | | | | | | | | | | | | |

# Figure 20-B: Lower Portion of ABC Worksheet

| | A | B | C | D | E | F | GH | I | JK | L | MN | O | P |
|---|---|---|---|---|---|---|---|---|---|---|---|---|---|
| 38 | | FACTORY OVERHEAD: | | | | | | | | | | | |
| 39 | | Machinery, Cost Per Machine Hour.... | > | 1.00 | v | | > | 1.00 | v | | | | |
| 40 | | Machinery, Hours Per Batch.... | > | 100.00 | v | | > | 40.00 | v | | | | |
| 41 | | Machinery, Cost Per Batch.... | | | | | | | | | | | |
| 42 | | Machinery, Total Cost This Month.... | | | | | | | | | | | |
| 43 | | Purchasing, Cost Per Purchase Order.... | > | 13.00 | v | | > | 13.00 | v | | | | |
| 44 | | Purchasing, Purchase Orders Per Batch.... | > | 3.00 | v | | > | 4.00 | v | | | | |
| 45 | | Purchasing, Cost Per Batch.... | | | | | | | | | | | |
| 46 | | Purchasing, Total Cost This Month.... | | | | | | | | | | | |
| 47 | | Production Line Set-Up, Cost Per Hour.... | > | 25.00 | v | | > | 25.00 | v | | | | |
| 48 | | Production Line Set-Up, Hours Per Batch.... | > | 3.00 | v | | > | 3.00 | v | | | | |
| 49 | | Production Line Set-Up, Cost Per Batch.... | | | | | | | | | | | |
| 50 | | Production Line Set-Up, Total Cost Per Month.... | | | | | | | | | | | |
| 51 | | Inspection, Cost Per Hour.... | > | 18.00 | v | | > | 18.00 | v | | | | |
| 52 | | Inspection, Hours Per Batch.... | > | 6.00 | v | | > | 2.00 | v | | | | |
| 53 | | Inspection, Cost Per Batch.... | | | | | | | | | | | |
| 54 | | Inspection, Total Cost This Month.... | | | | | | | | | | | |
| 55 | | Other Factory Overhead, Cost Per Handbag.... | > | 1.25 | v | | > | 1.25 | v | | | | |
| 56 | | Other Factory Overhead, Handbags Per Batch.... | | | | | | | | | | | |
| 57 | | Other Factory Overhead, Cost Per Batch.... | | | | | | | | | | | |
| 58 | | Other Factory Overhead, Total Cost This Month.... | | | | | | | | | | | |
| 59 | | | | | | | | | | | | | |
| 60 | | TOTAL COST PER BATCH OF HANDBAGS.... | | | | | | | | ===== | | | |
| 61 | | | | | | ===== | | | | ===== | | | |
| 62 | | TOTAL COST PER HANDBAG.... | | | | | | | | ===== | | | |
| 63 | | | | | | ===== | | | | | | | |
| 64 | | TOTAL MANUFACTURING COSTS THIS MONTH.... | | | | | | | | | | ===== | |
| 65 | | | | | | | | | | | | ===== | |

20-3

Note: Since this activity-based costing worksheet is an internal document, it can contain notes on it like the one on rows 7 through 9. Notes like this are important in worksheets because they give other people some guidance on how to enter new amounts.

3. You can tell from the information in the General Data Input section that Star Handbags, Inc. produces name brand-handbags in batches of one gross each. The company produces private-label handbags in batches of two dozen each. The two Total columns represent totals per month for the name-brand handbags and the private-label handbags. The Totals This Month column contains the amounts for all the batches combined.

The two Total columns are used differently starting with the Raw Materials section. Starting with row 19, the totals indicate per-batch amounts rather than per-month amounts.

4. Enter the formulas in the General Data Input section by doing the following:

Type  =d12+i12  in cell **O12** and press **<Enter>**
Type  =d12*d13  in cell **F14** and press **<Enter>**
Type  =i12*i13  in cell **L14** and press **<Enter>**
Type  =F14+L14  in cell **O14** and press **<Enter>**

The amounts in the Totals This Month column should be 160 in cell O12 and 11,040 in cell O14. Format the numbers so that the commas are in the appropriate position (see Figure 20-C on page 20-6).

5. The Raw Materials section contains rows labeled *cost per batch* and *total cost this month* for each type of material used. Notice that the company reduces the cost of the private-label handbags by substituting synthetic materials.

Enter the formulas by using cell locations in the two Totals columns as you did in step 4. Compare your answers with those in the upper portion of the tutorial worksheet illustrated in Figure 20-C on page 20-6.

The formulas in the Totals This Month column are a bit more complicated. For example, the total cost of the leather in cell O20 is total per batch of the name-brand handbags times the number of name-brand batches PLUS the total per batch of the private-label handbags times the number of private-label batches. Enter the formula in cell O20 by doing the following:

Type = in cell **O20**
Arrow to cell **B19** (to pick up the description)
Arrow to cell **F19** and type *
Arrow to cell **B12** and arrow to cell **D12**
Type + and arrow to cell **B19** and arrow to cell **L19**
Type * and arrow to cell **B12**
Arrow to cell **I12** and press **<Enter>**

The rest of the formulas in the Raw Materials section should be entered in a similar manner. Format the numbers in the Raw Materials section as is illustrated in Figure 20-C on page 20-6.

6. Enter the formulas in the Direct Labor section the same way as you did in the Raw Materials section. The cost driver here is direct labor. The Total Cost This Month in cell O37 is the cost per batch of name-brand handbags times the number of batches PLUS the cost per batch of private-label handbags times the number of batches.

7. In the Factory Overhead section, a variety of drivers are used to allocate cost. A cost driver is "a factor that creates or influences cost" (source: James A. Brimson, *Activity Accounting, An Activity-Based Costing Approach*, John Wiley & Sons, Inc., 1991).

The cost of running factory machinery influences the cost of goods manufactured as does the cost of the activities of the purchasing department. The set-up time it takes for each new batch of handbags costs money. So do the inspectors. This worksheet is used to allocate factory overhead by the activities responsible for each cost.

Enter your formulas as you did for the Direct Labor section. There is one exception: The information in row 56 comes from row 13. Did you notice that there are no > < (arrows) in row 56?

8. The Total Cost per Batch of Handbags is equal to the sum of the costs for Raw Materials, Direct Labor, and Factory Overhead:

Type = sum(f16:f58) in cell **F60** and press **<Enter>**
Type = sum(L16:L58) in cell **L60** and press **<Enter>**

# Figure 20-C: Upper Portion of Completed Tutorial

Student Name
999-99-9999
Acct150
Chapter 20
15-Sep-93

STAR HANDBAGS, INC.
ABC WORKSHEET
FOR THE MONTH ENDED
APRIL 30, 1993

NOTE: ENTER NUMBERS BETWEEN THE > < (ARROWS).
ALL OTHER NUMBERS COME FROM FUNCTIONS AND FORMULAS.

| | NAME BRAND HANDBAGS | | PRIVATE LABEL HANDBAGS | | TOTALS THIS MONTH |
|---|---|---|---|---|---|
| | DETAIL | TOTAL | DETAIL | TOTAL | |
| **GENERAL DATA INPUT:** | | | | | |
| Batches This Month............ | > 60 < | | > 100 < | | 160 |
| Handbags Per Batch........... | > 144 < | | > 24 < | | ========= |
| Handbags This Month......... | | 8,640 | | 2,400 | 11,040 |
| | ======== | ========= | ======== | ======== | ========= |
| **RAW MATERIALS:** | | | | | |
| Leather, Cost Per Yard........ | > 16.00 < | | > 16.00 < | | |
| Leather, Yards Per Batch...... | > 144.00 < | | > 12.00 < | | |
| Leather, Cost Per Batch....... | | 2,304.00 | | 192.00 | 157,440.00 |
| Leather, Total Cost This Month.. | | | | | |
| Synthetic, Cost Per Yard...... | > 0.00 < | | > 6.00 < | | |
| Synthetic, Yards Per Batch.... | > 0.00 < | | > 12.00 < | | |
| Synthetic, Cost Per Batch..... | | 0.00 | | 72.00 | 7,200.00 |
| Synthetic, Total Cost This Month.. | | | | | |
| Fabric, Cost Per Yard......... | > 4.50 < | | > 4.50 < | | |
| Fabric, Yards Per Batch....... | > 144.00 < | | > 24.00 < | | |
| Fabric, Cost Per Batch........ | | 648.00 | | 108.00 | 49,680.00 |
| Fabric, Total Cost This Month... | | | | | |
| Buckles & Snaps, Cost Per Set.... | > 2.00 < | | > 2.00 < | | |
| Buckles & Snaps, Sets Per Batch.. | > 144.00 < | | > 24.00 < | | |
| Buckles & Snaps, Cost Per Batch.. | | 288.00 | | 48.00 | 22,080.00 |
| Buckles & Snaps, Total Cost This Month.. | | | | | |
| **DIRECT LABOR:** | | | | | |
| Direct Labor, Cost Per Hour....... | > 14.00 < | | > 14.00 < | | |
| Direct Labor, Hours Per Batch..... | > 80.00 < | | > 8.00 < | | |
| Direct Labor, Cost Per Batch...... | | 1,120.00 | | 112.00 | 78,400.00 |
| Direct Labor, Total Cost This Month.. | | | | | |

Figure 20-D: Lower Portion of Completed Tutorial

| FACTORY OVERHEAD: | Left | | Right | | Total This Month |
|---|---|---|---|---|---|
| Machinery, Cost Per Machine Hour........ | ^ 1.00 | | ^ 1.00 v | | |
| Machinery, Hours Per Batch............. | ^ 100.00 | | ^ 40.00 v | | |
| Machinery, Cost Per Batch............. | 100.00 | | 40.00 | | |
| Machinery, Total Cost This Month...... | | | | | 10,000.00 |
| Purchasing, Cost Per Purchase Order.... | ^ 13.00 | | ^ 13.00 v | | |
| Purchasing, Purchase Orders Per Batch.. | ^ 3.00 | | ^ 4.00 v | | |
| Purchasing, Cost Per Batch............ | 39.00 | | 52.00 | | |
| Purchasing, Total Cost This Month..... | | | | | 7,540.00 |
| Production Line Set-Up, Cost Per Hour.. | ^ 25.00 | | ^ 25.00 v | | |
| Production Line Set-Up, Hours Per Batch | ^ 3.00 | | ^ 3.00 v | | |
| Production Line Set-Up, Cost Per Batch. | 75.00 | | 75.00 | | |
| Production Line Set-Up, Total Cost Per Month | | | | | 12,000.00 |
| Inspection, Cost Per Hour............. | ^ 18.00 | | ^ 18.00 v | | |
| Inspection, Hours Per Batch........... | ^ 6.00 | | ^ 2.00 v | | |
| Inspection, Cost Per Batch............ | 108.00 | | 36.00 | | |
| Inspection, Total Cost This Month..... | | | | | 10,080.00 |
| Other Factory Overhead, Cost Per Handbag.. | ^ 1.25 | | ^ 1.25 v | | |
| Other Factory Overhead, Handbags Per Batch... | 144.00 | | 24.00 | | |
| Other Factory Overhead, Cost Per Batch...... | 180.00 | | 30.00 | | |
| Other Factory Overhead, Total Cost This Month.. | | | | | 13,800.00 |
| TOTAL COST PER BATCH OF HANDBAGS...... | 4,862.00 | | 765.00 | | |
| TOTAL COST PER HANDBAG............... | 33.76 | | 31.88 | | |
| TOTAL MANUFACTURING COSTS THIS MONTH.. | | | | | 368,220.00 |

9. To find the Total Cost per Handbag, divide the sums in cells F60 and L60 by the number of handbags per batch:

Type  = f60/d13  in cell **F62** and press **<Enter>**
Type  = **L60/i13**  in cell **L62** and press **<Enter>**

10. Enter the following for the Total Manufacturing Costs This Month column:

Type  = sum(o16:o62)  in cell **O64** and press **<Enter>**

11. Format the numbers so that they look similar to the amounts illustrated in Figure 20-D on page 20-7. Save your tutorial as **a:\tut20** and print it in a portrait orientation using a condensed type font. Exit the program.

# Project:

Ms. Star Kwalatee, president of Star Handbags, Inc., is pleased with your first effort at creating an activity-based costing worksheet. You produced total costs per handbag that were more realistic than the ones provided by using direct labor as a single cost driver.

|  | Multiple Driver Costs | Single Driver Costs |
|---|---|---|
| Name-Brand Handbags | $33.76 | $35.58 |
| Private-Label Handbags | $31.88 | $25.33 |

There are, however, some errors on the tutorial worksheet that she wants you to correct. She also wants you to "sharpen your pencil" and get those per unit costs closer to $30.00.

1. Do the following in accordance with the instructions in the Introduction chapter:

Load  **Microsoft® Excel** and open  **a:\tut20.xls**

2. Ms. Kwalatee notices that the Machinery Hours per Batch of private-label handbags is too high. Make the change to 16 machine hours.

A different quality of leather can be used for the private-label handbags. It sells for $14.50 per yard. Make the appropriate change.

The Direct Labor, Hours per Batch, for private-label handbags should be changed from 8 to 16.

3. When all of the changes are made, the total cost per name-brand handbag should remain at $33.76 and the total cost per private-label handbag should increase to $34.79. (So much for moving towards $30.00 per handbag.) The Total Manufacturing Costs This Month column amount is now $375,220.00. Save your project as **a:\proj20a** and print it in a portrait orientation using a condensed type font.

4. Ms. Kwalatee is considering the use of robotics on the assembly line. If she were to install certain computerized machines, the total machinery cost per month would increase to 300% of the present amount. However, certain costs would decrease. Total direct labor hours per batch would decrease by 25%. The yards per batch of leather, synthetic materials and fabric would decrease by 15%.

Change the PROJ20A worksheet to reflect the above changes. Save it as **a:\proj20b** and print it.

5. (Optional) Send Ms. Kwalatee a typed report indicating the impact of the new machines on the cost per handbag. Support your report with printouts of the ABC worksheets.

## Assignment:

Do the chapter project by hand.

# Chapter Twenty Transmittal Sheet for Excel

A. Hand in this page in your instructor with the following items attached in the order requested:

1. PROJ20A ABC worksheet
2. PROJ20B ABC worksheet
3. Hand-written assignment
4. Project step 5 report (optional)

B. Use the figures in the PROJ20A ABC worksheet to compute the per-unit cost of the handbags using direct labor hours as the only cost driver.

|  | Name Brand Handbags | Private Label Handbags |
|---|---|---|
|  | ---------- | ---------- |
| Raw Materials |  |  |
| Direct Labor |  |  |
| Factory Overhead | ---------- | ---------- |
| Total Unit Cost |  |  |

C. What is the cell-location based formula in cell F23 of the PROJ20B worksheet?

D. Only one column D cell in the PROJ20B worksheet has a formula in it. Name the cell location.

# Chapter Twenty-One

# Flexible Budgets

---

## Chapter Objectives:

A.  Prepare a flexible budget worksheet that includes standard costs per unit of production and variance analysis.

B.  Use the worksheet to compare budget amounts at different levels of capacity with actual costs at month end.

C.  Compute variances for direct materials, direct labor, and factory overhead.

## Tutorial:

When Karl Krusher graduated from college he was full of idealism.  He discovered reality in short order when he couldn't find a job that matched his major in sociology and minor in economics.  He decided to work for himself. He put together an environmentally sensitive company called Recycled Anti-Theft Devices Corporation (RAD Corp.).  His company, started with loans from friends and relatives, recycles waste materials into devices that would prevent crooks from stealing cars.   He sells them through nonprofit organizations that help the homeless.

Assume you have been hired by this young company to work in the accounting department.

1.  Do the following:

**Load Microsoft® Excel and run the Info Macro**

# Figure 21-A: Data Input Area

| | A | B | C | D | E | F | G | H |
|---|---|---|---|---|---|---|---|---|
| 1 | Student Name | | | | | | | |
| 2 | 999-99-9999 | | | | | | | |
| 3 | Acct150 | | | | | | | |
| 4 | Chapter 21 | | | | | | | |
| 5 | 15-Sep-93 | | | | | | | |
| 6 | | | | | | | | |
| 7 | | | RAD CORPORATION | | | | | |
| 8 | | | FLEXIBLE BUDGET WORKSHEET | | | | | |
| 9 | | | FOR THE MONTH ENDED | | | | | |
| 10 | | | JUNE 30, 1993 | | | | | |
| 11 | | | | | | | | |
| 12 | | DATA INPUT AREA: | | | | | | |
| 13 | | | | BUDGET | | | | |
| 14 | | | | AMOUNTS | | | | |
| 15 | | | | --------- | | | | |
| 16 | | Units Of Production At 100% Capacity............. | | 40,000 | | | | |
| 17 | | Direct Materials, Cost Per Pound............. | | 1.20 | | | | |
| 18 | | Direct Materials, Pounds At 100% Capacity............. | | 20,000 | | | | |
| 19 | | Direct Labor, Rate Per Hour............. | | 16.00 | | | | |
| 20 | | Direct Labor, Overtime Rate Per Hour............. | | 24.00 | | | | |
| 21 | | Direct Labor, Hours at 100% Capacity............. | | 5,000 | | | | |
| 22 | | Indirect Factory Labor, Rate Per Direct Labor Hour............. | | 3.20 | | | | |
| 23 | | Indirect Factory Labor, Overtime Rate Per Direct Labor Hour............. | | 4.80 | | | | |
| 24 | | Gas, Electricity & Water............. | | 1.40 | | | | |
| | | Indirect Materials............. | | 0.80 | | | | |
| | | Repairs and Maintenance............. | | 0.60 | | | | |
| | | Management Salaries............. | | 5,500 | | | | |
| | | Plant & Equipment Depreciation............. | | 4,500 | | | | |
| | | Property Insurance and Taxes............. | | 2,000 | | | | |

# Figure 21-B:  Flexible Budget and Standard Costs

| | B | C | D | E | F | G | H |
|---|---|---|---|---|---|---|---|
| 24 | | | | | | | |
| 25 | FLEXIBLE BUDGET AT DIFFERENT PRODUCTION LEVELS: | | | | | | |
| 26 | | | | | | | |
| 27 | PERCENT OF PRODUCTIVE CAPACITY | | 80.00% | 90.00% | 100.00% | 110.00% | |
| 28 | | | | | | | |
| 29 | DIRECT MATERIALS | | 19,200 | 21,600 | 24,000 | 26,400 | |
| 30 | | | | | | | |
| 31 | DIRECT LABOR | | 64,000 | 72,000 | 80,000 | 92,000 | |
| 32 | | | | | | | |
| 33 | FACTORY OVERHEAD: | | | | | | |
| 34 | Variable Cost: | | | | | | |
| 35 | Indirect Factory Wages | | 12,800 | | | | |
| 36 | Gas, Electricity & Water | | 5,600 | | | | |
| 37 | Indirect Materials | | 3,200 | | | | |
| 38 | Repairs and Maintenance | | 2,400 | | | | |
| 39 | | | | | | | |
| 40 | Total Variable Cost | | 24,000 | | | | |
| 41 | | | | | | | |
| 42 | Fixed Cost: | | | | | | |
| 43 | Management Salaries | | 5,500 | | | | |
| 44 | Plant & Equipment Depreciation | | 4,500 | | | | |
| 45 | Property Insurance & Taxes | | 2,000 | | | | |
| 46 | | | | | | | |
| 47 | Total Fixed Cost | | 12,000 | | | | |
| 48 | | | | | | | |
| 49 | TOTAL FACTORY OVERHEAD | | 36,000 | | | | |
| 50 | | | | | | | |
| 51 | TOTAL COST OF PRODUCTION | | 119,200 | | | | |
| 52 | | | | | | | |
| 53 | | | | | | | |
| 54 | STANDARD COSTS PER UNIT OF PRODUCTION: | | | | | | |
| 55 | Direct Materials | | 0.6000 | | | | |
| 56 | Direct Labor | | 2.0000 | | | | |
| 57 | Factory Overhead | | 1.1250 | | | | |
| 58 | | | | | | | |

2. Create a worksheet that is similar to the one illustrated in Figures 21-A and 21-B on the previous two pages. Be careful when you enter the numbers in the Data Input Area. They should be entered as numbers (without commas) and formatted to look like the amounts in figure 21-A.

DO NOT ENTER the numbers shown in rows 29 through 57. They all are the result of formulas.

3. The direct materials amount in cell D29 is the percent of productive capacity times the cost per pound times the number of pounds used.

> Type  =  in cell **D29** and arrow to cell **D27**
> Type  *  and arrow to cell **B11** and arrow to cell **D11**
> Type  *  and arrow to cell **B12** and arrow to cell **D12**
> Press <**Enter**>

> Note: Arrowing to cell B11 before cell D11 helps you to identify the cost per pound of the direct materials.

You should end up with 19200 in cell D29. Use a similar method for putting the numbers in cells E29 through G29.

4. The direct labor amount in cell D31 is the percent of productive capacity times the rate per hour times the number of hours at 100% capacity. Use the same method as you did in step 3 for cells D31 through F31.

The formula that goes into cell G31 is different because the plant is running over capacity (the workers are being paid overtime wages).

> Type  =f31+(d14*d15*.1)  in cell **G31** and press <**Enter**>

In other words, the 92000 in cell G31 represents the regular pay at 100% capacity plus the overtime pay for 10% excess capacity.

5. The variable factory overhead costs in cells D35 through D38 are gotten using the same method as in step 2. Use the SUM function in cell D40 to find total variable cost.

6. The management salaries amount in cell D43 is the result of an absolute cell reference.

> Type  =$d$21  in cell **D43** and press <**Enter**>

Absolute cell references should also be used for cells D44 and D45. Use the SUM function in cell D47 to get the total fixed cost.

7. The total factory overhead in cell D49 is the total variable cost plus the total fixed cost.

Type  **=d40+d47** in cell **D49** and press **<Enter>**

8. The total cost of production in cell D51 is the raw materials plus the direct labor plus the factory overhead.

Type  **=d29+d31+d49**  in cell **D51** and press **<Enter>**

9. The standard costs per unit of production will be different at each percent of productive capacity. For example, the unit cost for direct materials is the budgeted cost in cell D29 divided by product of the units of production times the percent of productive capacity. Notice the absolute cell reference for the units of production.

Type  **=d29/$d$10*d27**  in cell **D55** and press **<Enter>**

The formulas that go into cells D56 and D57 have the same denominator as the formula you typed for cell D55. The numerators are different.

For cell **D56** the numerator is **D31**
For cell **D57** the numerator is **D49**

10. Format the numbers in cells G29 through D51 to look like the amounts in figure 21-B. The numbers in cells D55 through D57 are carried to four decimal places.

Drag **Format** to **Number** and click on **#,##0.00**
Move the icon to the right of **#,##0.00** in the **Format** box
Click the icon once and type  **00**  (two zeros)
Click on **OK**

11. Save your partially completed worksheet as **a:\tut21** and print it in a portrait orientation using a compressed type font. Exit the program.

# Project:

Karl Krusher, RAD Corp. president, notices the work you did on the tutorial worksheet (he's a "hands on" entrepreneur). He wants you to change some of the numbers in the data input area and to complete the flexible budget worksheet.

1. Do the following:

    Load **Microsoft**® **Excel** and open **a:\tut21.xls**

2. Make the following changes in the data input area:

| | |
|---|---:|
| Units of production at 100% capacity | 44,000 |
| Direct material, pounds at 100% Capacity | 88,000 |
| Management salaries | 7,000 |

3. Complete the worksheet. Save it as **a:\proj21** and print it. Exit the program and type the answers to the following questions on a piece of paper:

> a. The board of directors of Karl Krusher's company approved a master budget in December 1992. At that time they expected production to run at 80% capacity. What was the expected total cost of production for June 1993 in the master budget?

> b. Demand for the anti-theft devices ran much higher than expected. At the beginning of June the managers decided to run the plant at 110% capacity. What was the expected total cost of production for June 1993 in the flexible budget?

> c. What was the actual total cost of production for June 1993 if the actual results at the end of the month were as follows:

>> Direct materials used: 97,000 lbs. @ $1.18 per pound

>> Direct labor used: 5,500 hours @ $18.00 per hour

>> Indirect labor used: 5,500 hours @ $3.40 per hour

> Note: The rates for direct labor and indirect labor include some overtime pay. The rest of the costs were identical to the amounts predicted in the flexible budget.

d. Compute the following variances:

> Direct Materials Unit Cost Variance
> Direct Materials Quantity Variance
> Direct Labor Time Variance
> Direct Labor Rate Variance
> Factory Overhead Volume Variance
> Factory Overhead Controllable Variance

4. (Optional) Type a memo to the data entry operator indicating the journal entries for the six variances above.

## *Assignment*

Do by hand the flexible budget worksheet with the changes suggested in the project step 2. A data input area is not necessary.

Student Name:_____

Date:_____

# Chapter Twenty-One Transmittal Sheet for Excel

A.  Hand in this page to your instructor with the following items attached in the order requested:

      1. PROJ21 flexible budget worksheet
      2. Answers to project questions
      3. Hand-written assignment
      4. Project step 4 memo (optional)

B.  The formula in cell G35 takes into account overtime wages of indirect labor.  What is the cell-location based formula?

C.  What is the cell-location based formula in G43?

D.  What is the cell-location based formula in cell F56?

# Chapter Twenty-Two

# Capital-Budgeting Alternatives

## Chapter Objectives:

A.  Prepare a capital-budgeting worksheet which contains a six-year pro forma income statement with cash flow.

B.  Use what-if analysis to rank three projects using three capital-budgeting methods.

## Tutorial:

Assume that you work in the Finance Department at Smart & Honest Corporation.  Your boss has given you the job of ranking three capital-budgeting alternatives.  You are to prepare three worksheets and a one-page report that discusses the projects in terms of three capital-budgeting alternatives.

When you look at the worksheet illustrated in this tutorial, you'll notice that it may contain different assumptions than your accounting principles (or managerial accounting) textbook. The Sales account balance varies each year as does the Net Income balance.  The worksheet also uses an IRS tax depreciation method called MACRS5 (Modified Accelerated Cost Recovery System depreciation for a five-year business asset).

1.  Do the following in accordance with the instructions in the Introduction chapter:

**Load Microsoft® Excel and run the Info Macro**

## Figure 22-A: Upper Section of Tutorial Worksheet

| | A | B | C | D | E | F | G | H | I |
|---|---|---|---|---|---|---|---|---|---|
| 1 | | Student Name | SMART & HONEST CORPORATION | | | | PROJECT NAME: | Denver#1 | |
| 2 | | 999-99-9999 | CAPITAL-BUDGETING WORKSHEET | | | | PROJECT COST: | 550,000 | |
| 3 | | Acct150 | NOVEMBER 23, 1993 | | | | | | |
| 4 | | Chapter 22 | | | | | | | |
| 5 | | 15-Sep-93 | | | | | | | |
| 6 | | | Year 1 | Year 2 | Year 3 | Year 4 | Year 5 | Year 6 | |
| 7 | | | | | | | | | |
| 8 | | Estimated Revenue: | | | | | | | |
| 9 | | Project Sales.......... | 300,000 | 450,000 | 400,000 | 300,000 | 250,000 | 200,000 | |
| 10 | | Estimated Expenses: | | | | | | | |
| 11 | | MACRS5 Depreciation........ | | | | | | | |
| 12 | | Other Variable Costs........ | | | | | | | |
| 13 | | Other Fixed Costs........ | | | | | | | |
| 14 | | | | | | | | | |
| 15 | | Total Expenses........ | | | | | | | |
| 16 | | | | | | | | | |
| 17 | | Project Income Before Taxes........ | | | | | | | |
| 18 | | Less: Corp. Inc. Tax Prov........ | | | | | | | |
| 19 | | | | | | | | | |
| 20 | | Estimated Project Net Income.......... | | | | | | | |
| 21 | | | | | | | | | |
| 22 | | Net Cash Flow: | | | | | | | |
| 23 | | Estimated Project Net Income........ | | | | | | | |
| 24 | | Add Back Depreciation........ | | | | | | | |
| 25 | | | | | | | | | |
| 26 | | Total Cash Flow........ | | | | | | | |
| 27 | | | | | | | | | |
| 28 | | | | | | | | | |

22-2

# Figure 22-B:  Lower Section of Tutorial Worksheet

| | A | B | C | D | E | F | G | H | I |
|---|---|---|---|---|---|---|---|---|---|
| 28 | | | | | | | | | |
| 29 | | PAYBACK METHOD: | This Year Cash Flow | Accum. Cash Flow | Selected Year | | | | |
| 30 | | | ---------- | ---------- | ---------- | | | | |
| 31 | | | | | | | | | |
| 32 | | End of Year 1............. | | | | | | | |
| 33 | | End of Year 2............. | | | | | | | |
| 34 | | End of Year 3............. | | | | | | | |
| 35 | | End of Year 4............. | | | | | | | |
| 36 | | End of Year 5............. | | | | | | | |
| 37 | | End of Year 6............. | | | | | | | |
| 38 | | | | | | | | | |
| 39 | | RETURN ON AVERAGE INVESTMENT METHOD: | | | | | | | |
| 40 | | | | | | | | | |
| 41 | | A. Original Project Cost........... | | | | | | | |
| 42 | | B. Salvage Value of Project........ | | | | | | | |
| 43 | | | ---------- | | | | | | |
| 44 | | C. Average Investment ((A+B)/2).... | | | | | | | |
| 45 | | | ---------- | | | | | | |
| 46 | | D. Six Years Net Income............ | | | | | | | |
| 47 | | | ---------- | | | | | | |
| 48 | | E. Average Net Income.............. | | | | | | | |
| 49 | | | ========= | | | | | | |
| 50 | | F. Return on Investment  (E/C)..... | | | | | | | |
| 51 | | | | | | | | | |
| 52 | | DISCOUNTED CASH FLOW METHOD: | | | PV of $1 | | | | |
| 53 | | | | | @ 16% Rate | | | | |
| 54 | | Cash Outflow for Project......... | | | ---------- | | | | |
| 55 | | PV of Year 1 Cash Inflow......... | | | 0.862 | | | | |
| 56 | | PV of Year 2 Cash Inflow......... | | | 0.743 | | | | |
| 57 | | PV of Year 3 Cash Inflow......... | | | 0.641 | | | | |
| 58 | | PV of Year 4 Cash Inflow......... | | | 0.552 | | | | |
| 59 | | PV of Year 5 Cash Inflow......... | | | 0.476 | | | | |
| 60 | | PV of Year 6 Cash Inflow......... | | | 0.410 | | | | |
| 61 | | | | | ---------- | | | | |
| 62 | | Net Present Value of Project..... | | | | | | | |
| 63 | | | | | ========= | | | | |
| 64 | | | | | | | | | |

22-3

2. Create a worksheet according to Figures 22-A and 22-B. Make sure you enter the numbers without commas and then format them. For example, the project cost in cell H3 should be entered as 550000 and formatted to look like 550,000.

3. You have entered the estimated revenue from project sales. Now you should enter estimated expenses. The first one is depreciation. The corporate management team wants to use an accelerated method of depreciation rather than straight line. You suggest MACRS5, provided by the IRS, with the factors in the following table:

| Year 1 | .2 | Year 4 | .1152 |
| Year 2 | .32 | Year 5 | .1152 |
| Year 3 | .192 | Year 6 | .0576 |

Enter a formula in cell C11 according to the following:

Type  =h3*.2  in cell **C11** and press **<Enter>**

Enter similar formulas in cells D11 through H11 using the factors in the table above.

4. Amounts in the row labeled Other Variable Costs are entered as a percentage of sales. Notice, however, that factors are used in the formulas instead of percentage amounts.

Type  =c9*.25  in cell **C12** and press **<Enter>**
Drag cell **C12** to cell **H12** and drag **Edit** to **Fill Right**

5. Notice that the other fixed costs start at $60,000, but are projected to increase each year at the rate of 6%.

Type  **60000**  in cell **C13** and press **<Enter>**
Type  =c13*1.06  in cell **D13** and press **<Enter>**
Drag cell **D13** to cell **H13** and drag **Edit** to **Fill Right**

6. The total expense amounts in row 15 are the sum of the amounts in rows 11 through 13:

Type  =sum(c11:c13)  in cell **C15** and press **<Enter>**
Drag cell **C15** to cell **H15** and drag **Edit** to **Fill Right**

7. The Project Income Before Taxes is the Sales amount minus the Total Expenses:

> Type  =c9-c15  in cell **C17** and press < **Enter** >
> Drag cell **C17** to cell **H17** and drag **Edit** to **Fill Right**

8.  The Provision for Income Taxes percentage is 34%.

> Type  =c17*.34  in cell **C18** and press < **Enter** >
> Drag cell **C18** to cell **H18** and drag **Edit** to **Fill Right**

9.  Get the Estimated Net Income by subtracting the number in cell C18 from the number in cell C17.

> Type  =c17-c18  in cell **C20** and press < **Enter** >
> Drag cell **C20** to cell **H20** and drag **Edit** to **Fill Right**

10. For planning purposes, assume that Depreciation is the only noncash expense and that the project Sales amounts are equal to the cash inflows. Copy the Net Income amounts from row 20 to row 23. Also, copy the Depreciation amounts from row 11 to row 24. Total cash flow can be computed, then, by adding the Depreciation Expense amounts to the Net Income amounts.

> Type  =c23+c24  in cell **C26** and press < **Enter** >
> Drag cell **C26** to cell **H26** and drag **Edit** to **Fill Right**

11. The Payback Method is the first of the capital-budgeting alternatives. It answers the question: In what year does the cash investment in the project get returned? First, transfer the cash inflows on row 26 to column C:

> Type  =c26  in cell **C32** and press < **Enter** >
> Type  =d26  in cell **C33** and press < **Enter** >

Enter the rest of the cash inflows in the same manner.

12. Next, accumulate the cash inflow amounts.

> Type  =c32  in cell **D32** and press < **Enter** >
> Type  =d32+c33  in cell **D33** and press < **Enter** >
> Drag cell **D33** to cell **D37** and drag **Edit** to **Fill Down**

# Figure 22-C: Upper Section of Completed Tutorial

Student Name
999-99-9999
Acct150
Chapter 22
15-Sep-93

SMART & HONEST CORPORATION
CAPITAL-BUDGETING WORKSHEET
NOVEMBER 23, 1993

PROJECT NAME: Denver#1
PROJECT COST: 550,000

| | Year 1 | Year 2 | Year 3 | Year 4 | Year 5 | Year 6 |
|---|---|---|---|---|---|---|
| Estimated Revenue: | | | | | | |
| Project Sales......... | 300,000 | 450,000 | 400,000 | 300,000 | 250,000 | 200,000 |
| Estimated Expenses: | | | | | | |
| MACRS5 Depreciation....... | 110,000 | 176,000 | 105,600 | 63,360 | 63,360 | 31,680 |
| Other Variable Costs....... | 75,000 | 112,500 | 100,000 | 75,000 | 62,500 | 50,000 |
| Other Fixed Costs........ | 60,000 | 63,600 | 67,416 | 71,461 | 75,749 | 80,294 |
| Total Expenses.......... | 245,000 | 352,100 | 273,016 | 209,821 | 201,609 | 161,974 |
| Project Income Before Taxes........ | 55,000 | 97,900 | 126,984 | 90,179 | 48,391 | 38,026 |
| Less: Corp. Inc. Tax Prov....... | 18,700 | 33,286 | 43,175 | 30,661 | 16,453 | 12,929 |
| Estimated Project Net Income....... | 36,300 | 64,614 | 83,809 | 59,518 | 31,938 | 25,097 |
| Net Cash Flow: | | | | | | |
| Estimated Project Net Income....... | 36,300 | 64,614 | 83,809 | 59,518 | 31,938 | 25,097 |
| Add Back Depreciation........ | 110,000 | 176,000 | 105,600 | 63,360 | 63,360 | 31,680 |
| Total Cash Flow........ | 146,300 | 240,614 | 189,409 | 122,878 | 95,298 | 56,777 |

22-6

## Figure 22-D: Lower Section of Completed Tutorial

| PAYBACK METHOD: | This Year Cash Flow | Accum. Cash Flow | Selected Year |
|---|---|---|---|
| End of Year 1................ | 146,300 | 146,300 | |
| End of Year 2................ | 240,614 | 386,914 | |
| End of Year 3................ | 189,409 | 576,323 | <------ |
| End of Year 4................ | 122,878 | 699,202 | |
| End of Year 5................ | 95,298 | 794,500 | |
| End of Year 6................ | 56,777 | 851,277 | |

### RETURN ON AVERAGE INVESTMENT METHOD:

| | |
|---|---|
| A. Original Project Cost............ | 550,000 |
| B. Salvage Value of Project.......... | 0 |
| C. Average Investment ((A+B)/2)......... | 275,000 |
| D. Six Years Net Income........ | 301,277 |
| E. Average Net Income.......... | 50,213 |
| F. Return on Investment E/C....... | 18.26% |

### DISCOUNTED CASH FLOW METHOD:

| | | PV Of $1 @ 16% Rate |
|---|---|---|
| Cash Outflow for Project........ | (550,000) | |
| PV of Year 1 Cash Inflow........ | 126,111 | 0.862 |
| PV of Year 2 Cash Inflow........ | 178,776 | 0.743 |
| PV of Year 3 Cash Inflow........ | 121,411 | 0.641 |
| PV of Year 4 Cash Inflow........ | 67,829 | 0.552 |
| PV of Year 5 Cash Inflow........ | 45,362 | 0.476 |
| PV of Year 6 Cash Inflow........ | 23,279 | 0.410 |
| Net Present Value of Project........ | 12,768 | |

13. The last step for the Payback Method is to set up IF and Nested IF functions that will automatically place an arrow next to the year during which the cash invested in the project is fully recovered. Remember the IF function has in it two actions to take depending upon the results of a test.

> Type  = if(d32 > h3,"< ------"," ")  in cell **E32** and press <**Enter**>
> Type  = if(d33 > $h$3,if(d32 < $h$3,"< ------"," ")," ")
>       in cell **E33** and press <**Enter**>
> Drag cell **E33** to cell **E37** and drag **Edit** to **Fill Down**

Cash invested in Denver #1 is expected to be paid back during year 3.

14. The next method computes the Return on Average Investment for the six-year period. The original project cost is the amount found in cell H3. There will be no salvage (or residual) value for the project.

> Type  = h3  in cell **C41** and press <**Enter**>
> Type  **0**  (zero) in cell **C42** and press <**Enter**>
> Type  = (c41+c42)/2  in cell **C44** and press <**Enter**>

15. The Six-Years Net Income is the sum of the amounts in row 20.

> Type  = sum(c20:h20)  in cell **C46** and press <**Enter**>
> Type  = c46/6  in cell **C48** and press <**Enter**>
> Type  = c48/c44  in cell **C50** and press <**Enter**>

Format the amount in cell C50 as a percent carried to two decimal places.

16. The Discounted Cash Flow Method is also called the Net Present Value Method. Assume that there is a $550,000 cash outflow on day one of the project. Also, assume that all of the cash inflows occur on the last day of their respective years.

> Type  = -h3  in cell **C54** and press <**Enter**>
> Type  = e55*c26  in cell **C55** and press <**Enter**>
> Type  = e56*d26  in cell **C56** and press <**Enter**>

Enter formulas in cells C57 through C60 in a similar manner. The Net Present Value of the project is the sum of the amounts in cells C54–C60.

> Type  = sum(c54:c60)  in cell **C62** and press <**Enter**>

17. Check your worksheet with the one illustrated in Figures 22-C and 22-D. Format your numbers. Save your worksheet as **a:\tut22** and print it in a portrait orientation with a regular-sized type font. Exit the program.

# Project:

Assume that your boss likes the organization of the tutorial worksheet. Now it is going to be used for some what-if analysis. The board of directors of Smart & Honest Corporation is looking at projects in three different cities. You are to change the numbers in the tutorial worksheet according to the schedule prepared by the board members.

1. Do the following in accordance with the instructions in the Introduction chapter:

Load **Microsoft® Excel** and open **a:\tut22.xls**

2. Change your worksheet to reflect the information in the schedule on the next page. Save and print each project separately. Exit the program.

3. (Optional) Type a one-page report to the board of directors that discusses the three projects and the three capital-budgeting alternatives. Give your opinion as to which project is the best and explain why.

# Assignment:

Prepare the three project worksheets by hand using the format shown in the tutorial.

## Figure 22EE: Key Numbers From Three Projects

| Proj. Name: | Seattle#2 | Houston#4 | Miami#1 |
|---|---|---|---|
| Proj. Cost: | 530,000 | 540,000 | 560,000 |
| Year 1 Sales | 280,000 | 260,000 | 240,000 |
| Year 2 Sales | 430,000 | 320,000 | 340,000 |
| Year 3 Sales | 410,000 | 360,000 | 390,000 |
| Year 4 Sales | 320,000 | 410,000 | 460,000 |
| Year 5 Sales | 220,000 | 460,000 | 350,000 |
| Year 6 Sales | 190,000 | 255,000 | 340,000 |
| Var. Cost % | 30% | 29% | 28% |
| Year 1 Fixed | 50,000 | 60,000 | 62,000 |
| Save As: | a:\proj22a | a:\proj22b | a:\proj22c |

Assume a 6% increase in fixed cost as
   in the tutorial.

# Chapter Twenty-Two Transmittal Sheet for Excel

A. Hand in this page to your instructor with the following items attached in the order requested:

1. PROJ22A Seattle #2 worksheet
2. PROJ22B Houston #4 worksheet
3. PROJ22C Miami #1 worksheet
4. Hand-written assignment
5. Project step 3 report to board (optional)

B. What is the cell-location based formula or function in cell E23?

C. If the number in cell C62 is positive, what does it mean?

D. Rank the three projects (first, second, third) for each of the three capital budgeting methods:

| Project Name | Seattle#2 | Houston#4 | Miami#1 |
| --- | --- | --- | --- |
| Payback Year | 1st | | |
| ROA % | | | |
| Net P.V. | | | |

Notes:

## Chapter Twenty-Three

# Corporation Income Tax Worksheet

---

## Chapter Objectives:

A.  Prepare a worksheet that reconciles financial statement net income with corporation tax return income.

B.  Compute and record corporation income tax based on various levels of income.

## Tutorial:

Federal Form 1120, U. S. Corporation Income Tax Return, is one of the more unusual forms designed by the Internal Revenue Service. It contains information that comes from two balance sheets that are usually prepared in accordance with generally accepted accounting principles (GAAP). On the other hand, the return's version of an income statement contains numbers that are in accordance with the federal tax laws. This tutorial shows how the two balance sheets are connected and how net income, according to GAAP, is reconciled with taxable income.

1.  Assume that you are an enrolled agent who prepares the corporate tax returns for your client, Junk Food Charlies, Inc., every year. You work from financial statements prepared by the company controller.

Load **Microsoft₈ Excel** and run the **Info Macro**

2.  Format a single worksheet that looks similar to the illustrations on the following two pages.

# Figure 23-A: Upper Portion of Worksheet

| | A | B | C | D | E | F | G | H |
|---|---|---|---|---|---|---|---|---|
| 1 | | Student Name | | JUNK FOOD CHARLIES, INC. | | | | |
| 2 | | 999-99-9999 | | TAX RETURN WORKSHEET | | | | |
| 3 | | Acct150 | | FOR THE YEAR ENDED | | | | |
| 4 | | Chapter 23 | | DECEMBER 31, 1993 | | | | |
| 5 | | 15-Sep-93 | | | | | | |
| 6 | | | LAST YEAR | THIS YEAR | | | | |
| 7 | | ACCOUNT NAMES | BAL SHEET | BAL SHEET | | | | |
| 8 | | --------------------------------- | ----------------- | ----------------- | | | | |
| 9 | | Cash................................... | 80,250 | 75,000 | | | | |
| 10 | | Accounts Receivable................. | 144,000 | 150,000 | | | | |
| 11 | | Less: Allow for D/A................... | (5,000) | (4,000) | | | | |
| 12 | | Inventories............................. | 242,000 | 250,000 | | | | |
| 13 | | Land..................................... | 100,000 | 100,000 | | | | |
| 14 | | Building & Equipment............... | 280,000 | 280,000 | | | | |
| 15 | | Less: Accum Deprn................... | (15,000) | (30,000) | | | | |
| 16 | | | ----------------- | ----------------- | | | | |
| 17 | | TOTAL ASSETS...................... | | | | | | |
| 18 | | | ============ | ============ | | | | |
| 19 | | Accounts Payable..................... | 134,000 | 138,000 | | | | |
| 20 | | Corp Income Tax Pay................. | 13,000 | 12,000 | | | | |
| 21 | | Deferred Taxes Pay................... | 0 | 0 | | | | |
| 22 | | Curr Port LT Debt..................... | 4,000 | 3,000 | | | | |
| 23 | | Mortgage Payable..................... | 183,000 | 180,000 | | | | |
| 24 | | Common Stock........................ | 100,000 | 100,000 | | | | |
| 25 | | Paid-in Capital......................... | 250,000 | 250,000 | | | | |
| 26 | | Retained Earnings.................... | 142,250 | 138,000 | | | | |
| 27 | | | ----------------- | ----------------- | | | | |
| 28 | | TOTAL LIAB & EQUITY............. | | | | | | |
| 29 | | | ============ | ============ | | | | |
| 30 | | | | THIS YEAR | TAX RETURN | | TAX RETURN | |
| 31 | | | | INC STMT | ADJUSTMENTS | | BALANCE | |
| 32 | | | | ----------------- | ----------------- | | ----------------- | |
| 33 | | Sales................................... | | 1,200,000 | | | | |
| 34 | | | | ----------------- | | | ----------------- | |
| 35 | | Cost of Goods Sold................... | | 800,000 | | | | |
| 36 | | Officers' Salaries..................... | | 90,000 | | | | |
| 37 | | Salaries and Wages................................ | | 120,000 | | | | |
| 38 | | Repairs................................. | | 15,000 | | | | |
| 39 | | Bad Debts Exp......................... | | 5,000 | | | | |
| 40 | | Taxes Exp.............................. | | 20,000 | | | | |
| 41 | | Interest Expense...................... | | 19,000 | | | | |
| 42 | | Depreciation Expense................. | | 15,000 | | | | |
| 43 | | Travel & Entertainment................ | | 8,000 | | | | |
| 44 | | Corp Income Tax Exp................. | | 22,250 | | | | |
| 45 | | | | ----------------- | ----------------- | | ----------------- | |
| 46 | | TOTAL EXPENSES................... | | | | | | |
| 47 | | | | ----------------- | ----------------- | | ----------------- | |
| 48 | | NET INCOME/TAXABLE INCOME.................. | | | | | | |
| 49 | | | | ============ | ============ | | ============ | |

## Figure 23-B: Lower Portion of Worksheet

| | A | B | C | D | E | F | G | H |
|---|---|---|---|---|---|---|---|---|
| 50 | | SCHEDULE M-1--INCOME RECON | | | | | | |
| 51 | | Net income per books................................ | | | | | | |
| 52 | | Add federal income tax.............................. | | | | | | |
| 53 | | Add travel & entertainment......................... | | | | | | |
| 54 | | Add bad debt exp...................................... | | | | | | |
| 55 | | Deduct depreciation................................... | | | | | | |
| 56 | | | | ----------------- | | ----------------- | ----------------- | |
| 57 | | NET INCOME/TAXABLE INCOME...................... | | | | | | |
| 58 | | | | =========== | | ========== | =========== | |
| 59 | | SCHEDULE M-2--RET EARNINGS | | | | | | |
| 60 | | Balance at beg of year.................... | | | | | | |
| 61 | | Net income per books.................... | | | | | | |
| 62 | | Cash distributions......................... | | | | | | |
| 63 | | | ----------------- | ----------------- | | | ----------------- | |
| 64 | | BEG BALANCE/END BALANCE.. | | | | | | |
| 65 | | | =========== | =========== | | | =========== | |

3. The SUM functions should be entered in the following cells:

Type  =sum(c9:c15)  in cell **C17** and press **<Enter>**
Type  =sum(d9:d15)  in cell **D17** and press **<Enter>**
Type  =sum(c19:c26)  in cell **C28** and press **<Enter>**

Type  =sum(d19:d26)  in cell **D28** and press **<Enter>**
Type  =sum(d35:d44)  in cell **D46** and press **<Enter>**

4. Deduct the total expenses from sales to get this year's net income by doing the following:

Type  =d33-d46  in cell **D48** and press **<Enter>**

Notice that debits and credits are not used here. Debits and credits are neither used on financial statements nor on tax returns.

5. Start to make the adjustments to the Net Income account to get to the Taxable Income. The other side of these adjustments are reflected in Schedule M-1 on the tax return. Schedule M-1 is used to reconcile the Net Income per the books with the Taxable Income per the return.

Corporate income tax is one of the expenses that leads to Net Income per the books, but is not one of the expenses that leads to Taxable Income.

Do the following to remove corporate income tax as an expense and to add to net income in Schedule M-1:

> Type  -22250  in cell **F44** and press  < **Enter** >
> Type  +22250  in cell **F52** and press  < **Enter** >

Enter  (a)  in cells E44 and E52.  Remember that you are not debiting or crediting any accounts.  These adjustments will not find their way to the general ledger of Junk Food Charlies, Inc.

6.  The Travel and Entertainment Expense account contains expense for travel, lodging, meals, and entertainment.  A curious part of the tax law limits the deduction for meals and entertainment to 80% of the actual costs.  Travel and lodging expenses are fully deductible.

> Type  -1000  in cell **F43** and press  < **Enter** >
> Type  +1000  in cell **F53** and press  < **Enter** >

Make this adjustment (b).

7.  Depreciation Expense for financial statement purposes is often quite different from Depreciation Expense for tax purposes.  The rules under the Modified Accelerated Cost Recovery System (MACRS) allow for shorter lives, no residual or salvage values, and larger deductions during the early years for many of the assets.  In this case the expense for tax purposes is higher than for financial statement purposes:

> Type  +10000  in cell **F42** and press  < **Enter** >
> Type  -10000  in cell **F55** and press  < **Enter** >

Make this adjustment (c).

8.  An analysis of Allowance for Doubtful Accounts reveals that $4,000 was actually written off as Bad Debts Expense.  That is all you can declare for tax return purposes.  The tax law does not conform to GAAP in this circumstance.

> Type  -1000  in cell **F39** and press  < **Enter** >
> Type  +1000  in cell **F54** and press  < **Enter** >

Make this adjustment (d).

## Figure 23-C: Upper Portion of Worksheet Completed

```
Student Name                          JUNK FOOD CHARLIES, INC.
999-99-9999                           TAX RETURN WORKSHEET
Acct150                               FOR THE YEAR ENDED
Chapter 23                            DECEMBER 31, 1993
15-Sep-93
```

| ACCOUNT NAMES | LAST YEAR BAL SHEET | THIS YEAR BAL SHEET |
|---|---|---|
| Cash............................................. | 80,250 | 75,000 |
| Accounts Receivable.................. | 144,000 | 150,000 |
| Less: Allow for D/A...................... | (5,000) | (4,000) |
| Inventories.................................. | 242,000 | 250,000 |
| Land............................................ | 100,000 | 100,000 |
| Building & Equipment.................. | 280,000 | 280,000 |
| Less: Accum Deprn...................... | (15,000) | (30,000) |
| | | |
| TOTAL ASSETS......................... | 826,250 | 821,000 |
| | =========== | =========== |
| Accounts Payable........................ | 134,000 | 138,000 |
| Corp Income Tax Pay................... | 13,000 | 12,000 |
| Deferred Taxes Pay..................... | 0 | 0 |
| Curr Port LT Debt........................ | 4,000 | 3,000 |
| Mortgage Payable........................ | 183,000 | 180,000 |
| Common Stock............................. | 100,000 | 100,000 |
| Paid-in Capital............................. | 250,000 | 250,000 |
| Retained Earnings....................... | 142,250 | 138,000 |
| | | |
| TOTAL LIAB & EQUITY.............. | 826,250 | 821,000 |
| | =========== | =========== |

| | THIS YEAR INC STMT | TAX RETURN ADJUSTMENTS | | TAX RETURN BALANCE |
|---|---|---|---|---|
| Sales........................................................... | 1,200,000 | | | 1,200,000 |
| | | | | |
| Cost of Goods Sold...................................... | 800,000 | | | 800,000 |
| Officers' Salaries......................................... | 90,000 | | | 90,000 |
| Salaries and Wages..................................... | 120,000 | | | 120,000 |
| Repairs........................................................ | 15,000 | | | 15,000 |
| Bad Debts Exp............................................. | 5,000 | (d) | (1,000) | 4,000 |
| Taxes Exp.................................................... | 20,000 | | | 20,000 |
| Interest Expense.......................................... | 19,000 | | | 19,000 |
| Depreciation Expense.................................. | 15,000 | (c) | 10,000 | 25,000 |
| Travel & Entertainment................................ | 8,000 | (b) | (1,000) | 7,000 |
| Corp Income Tax Exp................................... | 22,250 | (a) | (22,250) | 0 |
| | | | | |
| TOTAL EXPENSES....................................... | 1,114,250 | | (14,250) | 1,100,000 |
| | | | | |
| NET INCOME/TAXABLE INCOME...................... | 85,750 | | 14,250 | 100,000 |
| | =========== | | ========== | =========== |

**Figure 23-D: Lower Portion of Worksheet Completed**

```
SCHEDULE M-1--INCOME RECON
Net income per books................................        85,750                              85,750
Add federal income tax..............................             (a)        22,250              22,250
Add travel & entertainment........................              (b)         1,000               1,000
Add bad debt exp......................................           (d)         1,000               1,000
Deduct depreciation..................................           (c)       (10,000)            (10,000)
                                                          ----------      ----------         ----------
NET INCOME/TAXABLE INCOME                                  85,750          14,250            100,000
                                                          ==========      ==========         ==========
SCHEDULE M-2--RET EARNINGS
Balance at beg of year.....................  142,250                                         142,250
Net income per books......................               85,750                               85,750
Cash distributions...........................           (90,000)                             (90,000)
                                             ----------   ----------                        ----------
BEG BALANCE/END BALANCE..   142,250         (4,250)                                         138,000
                             ==========     ==========                                      ==========
```

9. Finish the rest of the Tax Return Adjustments and Tax Return Balance columns so that they look like the columns illustrated in Figure 23-C. The formula in cell G33 should be  +d33+f33  and should be copied to cells G35 through G44.

10. Finish Schedule M-1. Rather than typing a number in cell D51, enter a formula to copy the amount from cell D48. The amount in cells F48 and F57 should be equal to but opposite from the amount in cell F46.

11. Schedule M-2 is an analysis of unappropriated Retained Earning. The beginning balance should equal the amount in cell C26. The Net Income per Books is the same amount as in Schedule M-1. The Cash Distributions are cash dividends paid during the year. Assume that the $90,000 came from the 12/31/93 Adjusted Trial Balance. The ending balance in cell G64 is the sum of the amounts in cells G60 through G62.

12. Format the numbers in the worksheet so that they look like the amounts in Figures 23-C and 23-D. Save your tax return worksheet as **a:\tut23**  and print it in a portrait orientation using compressed print. Exit the program.

# Project:

Assume that another year has passed and that it is time to do the income tax return for Junk Food Charlies, Inc., again. It has been the best year ever for the company because a new line of diet junk food products has been introduced and is doing extremely well. A new controller was hired. She has given you the Adjusted Trial Balance in Figure 23-E.

1. Do the following in accordance with the instructions in the Introduction chapter:

Load **Microsoft**® **Excel** and open **a:\tut23.xls**

### Figure 23-E: 12/31/94 Adjusted Trial Balance

| | | |
|---|---:|---:|
| Cash | 86,000 | |
| Accounts Receivable | 170,250 | |
| Allow for Doubtful Accounts | | 6,000 |
| Inventory | 255,000 | |
| Land | 100,000 | |
| Building | 110,000 | |
| Equipment | 170,000 | |
| Accumulated Depreciation | | 45,000 |
| Accounts Payable | | 119,000 |
| Corp Income Tax Payable | | 6,000 |
| Cur Port of L.T. Debt | | 3,000 |
| Mortgage Payable | | 180,000 |
| Less Cur Port of L.T. Debt | 3,000 | |
| Common Stock | | 100,000 |
| Paid-In Capital | | 250,000 |
| Retained Earnings | | 138,000 |
| Cash Dividends Paid | 110,000 | |
| Sales | | 1,680,000 |
| Cost of Goods Sold | 1,120,000 | |
| Officers Salaries | 108,000 | |
| Salaries and Wages | 168,000 | |
| Repairs Expense | 21,000 | |
| Bad Debts Expense | 7,000 | |
| Taxes Expense | 32,000 | |
| Interest Expense | 18,500 | |
| Depreciation Expense | 15,000 | |
| Travel & Lodging Expense | 6,000 | |
| Meals & Entertainment Exp | 5,000 | |
| Corp Income Tax Expense | 22,250 | |
| TOTALS | 2,527,000 | 2,527,000 |

2.   Move the This Year Balance Sheet numbers into the Last Year Balance Sheet column.  Clear (erase) the This Year Income Statement and the Tax Return Adjustment amounts.

3. Enter the information from the Adjusted Trial Balance on the previous page without changing the names formatted in column A.  Combine numbers to get the appropriate amounts for the purposes of this worksheet.

4.  The following information is for the tax return adjustments:

      a.  The bad debts actually written off is $1,500 less than the expense shown on the Adjusted Trial Balance.

      b.  The Depreciation Expense is $8,000 more than the expense shown on the Adjusted Trial Balance.

      c.  The Travel and Entertainment Expense for tax purposes is $1,500 less than shown on the Adjusted Trial Balance.

      d. Remove the Corporate Income Tax Expense amount.  The new controller hasn't allocated the correct amount for the year.

5.  It is time to compute the income tax for financial statement purposes and for the tax return.  These computations get complicated because of the provisions of FASB-96 which, as of this writing, should become effective for fiscal years beginning after December 15, 1992.  Under these complex rules *temporary differences* must be accounted for.  According to Appendix E of FASB-96, a temporary difference is defined as, "a difference between the tax basis of an asset or liability and its reported amount in the financial statements that will result in taxable or deductible amounts in future years when the reported amount of the asset or liability is recovered or settled, respectively."

This project has two temporary differences.  One is the adjustment for Bad Debts taken on Accounts Receivable.  The other is the adjustment for Depreciation taken on the Buildings and Equipment.

If the rules of FASB-96 are interpreted correctly, the Taxable Income for tax return purposes is $174,500 (as your worksheet should show).  To get the Corporate Income Tax Expense for financial statement purposes, you have to deduct the $8,000 Depreciation adjustment and add back the $1,500 Bad

Debts adjustment. That produces a Taxable Income for financial statement purposes of $181,000.

Compute the income tax on both amounts ($174,500 and $181,000) in accordance with the following schedule:

| Taxable Income Over: | But Not Over: | The Tax Is: | Of the Amount Over: |
|---|---|---|---|
| -0- | 50,000 | 15% | -0- |
| 50,000 | 75,000 | 7,500 + 25% | 50,000 |
| 75,000 | ___ | 13,750 + 34% | 75,000 |

Note: If a corporation has taxable income over $100,000, then the tax as determined under the above schedule is increased by 5% of the excess over $100,000 or $11,750, whichever is less. (Code Sec. 11(b)).

The difference between the two tax amounts should be $2,535. Put that into the Deferred Tax Payable account up in the Balance Sheet section of your worksheet.

6. The amount in the Corporate Income Tax Payable account should be changed from $6,000 to $35,055. The Corporate Income Tax Expense (and the tax return adjustment) should be changed to the tax amount you figured on $181,000. If you have done everything right, the amount in cell G64 should be equal to the amount in D26.

7. Save the worksheet as **a:\proj23** and print it in a portrait orientation. Exit the program.

8. (Optional) Fill out an actual tax return (provided by your instructor) with the numbers from your worksheet. Type a memo to the controller of Junk Food Charlies, Inc., recommending the adjusting entry for the corporate income tax. Advise her that this entry should be done before she closes the books for the year.

## Assignment:

Do by hand the tax return worksheet discussed in the project section of this chapter.

Student Name:_____

Date:_____

# Chapter Twenty-Three Transmittal Sheet for Excel

A. Hand in this page to your instructor with the following items attached in the order requested:

1. Project tax return worksheet
2. Hand-written assignment
3. Project step 8 tax return (optional)
4. Project step 8 memo (optional)

B. What is the cell-location based formula or function that produces the amount in cell D17?

C. Explain how you got the number that appears in cell D43.

D. If the amount in cell D28 is not equal to the amount in D18, please explain below:

*Appendix*

# Overview of Microsoft® Excel

---

This workbook has been written for **Microsoft® Excel Version 2.0** or later. The commands suggested in the workbook tutorials are intended for IBM® PS2's (or clones) that have a Hercules Graphics or VGA card. Virtually all of the commands will work just as well on Apple® computers. A lot of new features have been added with Excel Versions 3.0 and 4.0, but the basic features needed for analysis in accounting remain pretty much the same.

**Microsoft® Excel** has become a popular graphics oriented spreadsheet program since the introduction of Windows®. It is particularly useful for business applications.

Knowing Excel is not the same as knowing its applications. It's also not the same as knowing how to put numbers into some template or knowing how to follow a tutorial. Knowing Excel is being able to solve spreadsheet-style problems (thinking critically) while Excel is on the screen. The project in each chapter of this workbook is designed to help you exercise your critical thinking skills in accounting.

Excel is a three-in-one software program. It is a worksheet, a chart, and a database. First, a worksheet, it is like a paper pad with rows and columns that you can buy from an office supply store. On an electronic worksheet each intersection of a row and a column is called a cell.

Second, Excel software can also be used to create a chart. A chart is a pictorial representation of certain values from a range of cells in the worksheet. The most commonly used Excel charts are line, pie, and bar charts.

Third, it can be used to create a database. A database is a special kind of worksheet where the data are related. The data can be arranged in records (by row) and fields (by column). The data can be searched, sorted, and retrieved. Chapter 11 in this workbook utilizes the database features.

A typical screen display for **Microsoft® Excel** is illustrated in Figure A-1. It contains two menu bars, a formula bar and spreadsheet window.

# Figure A-1: Excel Worksheet Screen Display

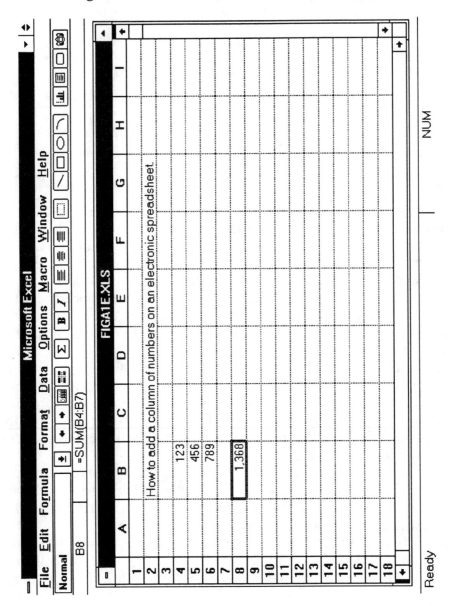

Along the top of the illustration is an area called the menu bar. It shows menu selections such as file, edit, formula, etc. When you use a mouse to click on one of the menu selections, a drop down menu will appear. Each drop down menu has various command options for your selection.

On Versions 3.0 and later there is a shortcut menu bar just below the main menu bar. It contains the menu commands most often selected.

The bar below the menu bar(s) is called the formula bar. It is where you can see the current cell information. You can see that the currently active cell is B8. The formula, =SUM(B4:B7), has been typed into the cell. Notice that the answer to the formula (1,368) is shown in the active cell location (highlighted in the worksheet area) rather than the formula.

In the lower left corner of Figure A-1 is the mode indicator. The main modes that you will see are Ready or Edit. The illustration indicates that the software is in a Ready mode. You cannot type in new information unless the software is in the ready mode.

The spreadsheet (or worksheet) window in Figure A-1 is bounded by column letters and row numbers. A *cell* is an intersection of a column and row. The currently active cell is highlighted.

In the bottom right corner is one of the keyboard indicators. The NUM indicator means the number lock light above the 10-key pad on the computer keyboard is on. It should always be on since you should be using the 10-key pad like your pocket calculator. There is also a CAPS indicator that will appear when the caps light is on. When the light is on, you will be typing all capital letters.

In each cell of a typical worksheet or database you can enter labels, numbers, formulas, or functions. A *label* is a string of text. In accounting such things as account names, column headings, or titles are labels.

*Numbers* are strings of any of the ten digits (0 through 9). You may use one . (period key) to establish the decimal point within the digit string. Numbers are assumed to be positive. If you begin a string of digits with the − (minus key), you will be entering a minus number in a cell location. If you use a , (comma key) within the string of digits, you will convert the numbers into a label. A label cannot be added, subtracted, multiplied, divided, or used in a formula.

The power of an electronic worksheet lies in its capability to perform calculations on formulas that you enter. That power is enhanced when you use cell locations in your formulas rather than the numbers in the cells. For example the illustration on the previous page shows the following:

| | |
|---|---|
| In cell B4 | 123 |
| In cell B5 | 456 |
| In cell B6 | 789 |

You could type the formula, +123+456+789, in cell B8 and get 1,368 for your answer. A better formula is +b4+b5+b6. The answer will be the same, but will come with a bonus. If you want to do some what-if analysis, you can change the numbers in cells B4 through B6. The answer will automatically show up in cell B8 if you used a cell-location based formula.

Functions are special, preconstructed formulas. If macros can be defined as automatic sequences of keystrokes, then functions can be called formula macros. Of the many functions offered in **Microsoft® Excel**, one that you will use a lot is the SUM function. Notice in the formula bar of Figure A-1 that the SUM function =SUM(B4:B7) is typed in cell B8.

Functions are preferred over formulas because they are more flexible. If, for example, you want to add some cells of numbers between B4 and B6, you could do it without having to retype the function in cell B8.

With **Microsoft® Excel Version 3.0** (or later), you don't even have to type the SUM function. You can click on a the SUM button in the shortcut menu bar instead.

This workbook doesn't give you specific instructions on how to print your worksheets and graphs. Those instructions, which depend on the type of equipment you are using, will be provided by your instructor.

It is not the intention of this workbook to teach you everything there is to know about **Microsoft® Excel**. It is a tremendously powerful program. This workbook aims, instead, to teach you how to use computer software to solve accounting problems and to teach you how to think with a computer in front of you.

# Index to Key Terms